# My Brig
## A Mother's True Story of Brilliance, Love and Suicide

**Rhonda Sellers Elkins**

Perfect Publishers Ltd

ISBN 978-1-905399-94-9

Cover Design by Duncan Bamford
http://www.insightillustration.co.uk

Edited by Jan Andersen
http://www.creativecopywriter.org

**PERFECT PUBLISHERS LTD**
23 Maitland Avenue
Cambridge
CB4 1TA
England
http://www.perfectpublishers.co.uk

## Book Title and Cover Explained

Ever since Kaitlyn was a little girl, until the time she took her own life, I always called her my bright shining star. She was - and always will be - the light of my life and this is why I chose this title.

I always told her that I loved her bigger than the universe, meaning that I had more love for her than even the universe could contain; it was endless. We both took an interest in astronomy. This is why I chose a picture taken from the Hubble Space Craft for the background to portray the vastness of the universe. On Kaitlyn's tombstone I had inscribed "I Love You Bigger than the Universe" and I always will.


## The Layout of this Book

At the end of some of the chapters, and sometimes within chapters, I include a number of my blog entries. I wanted to include them to portray some of the feelings I had at that point in time; feelings I still have now, but written at a time when I felt them so intensely.

# Dedication

To Kaitlyn,
You will always be my bright Shining Star.

*Tragedy should be utilized as a source of strength.*

*Dalai Lama XIV*

# Acknowledgements

Firstly, I would like to thank my husband Allyn Elkins who, even in his own tormented grief, still remained strong and helped me to carry on again after Kaitlyn's death. He has supported me endlessly in every way and I love him dearly.

I thank my eldest daughter Stephanie Elkins Alford for contributing her voice to this book and for knowing beyond a shadow of a doubt that I love both she and Kaitlyn the same. I thank her for all the times she has taken me out of this house and done things with me that we both enjoy to help us both feel better, in addition to the lengthy talks we have had, and continue to have. I thank Stephanie's husband Steve Alford for supporting her through this horrible loss and helping us as well.

I thank my wonderful mother, Lucille Sellers, who continues to call me every single day to make sure I'm ok; for the countless hours we have talked and cried together, for listening to me no matter how long I talked, and for understanding when I didn't want to talk at all.

To my father UV Sellers who always worries about us all.

I thank my three sisters Judy Herring, Gail Lynch and Sherry Smith who talk to me and let me talk and talk and talk, or not talk at all.

To my mother-in-law, Eunice Elkins, who is always there for us.

I thank all my nieces and nephews and all of our family and loved ones who have given us tremendous support through this horrific time in our lives.

To the endless Facebook and blog friends I have gained since my daughter's death, thank you for being there for me and encouraging me in writing this book.

Thank you to all of Kaitlyn's friends who gave me so much support in the aftermath of the tragedy, many of whom have also contributed their thoughts and feelings to my book. Kaitlyn chose her friends wisely, and it shows through each of their characters and the beautiful words some of them have graciously shared in this book.

Thank you to all my friends that comment on my blogs and the many people I have come to know through it, some of whom have contributed to my book.

Special thanks go to Jan Andersen, author of Chasing Death: Losing a Child to Suicide, a book that gave me so much comfort in knowing that I am not alone in my feelings; for becoming my good friend and for being a great guide and inspiration to me. Thank you for your friendship and encouragement and also for editing my book.

# Disclaimer

All of the articles quoted in this book have been used with permission from the original authors. All personal stories and writings were used by permission of the authors, whose real names have been used by permission unless otherwise indicated.

Self-Portrait by Kaitlyn Elkins 2008

# Foreword

*by Jan Andersen*
*Author of Chasing Death: Losing a Child to Suicide*

The positive side of shared tragedy is that it forms bonds between people who might not otherwise have met and beautiful friendships never realized.

Rhonda and I first connected just few weeks after her daughter Kaitlyn passed over. In those first few emails from Rhonda's home in the US to mine in the UK, I could feel her intense pain; the shock, the disbelief, the self-questioning, the crushing sense of loss and not knowing how she would be able to carry on. All these were emotions with which I could identify and which can only be truly understood by someone who has experienced the same, unthinkable loss.

There is no singular strategy for coping that will suit everyone, because we all grieve so differently. Our grieving process is not only based on personality type, or personal circumstances, but can be affected by so many other criteria; the relationship that we had with the person who has passed over, for example, or things we did or didn't say and did or didn't do prior to the tragedy.

In Rhonda's case, she found an outlet for her grief through writing and through which she also admonishes herself - albeit unfairly - for not noticing the signs of her daughter's depression, which were so well concealed. Kaitlyn was a talented writer and although Rhonda professes not to be a writer herself, she has managed to articulate with great skill the overpowering array of thoughts and emotions that accompany the aftermath of the totally unexpected loss of a child to suicide.

To make the transition from being an intensely private person to opening up your heart to the world - and consequently risk being criticized by an insensitive minority - takes an enormous amount of courage. However, Rhonda knew that the need to share Kaitlyn's story and potentially help many people in the process was far more important that the fear of disapproval from those who would rather close their eyes and ears to the heartbreaking issues of hidden depression and suicide.

I've always felt it important to be a voice for those who are unable to articulate their pain, but who still wish to raise awareness of depression and suicide. After all, if we all allowed ourselves to be bullied into silence, would this problem escalate? How would survivors cope if they felt they were isolated on an island of overwhelming grief?

No one can deny that Rhonda's book is heartrending, but how can it not be? It is only by being open about the truth behind such issues that we can ever hope to raise awareness, understanding and tolerance of mental illness and depression - and the grief that affects the families left behind after these illnesses mercilessly take their loved ones from them.

In editing this book, I felt it important to retain the author's voice and style, in order for the reader to gain an insight into Rhonda as a real person; a bereaved mother enduring the agony of the loss of her beautiful, talented and much loved daughter and the crippling emotions that ensue.

Kaitlyn would be extremely proud of her mom, not only for honoring her memory, but for turning her loss into something so positive.

# Contents

Kaitlyn aged 18

# Introduction

Before you begin reading this book, I want the reader to know that this is not a book about how to recover from the loss of a loved one to suicide. I am too new into this horrible journey to give any advice on how to recover, since I am still trying to discover that for myself. Perhaps in reading about my experiences, however, you may be able to relate and at least feel that you are not alone if you have suffered a similar loss.

This book is a warning; a warning to parents, teachers, counselors, social workers and to the many, many children, adolescents and young adults out there who suffer from depression and cannot bring themselves to tell anyone, so they suffer in silence; in deadly silence. These sufferers may appear totally in control of their lives and seem to adjust to every situation, so much so that even those closest to them have no clue as to how they are really feeling. The crucial message this book sends out is that the signs of serious depression are not always obvious.

This book is also a tribute to my daughter Kaitlyn, the memories of her, and the lives she touched in her short life.

This book chronicles my excruciatingly painful grieving journey; I have held nothing back. I can't imagine anything worse than losing a child; I don't think there is anything worse and it's an experience I wouldn't wish on anyone.

Many people who have taken their own lives have shown signs of depression. Perhaps they had sought mental health help, perhaps not. There is much material written about suicides of people who have been diagnosed with depression and, while this is a good thing, much more needs to be written about mental illness and suicide to pull it out of the shadows and into everyday awareness. However, there are those out there who never show signs of depression; high achievers who are the epitome of a life that is directed toward great success. All their lives they have been known as intelligent, sometimes brilliant, goal oriented, creative, driven and loving people. My daughter Kaitlyn, was one such person.

I want to tell the story of my wonderful daughter in the hope that it might help others. Since her death, I have learned so many things I did not know previously, even though I am a registered nurse. I had no clue that someone could be severely depressed, even suicidal, yet completely conceal it while continuing to lead a successful life. I am familiar with the signs of depression, so I assumed that someone suffering from severe depression would exhibit some - if not all - of these signs. Nothing I learned in nursing school, during my career, or in life taught me that someone could hide severe depression from everyone until the moment they end their life.

I want this book to teach others that the signs aren't always obvious; that the sinister side of depression is that it can remove someone from this life without any prior warning whatsoever. And when this happens, the families left behind are trapped in a sea of disbelief, confusion, overpowering grief and countless unanswered questions.

It is important to stress that in no way am I suggesting that high-achievers who suffer from depression are any more important than sufferers who come from any other type of background; they are not. All are equally important. Sadly, depression (whether obvious or not) can affect anyone, irrespective of socio-economic status. However, my wish is to write about a group who are rarely mentioned in any reading material I have come across. I have read a few articles, but hidden depression is not well documented.

I write a great deal about Kaitlyn's achievements and how intelligent she was, but I do this to give you a picture of what my daughter was like; I cannot gloss over the facts. My daughter was so much more than her achievements, but they were very much a part of her because she thrived on academic and creative success. I loved her for the person she was inside; a very caring, sweet, loving, unique and totally wonderful human being. She was my kindred spirit whom I loved more than life itself. I would have given my life a hundred times over if only I could have saved her, if only I had known that she was suffering. I know she was not perfect, no one is, but to me, and many others who knew her, she was amazing.

Kaitlyn was not my only child. She has an older sister, Stephanie, who is also a wonderful, intelligent and caring young woman whom I love every bit as much as I love Kaitlyn. Stephanie has contributed her own thoughts and feelings in this book. I don't delve into Stephanie's life in detail, nor do I reveal much about the lives of other family members, including my husband Allyn. It's not that I don't love them as much, but because I want to leave their private lives as private as possible. I open up Kaitlyn's life and my life for the sake of telling a story that needs to be told in order, hopefully, to make a difference in the lives of others. I don't have that right to do that to anyone else.

I hope this book in some way helps drive away the stigma of mental illness. I hope it educates other parents to realize that their highly intelligent "golden child" could be hiding a deep dark secret that could ultimately kill them. No one ever told me; I wish someone had. I hope this book also makes other young people out there know that it is ok to seek help and is nothing to be ashamed of.

I also want to make it clear that not all intelligent, creative, and successful people are depressed or suicidal. However, I have found that high-functioning people sometimes have the ability to hide depression most expertly. No one expects them to be depressed and, as a result, they are less likely to seek help.

Kaitlyn was the last person on this earth that I, or anyone that knew her, would think would take her life. As a result, I am driven to do as much as I can to call attention to this insidious problem that is taking away so many of our wonderful youth. I know Kaitlyn would want this; I feel her spirit moving within me to do this. I hope this book is taken in the way that I intend, to help and to reach as many people as possible.

For Kaitlyn, who for reasons unknown could not cry out for help, I cry out for her with the aim of helping others who suffer as she did. Alone and silent in her despair.

### *Dandelion*

*You know how you lost her:*
*letter by letter.*

*The poem of her unlaced;*
*like a chain of dandelions you whispered to,*
*blew away their tiny parachutes. Early,*
*too early. Not even in time to meet the honey bees.*
*And some of them flew, found a spring.*

*Walk through the meadow, dear;*
*wonder which were yours.*

### *Kaitlyn Elkins*

# Chapter 1

## The Call That Changed It All

*How much does a man live, after all? Does he live a thousand days, or one only? For a week, or for several centuries? How long does a man spend dying? What does it mean to say 'for ever'?*

*Pablo Neruda*

It was around 1:00 pm on Friday April 12, 2013 when I got the call on my cell phone. I had just finished my lunch break and had returned to my desk to resume my nursing notes for the company I worked for as a home health RN. It was a normal day and I was still feeling contentment from the recent visit that my 23-year-old daughter Kaitlyn had made back home during her Easter break from Wake Forest School of Medicine, where she was just beginning her third year of medical school. She lived three and a half hours away so visits home were not as often as I would have liked, but my husband Allyn and I understood. She was extremely busy. We would often visit her once a month so she would not have to use her precious study time for the long drive home and back to school again.

I took my phone out of my pocket and looked at the caller ID, which read "Private Caller". I had absolutely no idea who it might be. When I answered, a male voice asked, "Is this Rhonda Elkins?" "Yes," I replied. He said, "Is your daughter Kaitlyn Elkins?" Again, I said, "Yes."

He said he was from the Winston-Salem police department and that he needed to talk with me about my daughter. My immediate thought was, "Kaitlyn is in trouble! She has never been in trouble in her life!" Then, almost immediately, another thought went through my

1

mind sending chills down my back, draining the blood from my face.

I asked, "What's wrong? What's the matter? What happened?"

The officer said, "Mrs. Elkins, I can't talk to you about it on the phone; you will have to come here for me to talk with you."

"Oh my God!" I thought, "I wonder what has happened? Perhaps she's been in a wreck!"

I told the officer that I lived a three and a half hour drive away, so there was no way I could go that far without knowing what had happened to my daughter. Nevertheless, he still told me that I would have to go there. I pleaded with him to tell me what had happened, because I just couldn't wait that long to find out.

He then uttered the chilling words that would change my life.

"Mrs. Elkins, she is deceased."

At that very moment the world as I knew it ceased to exist. It felt as though my soul left my body and I was not the one talking on the phone. It couldn't possibly be real; I must have been dreaming some horrible nightmare.

I shouted, "WHAT!?? How did it happen?" My heart was beating wildly in my chest. I bent over my desk with my face buried into it as I sat there. No, this couldn't be. I believed I would wake up from the horrendous nightmare any moment. What he was telling me was not possible. I just visualized my daughter being involved in a car crash or some other horrible accident. It still didn't seem real.

The officer then delivered the horrifying news that my daughter had taken her own life.

What he said defied belief. Taken her own life? Kaitlyn??? Never; not her. This could not have happened. They had the wrong person. Kaitlyn was happy. I had only seen her a few days previously. She was a medical student making good grades. It wasn't possible.

Through my sobs, I managed to ask the officer how she did it. He said that she had put a bag over her head, put chemicals in the bag and inhaled them.

Everything was spinning, reality had ceased and it felt as though I had no blood left in my body. I was crying hysterically and during this time the only co-worker left in our building came from her office to see what was happening. She could tell by what I was saying that it was about my beloved youngest daughter.

I was still on the phone and the officer reiterated that I needed to get there as soon as possible. I told him we would be there just as soon as I could get home and tell my husband. I asked the officer whether Kaitlyn was still at her apartment and he said she was. I asked him if her body would still be there when I got there and he said no. I remember feeling relief; I could not bear to see my Kaitlyn dead. It felt as though someone else were talking to the officer. How could I be talking and asking these questions in the face of such a horrific situation? It was not I who was speaking; I was sure it was someone else.

My co-worker helped me gather my things, called our boss and helped me to my car because I could hardly walk. She then drove me home in her car. I sat in stunned silence, thinking all the while how this unthinkable tragedy could possibly have happened. What had happened to my child that would make her take her own life?

As I sat there riding in the car in some surreal plane of existence, numbness and disbelief, I wondered helplessly how such a young woman could end her life. Kaitlyn was a model daughter. Growing up she was so sweet and good, never got in trouble and made straight As in school. She was a model student, an artist and a talented poet and writer who won many awards for her works. She was in the band, was a Marshal and was in the National Honor Society. She was brilliant. She graduated valedictorian of her high school and was voted "Most Likely to Succeed" in her year

3

book by all her classmates. She graduated undergrad from Campbell University in two and a half years summa cum laude with a degree in biology. During her time in college and just after graduation, she worked for an oral surgeon as a surgical assistant. Her lifelong goal to become a doctor was set to be attained; she was accepted into Wake Forest School of Medicine in Winston-Salem, NC in 2011.

Kaitlyn had done very well in her studies at the medical school. She always told me that she loved it. The first year she came home and said, "Momma, this is what I was BORN to do!" She was always so happy when she talked about it.

Before she came home for Easter the last time, she had just had a 6 week break from the school, as all the students had, to study for the Step One Medical Board Exam. She studied so very hard and when the test was over, she called me and said she thought she had done very well on it and that she would come home the following day.

Before she came home, I asked her what kind of food she would like so I could buy it for her. She said that she would do it herself so I didn't have to, but I said I wanted to. You see, she was very careful about what she ate. She ate very healthy foods in several small servings a day. She had fruit, vegetables, lean grilled chicken, mix salads and similar. She was extremely health conscious and I wanted her to be able to eat as she had been doing, as we did not always eat those types of things at home.

So, off I went to a nice grocery store and I bought all the foods of her choice. I had never had so much fun buying food in my life. My baby was coming home and I had not seen her for a while. Since it was almost Easter, the grocery store had pretty flower arrangements there for sale. I bought Kaitlyn one with an attractive plastic egg on a stick in the middle of it for her room at home. I had never bought her flowers before, but I wanted everything just right for her homecoming.

4

A little over a year earlier, she decided she wanted to lose weight. To me, she did not need to lose any, but she thought she wanted to drop a few pounds, so she took up running. She had never been athletic before; none of us are in our family, but when she started running, she began to love it. She began running regularly and, never one to do anything halfheartedly, she dove into it with all she had. She learned about running, bought appropriate training clothes and learned how to run safely. With each day she was able to run farther. Within a few months she entered and finished a half marathon. The next month she entered and finished a full marathon of 26 miles. She loved it.

As I sat in the car with my eyes looking into space, I thought of her last visit home less than a week before. She was happy. She acted like usual self; smiling, making jokes with me, watching our favorite movies and talking. On Saturday we had a mother/daughter day and we went shopping in a town mall about an hour away, where she was looking for some business attire. She said that she would be starting orientation into her third year of medical school and would have to dress in business clothes on some of those days. After orientation, her clinical rotations would begin, with Pediatrics being her first rotation.

We went to a steakhouse for dinner and Kaitlyn actually ate a small steak and enjoyed it. She would go off her strict diet at times. She said she especially deserved it after six weeks of intense studying.

We finished there and we went to Victoria's Secret where she painstakingly shopped for beautiful underwear. She spent a lot of time in particular finding just the right bra and she finally settled on one of their newest editions; the most beautiful bra I've ever seen. At the checkout, she had spent enough to qualify for one of their pink and black umbrellas.

By this time, the movie we wanted to watch was getting ready to start, so we hurried to the theater in the mall. I bought Kaitlyn a drink and I can see her there now and hear her voice saying, "Thank you momma for buying me a $7.00 drink."

We enjoyed the movie and returned home. The next day we went to my side of the family and then my husband's side of the family to enjoy Easter meals. That afternoon, Kaitlyn took a flight to see her boyfriend for a week. We picked her up at the airport the following week and stopped at a Chinese restaurant on the way home.

I said, "Kaitlyn, are you happy about starting clinical?"

She replied, "Yes I am, but I'm also nervous. What if I'm not as smart as I think I am?"

I said, "Oh Kaitlyn, if you weren't smart you wouldn't be in medical school and you are just as smart as the rest of them."

She smiled and then we talked about other things.

When we arrived home, we watched two episodes of "Lost". She had told me about this series the week before as I had never seen it before. I loved it! After those shows, Kaitlyn said it was time for her to go. I hugged her neck and smelled her hair as I always did, and her daddy hugged her neck. She got her cat Gatito, whom we had been taking care of in her absence, and said goodbye to our Lab Savannah. She got into her black Honda Civic, backed out of the driveway, waved, drove down the road and disappeared.

We never saw her alive again.

The trees and the houses went by in a blur as I was driven home. I kept on asking myself how this could be. Kaitlyn had never once in her entire life displayed any obvious signs of depression, or admitted that she no longer wanted to live. To us, and to all who knew her, she had everything together. She was extremely intelligent, had a lot of common sense, was wise beyond her years, had her own apartment, her own car and was pursuing her dream of becoming a medical doctor. She had the world in the palm of her hands. As far as her father and I were concerned, she had her life mapped out perfectly; much more than anyone else we knew. She was contented and had a circle of loyal friends. She had also had a very stable upbringing. Her father and I had been happily married for 32 years. There were no drugs, no drinking and no smoking in our house. Now she had killed herself. It did not make sense. No one like this killed themselves.

The police officer said that she had left notes for her family and friends. Maybe I would understand something then. Something bad must have happened for her to do such a thing. Something dreadful.

On the way home I called her father, Allyn, to let him know. He did not work on Fridays and was just coming home from a doctor's appointment. I called him and asked him if he was driving. He said he was, so I asked him to pull over, which he did. It was so hard telling him. The horror and disbelief in his voice was indescribable.

I then called my oldest daughter Stephanie, Kaitlyn's sister, who is four and a half years her senior, married and living in another city. She started crying uncontrollably and when she wanted to know why, I told her that I just didn't know.

Finally, I called my mother. After that, I knew that the news would spread quickly to the others in my family so I called no one else.

As I did all of these things on the ride home, my mouth was so dry I could barely speak. I had this ghastly feeling of nausea and on many occasions almost asked my co-worker to pull over so I could vomit. But I could not even do that. I could find no release for any misery.

When I arrived home, Allyn was standing in the yard with a desperate look of disbelief on his face. He was crying and he hugged me saying, "Our baby is gone."

I looked at him in disbelief. I couldn't accept this. Why was she gone? How has she gone? What made her want to be gone? I was not ready for that phrase, that statement in all its finality. No, it was too early for that.

We went into the house and as is my husband's nature he buried his emotions inside somewhere and started thinking rationally. He had to cancel his colonoscopy scheduled for Monday. Cancel his colonoscopy? How could he even THINK that the appointment even existed? I told him not to worry about that then, but he insisted he had to or else we would forget about it. I sat there in the chair wondering how anyone could think rationally in that situation. Our baby whom we loved more than life was dead and I didn't know why. To heck with rationality! I couldn't move, I couldn't think; it felt as though I couldn't breathe. I was paralyzed.

My baby daughter was gone. The person I was so connected to, in whose life I wrapped myself up, who I loved so desperately with all my heart and soul, was gone. All I had thought I had known in this world was suddenly called into question. Apparently I knew nothing. I did not see this coming; how could I even think I knew anything to be true ever again?

A few minutes later, my mother-in-law Eunice and my brother-in-law Ande arrived. Both also had the ability to think rationally and calmly in the face of utter devastation. Plans were made for his brother to drive our car to Winston-Salem, so we could bring Kaitlyn's car home when we returned. My mother-in-law would also go with us.

I numbly got up out of my chair, changed out of my nursing scrubs and into a t-shirt, jeans and tennis shoes as if I were a robot. Did I look in the mirror to see if I looked alright like I normally do before I leave home? I can't remember, although I doubt it. I didn't care. I allowed others to tell me what to do because I could not think what

8

to do myself. They even remembered to bring our big cat carrier for Kaitlyn's cat Gatito, because the one she owned was too small for him. How can people remember such things in the midst of such a tragedy when their brain is not functioning normally?

As the commotion of all this activity was going on, I sat in one of the living room chairs near our front door. "Kaitlyn, oh Kaitlyn, what have you done my baby, what have you done?" played over and over in my mind. The only thing rational I did was change my clothes. If I had changed into my pajamas I would never have known it. Yes, maybe I could change into my pajamas, get into bed, pull the covers over my head and wait for this nightmare to end. But it wouldn't end.

We got into our car and began the excruciatingly long three and a half hour drive to Winston-Salem. I sat in the back seat with Allyn in a complete daze. Every now and then I would cry, but I was in a state of total shock. I watched the houses, fields, trees and landmarks as I always had when we used to go and see Kaitlyn. The feeling of happiness and anticipation of seeing her was not there. These were replaced by crucifying feelings of horror, disbelief, despair, grief and a sense of total disengagement from my body.

I had no idea why she had taken her own life. The police officer said she had left notes; I hoped I would find out all my answers then. Who had hurt her so badly that she felt she had to die? What had made her feel that her life was not worth living? Something awful had to have happened. As far as I was aware, everything had been so RIGHT in her life!

I also didn't really understand the method she used to end her life. The police officer told me she put a bag on her head and put some kind of chemical in there that caused her death. What kind of chemical? I'd never heard of such a thing.

As our journey continued, two of the medical school deans called to say they would meet us at her apartment, both sounding shocked.

The entire ride there I thought about how difficult it would be to go to the hospital to identify her body. I didn't want to see her dead. I couldn't bear the thought, but I felt as her mother I had to do it. My brother-in-law offered to do it and my husband begged me not to do it, but I insisted that I must. However, the thought of it turned my insides out.

When we arrived we went to the apartment manager's office as we had been instructed to do by the police officer. We were met by the police officer and the apartment manager. The apartment manager produced an email from Kaitlyn that he had printed out and I read it. In it, she had informed him of her death and the need for him to notify the authorities.

Once at Kaitlyn's apartment, I read her two page suicide note she had written to us. She told us that she had been depressed all her life and had hidden it from us to protect us, as well as to protect herself. She said there was not a time in her life when she didn't feel as though she was barely treading water; she had been depressed ever since she could remember. She said we might wonder why she hadn't sought help, but could not explain why not. She said she couldn't take being sad any longer and was exhausted by the weight of it; this was what made sense to her. She told us not to blame ourselves, or ever wonder what we could have done, because the only thing that was wrong was her. She said we were the best parents in the world and never to forget how very much she loved us. She said she would have died years ago, but could not bear hurting us like that. She asked us to please forgive her that she could wait no longer. She said so many other things; she loved us very much and she was sorry.

I sat in stunned silence after reading that note. I hastily gave it to my husband to read as the deans of the school, the police officer and the apartment manager stood around me in her apartment. She was depressed all her life? This could not be possible. I have watched this child ever since the day she was born and she never once displayed any signs of depression. Where did this come from? How could this be? I wanted to think that someone must have killed her because she certainly could not have done this to herself, but the evidence was all around me. Her notes to us and her friends were in her own handwriting. No signs of foul play were there. She did this. My Kaitlyn killed herself.

So, nothing traumatic happened to her. No one had hurt her. Nothing had happened to make her do this, except years and years of relentless depression that wore her down so much that she could take it no more. No one ever knew.

Kaitlyn was always very precise and methodical in everything she did. Though apparently (by her suicide note telling us so) she was very depressed, she had the presence of mind to do the following before taking her life.

She had emailed the apartment manager informing him that she had taken her own life and in which apartment she was. This email was received in his email inbox on Thursday 4-11-13 at 6:00 am. I discovered later that she had obtained an account that would enable you to send an email, but for it arrive with the recipient at a future date. She stated that she was so very sorry to inconvenience him and to hurt the apartment complex community in any way by her death, but she wanted to die in the comfort of her own home. She needed him to do many things. First of all, she wanted him to inform the proper authorities that could deal with deceased persons. She asked for the letters left beside her to be given to the addressed people, which could be best done by handing them over to the authorities. She said she also had a letter addressed to him, the apartment manager, and for him to make sure he read it. She asked him to please take care of her cat Gatito until her parents arrived to take him. She said she left plenty of water and food out for him and there was more food in the pantry. She said that this will have hurt him, but she wanted his distress to be as minimal as possible and that she loved him very much.

Unfortunately, the apartment manager did not see this email until Friday 4-12-13.

In the letter that she left for the apartment manager, she wrote that she was so very sorry that she had to break her lease and she left a check for the remaining months of her contract, which was over $2,000. The apartment manager said there was no way he was going to keep that check and gave it back to us. What a wonderful man he was to do that. He was so very sad and kept petting and comforting her cat Gatito, saying that he had a cat just like him.

The police officer told me I didn't have to ID Kaitlyn's body and that I only had to call the medical examiner so she could talk to me. She explained how Kaitlyn died by helium, telling me you could easily find how to do it on the internet and that it has been increasing in the last 10 years.

I didn't have to go and see her body; I didn't have to go to the hospital at all. I feel guilty in saying that I was relieved, but I do think I would have died if I had seen her then. I had thought that maybe they would send me her clothes she was wearing. That thought didn't occur to me at the time, otherwise we would have requested them. I'm sure that before she died she dressed in the beautiful new undergarments that she bought on our last visit to Victoria's Secret. She must have had them on, for I never found them. I also never found most of her new clothes she bought that day. So I assume she was wearing them, looking her best for her last moments of life. Oh how I wish I had asked for them. I would have buried her in them.

We talked with the two deans of the medical school that had met us at her apartment. These men had a look of pure despair on their faces and they were so genuinely devastated by Kaitlyn taking her life. One of them said that she was the kind of student that they always wished for there. They stated they had already paid for a room at a motel for the night for us, but we thanked them and declined, knowing that we would have to go back home and be with our family and make arrangements. We would go back later in the week and clean out her apartment.

As I sat in Kaitlyn's apartment on that pretty green couch that had been picked out by her over 3 years previously, I noticed some things. On the table in front of her couch was her laptop computer, a partially full glass of wine and an almost empty bottle of wine. There were also two new books of poetry by Sylvia Plath and Plath's book, "The Bell Jar". I later learned that she had only bought these books the week before because I found the receipt in them. Sylvia Plath was plagued by depression during her life, was a brilliant writer and poet, had attempted suicide once and failed. However, years later she was successful in completing suicide, just after her book was published. I had read Plath's book two years before and it is not one to read while depressed.

I pictured Kaitlyn dying on that couch and I asked the police officer if that was where she died. He said no, that she was in her bed laying down, just looking as though she were asleep.

I can see her in my mind, sipping the wine and eating the dessert she bought especially for this occasion, as she wrote her suicide notes to her family and those to whom she was closest at the time; notes that were neatly written and carefully thought out. I imagine she had written these words in her mind many times over the years, and researched her method of death methodically and carefully, as she did with everything else.

My mother-in-law reminded me that Kaitlyn would need clothes in which to be buried. I had called the funeral home at the town we lived near to tell them about her and how arrangements needed to be made to pick her up. The lady said she would need clothes for Kaitlyn's burial and a picture of her.

I looked in the closet and there before me were pieces of Kaitlyn's life in her clothes, her scent permeating everything. I almost fainted from the realization that my precious daughter who so recently wore all these clothes would never wear them again. She was dead. I went through her clothes, but it was so excruciatingly painful. I couldn't find her new clothes or the undergarments she had just bought. The dresses she had were too dressy to bury her in. She had nice dresses to be worn at symphonies, plays and operas or tiny strappy little dresses that didn't seem adequate enough to cover her body and keep her warm. Yes, I even thought about keeping her warm. I looked and I looked over and over again. I saw all the scrubs that she wore at her surgical assistance job, with the brutal fact hitting me that she would never wear another scrub. I continued to search. I told my mother-in-law I just couldn't choose; it was too hard. Finally, I chose a pretty blouse and nice dress pants, not really knowing whether or not they were items she had recently worn. No shoes; she did not need them. No socks either, but I regretted not getting socks even though they didn't go with dress pants. Her feet would be cold. Yes, I thought of her feet getting cold, even though she was no longer living. I thought I would go insane or die; I didn't know which. I didn't care which.

Before we left, I put her cat Gatito in his cat carrier, which was a chore because he hated it. He seemed so glad to see us when we arrived and was uncharacteristically oblivious to all the people that were present, which was strange for a very timid cat. When he saw me walk in, he walked right up to me.

I grabbed Kaitlyn's laptop computer and the rust colored Afghan that I knew she snuggled in every night, as I am an Afghan snuggler myself. It smelled like her. It would be my companion at home from then on. My Afghan would be put away. I also grabbed her pocket book and cell phone.

The ride home was occupied with calling the friends for whom she had left letters, as this was her request. They could not believe what had happened. One of her friends was so overwhelmed that he could barely talk for crying. The rest were stunned and did not even know how to react.

She left four or five letters for her most recent closest friends and her sister Stephanie, complete with addresses and phone numbers. I called them all on the way home. The rest of the trip was filled with reality hitting me so hard I could barely stand it. Allyn asked me whether I wanted him to take me to the ER. I didn't. What could they do?

Allyn was somehow able to drive us home. His brother drove Kaitlyn's car and his mother rode with him. All I did on the way home was alternately sit in stunned silence or cry and say over and over again, "My poor baby! My poor baby!"

How could someone with this much potential, this much success, who was so full of life, laughed and joked and seemingly had all she ever wanted, feel so sad that she wanted to kill herself? It made no sense, no sense whatsoever.

High School Graduation 2008. My husband Allyn, Kaitlyn and me

# Chapter 2

## My Kindred Spirit and Golden Child

*Loneliness is the human condition. Cultivate it. The way it
tunnels into you allows your soul room to grow. Never
expect to outgrow loneliness. Never hope to find people
who will understand you, someone to fill that space. An
intelligent, sensitive person is the exception, the very great
exception. If you expect to find people who will understand
you, you will grow murderous with disappointment. The
best you'll ever do is to understand yourself, know what it
is that you want.*

*Janet Fitch (White Oleander)*

I feel that I must allow you to get to know my daughter
Kaitlyn, because if you do not know what she was like, you
will not realize the importance of this book, or understand
the utter disbelief that she could ever be depressed, much
less take her own life. I'd like you to have a brief glimpse
into her life, which began on 1-19-90.

My husband Allyn and I had been married nine years
when Kaitlyn was born. He worked in industrial
construction as a welder/electrician. I was an office worker
in our local hospital in the outpatient department. Her sister
Stephanie was four and a half. Stephanie was a beautiful
child with dark brown hair and dark complexion; she
looked like her father. When Kaitlyn was born, I remember
thinking, "She looks just like Stephanie did when she was
born; dark hair and dark complexion. Both my children
look so alike."

As the weeks passed by, I noticed that Kaitlyn's skin
began to lighten and her hair started falling out. Eventually
it was replaced by bright blonde hair. She looked like me.
My two daughters now looked nothing alike. I marveled at

the transformation. Like Stephanie, Kaitlyn was also beautiful, but with blue eyes, fair skin and blonde hair.

My daughter Stephanie took on the big sister role and adored Kaitlyn, always wanting to hold her. On one occasion, I was videotaping them and she wanted to hold Kaitlyn. However, being too much of a worrywart, I just let her hold part of her while I held the rest. Stephanie said, "I want to hold the whole THING of her!" That made us laugh and will be imprinted on our minds forever more.

Kaitlyn was a good baby. The first night she was home, she slept through the night. I woke up horrified the next morning wondering whether or not something was wrong, but there she was, sleeping soundly. I called her doctor, concerned that she had gone so long without a bottle. He told me to count my blessings and reassured me that there was nothing wrong with her. So that's the way she was all her life; never any trouble at all.

When she was six-months-old, I started nursing school to become an RN. It was an extremely difficult and demanding course of study, but I was determined to give it all I had. Fortunately, our car was paid off at the time, enabling me to quit my job when I started college. My husband and I worked as a team to make this happen. I would go to school all day while he was at work. I would pick up the children, cook supper, wash dishes and give them a bath, so that between 7pm and 11pm I could devote my time to studying. My husband would then tend to the children's needs.

Though much of my time was filled with studying, I still gained so much pleasure from my children and spent as much time with them as possible. I was young and motivated, so I just did it. I graduated in 1993 when Kaitlyn was three-years-old and I was 33.

When Kaitlyn was almost a year old, we noticed that one of her eyes was turning in. We took her to the ophthalmologist who said that it was due to a weak eye muscle and that she would need to wear glasses to correct it. She still looked very much like a baby and I was concerned about her having to wear glasses at such a young age. I also worried that she would pull them off and stomp on them, or lose them constantly, as I would expect any baby to do. However, when she got those glasses, she never once took them off before bedtime. I imagine she could see so much better with them on that she knew not to take them off. I think she had double vision without them. She looked really cute in her glasses.

As she developed into a toddler, I began to notice how very smart she was. She was always so quick to learn anything and you never had to tell her twice how to do something.

When she was older, I liked to tell her, "I love you so much more than you love me," just to see what she would say. She would look at me with feigned horror and drew in her breath as if I had said something unthinkable. She'd say, "Momma, that's not true; I love YOU more!" We then agreed to compromise and never say one loved the other one more, because we decided we loved each other just the same. It was never supposed to be said again. It was the rule. As she continued to grow, I would sometimes say, "I love you so much m....." and I would stop before I got to the "more" part, but always act like I was getting ready to finish that sentence and she would say, "No, don't you dare say it!!" We would laugh and I would never finish the "more" part.

As the years passed and Kaitlyn entered high school, then college and eventually medical school, I would still do this with her. I would always say, "Now Kaitlyn, you're old enough to admit to the truth. You know I love you m........" and she would always shake her head retorting, "NO! Don't say it!" I'd say, "Well, you're a grown woman now, it's time you admit the truth." She would still act horrified and say, "NO!" We did this the last time she was home. This beautiful, brilliant medical student allowed her mother to joke with her in this way until she died. She loved it and I did too. Most of the time we talked about the ways of the world, books, school and spending good times together, but she allowed me to continue the inside jokes we always had, right up until she took her life.

When Kaitlyn was in grade school, she entered a geography bowl contest. I had just secured a new job as an RN and I was scared to request time off to attend the contest, but Allyn was off, so he went. He came home and said, "Rhonda, you'll never believe it. She was up there being asked questions with a bunch of other students and she kept answering the questions correctly. The rest of the students dropped out like flies and then Kaitlyn was the only one left. She won the geography bowl!" I regretted not going to see this, but I was so proud of her. That was when I really began to comprehend the depth of her intelligence.

Even when Kaitlyn was still young, I noticed how wise she was. She seemed to me to be what is termed an "old soul". I don't mean that she acted like an old person; she just had so much more wisdom, common sense and intelligence than anyone else her age. She was basically a quiet child; an introvert like me, but she always had friends whom she chose carefully. We would always have wonderful discussions and her maturity never ceased to amaze me. She seemed like an ethereal being to me.

She would spend time with her Grandmother Elkins, whom the grandchildren called "Nanny". Nanny had always been gifted with her hands; she could crochet, sew, weave baskets and that sort of thing. At an early age, Nanny would teach Kaitlyn her crafts and she would catch on incredibly fast and create beautiful works of art.

Nanny also taught her how to play games such as Scrabble, checkers and a variety of card games. I was never able to beat Kaitlyn at any game at all, except for one game of Monopoly. Her uncle Ande also taught her to play chess, which would become her lifelong love. In high school, she came second in a chess tournament between many competing schools and was president of the chess club.

That one game of Monopoly that I won though gave me some worry. As we were playing, she bought too much property and I tried to tell her she would go bankrupt if she was not careful. But she continued to do it and of course went bankrupt and lost. She was probably about seven-years-old at the time. When she lost, she became upset and started crying. She didn't cry in anger, but because losing seemed to genuinely hurt her inside in some way. I tried to tell her that she would not always win at everything and it was very important to be a good sport and accept loss with dignity. It's just that it was so seldom she lost at anything, she just could not cope with it. She did get better in time, but I still worried.

My husband, my mother, my husband's mother and I always read to our children from the time they were babies until they were able to read for themselves. Both my girls had a love for reading that continued into adulthood.

Kaitlyn was not only wise, but was also very sweet and loving. I remember one time in particular when we were in the bathroom and she had not yet taken her clothes off to take a bath and I said, "Give me a hug." She hugged me so tightly and rather than pull away quickly like so many small children do, she continued to hold onto me. She always let me know how very much she loved me and she stole my heart. Our bond grew with each passing day.

She and her sister also took lessons in ballet, jazz and gymnastics, with so many practices and recitals at the end of each year. That continued until years later when they lost interest.

From the time she was a toddler until she left home, Kaitlyn would always come to my bed on Saturdays before I got up and we would talk. She was so easy to talk to and sometimes we would lie there and talk for an hour.

As a family, we began going to Disney World when the girls were very little. It was our favorite place in the world. Every time we asked them where they wanted to go on vacation they would always say Disney World. Kaitlyn was not scared of any ride whatsoever. If there had been a ride to the moon she would have happily stood in line. She was absolutely fearless. I could not say the same for myself. Sometimes her sister and I would let Kaitlyn and Allyn "test" a ride before we got on. She was always so full of life and adventure. Many, many summer weeks were spent with our girls at Disney World.

In her 3rd grade year, Kaitlyn was placed in the academically and intellectually gifted classes and remained in them until high school where they didn't have this system. Instead, students could take AP (advanced placement) classes, which she took until she graduated. She achieved all As in all her school years before graduating.

One day, however, when she was small, Kaitlyn came to me with her little forehead all wrinkled up, like it would always do when she was concerned or worried. When she did this I would always take my fingers and try to smooth out the wrinkles as though I was taking the worry away. She said to me, "Momma, everyone at school always expects me to be the best at everything all the time and that bothers me." I told her, "Kaitlyn, you do not have to be the best at everything all the time and, as long as you do your best that is all we expect." With that, her little forehead smoothed out, she smiled and it never seemed to bother her again. Throughout the years we would talk of that conversation and I always asked her if it helped her. She said it did.

As the years passed, she became interested in writing poetry and she won some awards for her writing. This is a poem she wrote when she was 11-years-old. I thought nothing of it at the time, just a sweet little poem about angels. Now that Kaitlyn is gone, I put all kinds of meaning into her poems:

### Angels

*Angels*
*Are always looking down on us.*
*They see everything from up there.*
*They live on clouds,*
*And they always care.*

*Angels*
*Are perfect, in every way.*
*They love to make you smile,*
*And when you're very sad,*
*They go the extra mile.*

*Angels*
*Wings are made of silver,*
*Their harps are made of gold*
*Their castle is made of sunflowers,*
*As we are told.*

*Angels*
*Come and fly around us.*
*They swirl around every day.*
*And every time they visit,*
*They make things okay.*

*Angels*
*Love everyone on Earth,*
*And they will come to meet me,*
*Then we will be*
*Forever in eternity.*

*Kaitlyn Elkins 5th grade, 2001*

One day, Kaitlyn's teacher in the 7th grade called me and told me that because Kaitlyn's IQ was so high (I didn't even know she had been tested), she was eligible to take the SAT test that high school children take in order to identify academically gifted children through the Duke Talent Identification Program. She took the SAT and performed better than most high school children could ever hope to do. She was awarded a medal for this.

Kaitlyn's talents were continually emerging and she began to demonstrate a gift for art. This was inherited from my mother Lucille Sellers, as she is also an artist. During her years in high school, she took art courses and won many awards for her work. In junior high school and high school, she was in the band and played the flute. We spent many hours watching her in parades, at ballgames, competitions and concerts. She was inducted into the National Honor Society and continued to excel beyond belief in her studies and creative pursuits.

When she was 14-years-old, she heard of The North Carolina School of Science and Math. It was a free state boarding school for the academically gifted in science and math where the students would spend their junior and senior years in high school. It was completely free. If you graduated from this school, you would have your tuition paid for at any university in the NC college system you were accepted to attend.

Kaitlyn wanted this so badly. They offered courses of study that are not given in regular high schools and were very advanced. She had a new goal and that was to be accepted there. I didn't like the thought of her living away from home at the young age of 16, but I was willing to make the sacrifice for her education if that was what she wanted to do.

This was a very competitive school to get into. There are thousands of applicants across NC and there were only around 300 slots available each year. Applying for this school was just as complicated and involved as any college application, if not more so. We went there several times for tours and information workshops etc. Just one look at the campus and seeing all the students there, she just knew this was what she wanted.

After all the jumping through hoops of the application process were finished, she waited nervously for the announcements to be made. One day, a large envelope arrived in the mail informing her that she had been accepted. She was SO very happy!

Her daddy and I moved her in and made her little dorm nice and cozy with all the things she had picked out to bring. She had a lovely roommate. We got her settled and said goodbye. It was very hard for me; I didn't want to be without her, although I didn't tell her how much.

About two weeks later, Kaitlyn called me crying and said she didn't like it there and wanted to come home. I asked her why and she said it was a good school but she felt she didn't belong there. Being very concerned, I called the lady who was head over her hall and told her about this and asked if she could tell me what kind of problem Kaitlyn was having. She said she didn't realize anything was wrong, but that Kaitlyn would not come out of her room much during social time to "let others see her wonderful personality."

I called Kaitlyn back and I told her to think about it until the weekend and if by then if she still wanted to leave, I would go and pick her up. By the weekend she still wanted to come home, so I went and collected her myself.

When I went to pick her up, she looked so pale and appeared as though she had lost weight. There were several students that came in said goodbye to her, but when some of them left Kaitlyn said, "Momma that is the first time some of them have even spoken to me." However, one sweet little girl came in to say goodbye and she was sincere. She said she wanted to leave too but could not bear to tell her parents because she thought they would be disappointed with her. I felt terrible for her because there was no way I was going to make Kaitlyn stay somewhere she did not like.

This turn of events shocked me because never in Kaitlyn's past had she ever admitted not feeling part of any group. Kaitlyn was popular at school and always seemed so well adjusted and confident. She was very smart but was well respected by her classmates and had a wonderful circle of friends. Kaitlyn stopped wearing glasses at around 10 or 11 years of age in favor of contact lenses and took care of them herself so well. She was such a pretty girl.

On the way home from the school, I tried to encourage Kaitlyn to tell me, in a way that I could understand, why she didn't like it. I was extremely surprised that she did not like it after two years of wishing for it with all her might. She said that it was not that it was a bad school at all, but that it just wasn't for her and she was homesick. I figured she missed her boyfriend she left at home too, so I didn't worry about it too much.

She went back to her regular high school and took up where she left off. She was not the only one who had left the school, changed their mind and had come home, so I didn't worry about it anymore. I received the grades from the school from the time she spent there and she had made all As, so that was not the problem.

Totally undaunted by this disappointment, Kaitlyn continued to accomplish a great deal. She had a good little group of friends that were all like-minded and intelligent young people. I very much liked all the friends that she ever had. She usually always had a boyfriend and never seemed lonely or depressed.

In all of her years she never became rebellious and sulky like some teenagers do. She didn't drink, smoke, or get into any trouble. I couldn't have asked for a more wonderful daughter.

She was voted "Most Likely to Succeed" along with her best friend Ian McPherson by her high school class in her senior year. She graduated from her high school Valedictorian and her friend Ian graduated Salutatorian. Her speech was brilliant and full of wisdom. How very proud we were.

She was accepted into Campbell University in a tiny town two hours away from our home. She received a partial scholarship for it. She had been accepted into many other colleges, including UNC at Chapel Hill, which I thought would be her choice. But she told me she did not like the party and sports' atmosphere and chose to go with a quieter college in a small town. I struggled to understand her decision, but accepted it. She would have been awarded a larger scholarship had she chosen Chapel Hill because she had the highest GPA of her graduating class, but I accepted her decision. It also didn't hurt that her friend Ian McPherson also chose to go to Campbell University. Kaitlyn and Ian maintained a great friendship during the time she was there. He and she had so much in common.

Kaitlyn, who was always in a rush, vowed before her first day of class that she would graduate early. I tried to tell her, "Kaitlyn, take your time. Take the whole four years and enjoy your time at college, have fun and take advantage of it." Kaitlyn, who was always driven and in a hurry to move forward and get into medical school as fast as she could, did not listen to me at all and graduated summa cum laude in two and a half years with a degree in biology.

Before she had graduated from Campbell, Kaitlyn had acquired a job she loved as an intern surgical assistant at an oral surgeon's office.

About a year before her graduation, she called me with a proposal. She wanted to move into her own apartment. She had calculated that rent for an apartment would actually be less than room and board and a meal plan at college, and she was right. She said she wanted to move to Cary, NC, where her job with the oral surgeon was located. This would mean a 50 minute drive to school each day, but she said she did not mind. So the decision was made that she could get an apartment on her own; no roommates.

Kaitlyn came home and we took part of the money we had set aside for her college education and she and I went on a wonderful shopping spree for her apartment in Wilmington, NC. We shopped all day and she painstakingly picked out a couch, tables, kitchen table and chairs, a bedroom suite and other items. I have never had so much fun shopping in my life and Kaitlyn was SO happy.

I remember that day vividly. It was spring and her black Honda Civic was covered in pollen. I remember her putting her arms around my waist as we walked, telling me she was so happy and that she loved me. It was a day I would never forget. On another day, we spent all day helping her look for an apartment. Finally, she settled on something beautiful that we could afford. It was a safe, beautiful apartment complex and the apartment itself was really nice. Soon after, we helped her move in.

28

Then the business of applying to medical schools began. Since Kaitlyn graduated in two and a half years from college, she left in December, so she worked full time while she applied to many medical schools.

Applying to medical schools is a daunting, draining, time consuming and expensive task. The applications are expensive. Then, once you apply, if they are interested in you at all, they ask you to fill out a secondary application that costs even more money. Multiple essays have to be written and you have to jump through unimaginable hoops. The competition for medical schools is fierce. You have the brightest of the bright from all over the world competing against each other and you almost have to be able to walk on water or have taken a trip on the space shuttle to qualify.

After the application process was completed, the stressful interviews began. You are on display and you have to sell yourself as a worthy future medical school student. When all of these stages are over, you wait. Kaitlyn waited and waited. She was turned down by some and waitlisted by others before she received her acceptance to Wake Forest School of Medicine right here in NC, only three and a half hours away from home.

I remember vividly when she called me to tell me the news. I was at work taking my hour lunch break sitting on the office couch reading a book on my Kindle. She said, "Guess what? I got accepted!!!!" We both squealed, shouted and celebrated and were so happy. Her dream was finally going to come true. She had wanted to be a doctor all her life.

Thereafter followed a whirlwind of activity. She was accepted in June and had to start in July. She went on her own and picked out a new apartment in Winston-Salem where the medical school was based. She applied for her student loans and received them.

We rented the U-haul and helped her move into the beautiful apartment complex that she had picked out. All was right with the world.

Kaitlyn adapted to school very well and loved her coursework. They immediately had the students dissecting cadavers. I guess if you can stand that, you can stand just about anything. This did not bother her at all. As a matter of fact, she was fascinated by what she learned.

Nowadays, many lectures in medical school can be watched online and there were many days during the week when she did not have to attend school. Nevertheless, she would still set a strict schedule for herself and study a certain number of hours a day.

Medical school is demanding, but Kaitlyn did extremely well. They don't grade you in letter grades; their grading system is fail, pass, high pass and honors pass. She usually fell into the pass, high pass range, with which she was totally satisfied.

After about a year at medical school, Kaitlyn felt she wanted to lose weight. She was small boned and short like me, but she still felt she needed to shed a few pounds. Actually, she looked perfectly proportioned and certainly not fat at all. She was 5ft 2in and probably weighed about 115 to 120 pounds.

The running, dieting and the exercising began in earnest, as I mentioned earlier. I worried that she was running too much and that she should not run all those miles every day in addition to studying, but she said that she loved it and it helped her handle stress.

The winter before she died, Kaitlyn decided to cut her long blonde hair. She said she was ready for a change and she cut it very short. It looked good on her though and she loved it.

She continued to do well in medical school. Sometimes I would call her and she would sound a little down, but would say she was just tired, which she had every reason to be.

All appeared to be going well. Christmas arrived and she spent an enjoyable time at home with us. The following March she took the First Step Medical Board exam and felt she did very well. She came home for Easter, spent time with her boyfriend and then returned to school.

She did perform well on the Step One exam, but tragically did not live long enough to see the results.

Kaitlyn had so much potential. She was gifted in so many ways. She was an artist, a poet, a writer, a science and math whiz; successful in everything she ever did. She was driven, ambitious, sweet, goal oriented, organized and so very loving. In all her years of life, I must say that neither I, her father, nor any of her family, friends, or acquaintances ever noticed any signs of depression in her. She was independent, seemed so very self-assured and was the last person in the world anyone would have thought would take their own life.


**Blog Entry 5-13: My Kindred Spirit is Gone**

*I often thought that if I ever lost one of my children, my suffering would be unbearable, but that it would be brief. I thought I would just lie down in my bed, never eat or drink again, never bathe or change clothes and just simply die because my two girls were my world.*

*However, I did get out of bed, in addition to eating, drinking, bathing and working through my daily routine. This is so much worse, because I do everything while the tears and gut wrenching sobs come from the depths of my soul, so fiercely that I think my heart will burst from the pain of it all.*

*Oh Kaitlyn, you knew what great store I set in you and I admired you so deeply, not only because I was your mother, but because you were one of the best human beings I have ever known. You were so special. You made me feel like you always enjoyed being with me, talking, catching a movie or shopping and we always managed to fit this in during the brief times you were home from school and the times we went to see you. I sensed how much you enjoyed it and the depth of your love for me.*

*My heart is so broken; I just don't even know where to go from here. I miss you so much and though I tried as mothers do to guide you as best I could, you were also my friend and we were kindred spirits, as Anne of Green Gables always said (one of our very favorite movies). But she also said that they were not as hard to find as she once thought, but oh Kaitlyn, they are hard to find.*

*I find it so difficult to realize you're not here anymore. You're not in Winston-Salem sitting in your apartment studying; you're not out running at least every other day; you're not posting on Facebook how many miles you ran and on what days; you're not on Facebook voicing your strong opinions and beliefs and you're not sitting on the couch with your cat Gatito purring in your lap. You're not there walking around Baptist Hospital in your white coat. (In such horrible irony, that is where your body was taken, the very hospital you were to practice your clinical). You're not watching Netflix, or Grey's Anatomy or House anymore in the few moments of free time you had; you're not there inhabiting that beautiful apartment of yours filled with the things you so carefully chose.*

*You had so many talents. I use to tease you when you were growing up that in heaven, before you were born and they were passing out talents to each individual, you got in more lines than you were supposed to and possibly pushed some people out of line. (Just a joke I had). And you did; you had a multitude of talents. Some were passed down from your grandparents, but Kaitlyn, you were gifted with your own self-possessing talents and I have no idea from where they came.*

*You were born to be different, to go far and to travel far away from here to live your life. I happily accepted that because I wanted you to fulfill your passion wherever it took you. Perhaps you were too special for this world. When I was always depressed, the prevailing thought in my mind was how hard this world was to live in and how cruel so many people are. That was my sadness. But Kaitlyn, what was yours? You wrote that you were sad, but HOW were you sad?*

*I often love to reflect on movies where spirits of loved ones would visit them in their dreams or they would experience some sign of their presence. I would love for that to happen, for I know your spirit is all around me and I guess that will have to suffice.*

*I love you so much.*

Kaitlyn and I when she was little. She always loved
flowers

Stephanie and Kaitlyn

# Chapter 3

## Bringing Her Back Home

### *Last Move*

*I wake in a panic, feeling the need to do something so vital... If I could turn back the clock, it would be true. Instead, my utter helplessness in the face of time has me spinning in fear and confusion. It spurs me to adrenaline-charged action, and now more than ever I want to somehow do something important, helpful, productive; but time is unmoved by my potency, and the foolishness of my railing against such a silent foe reveals my true impotence. Why would time defend such an untimely thing? I feel lost and meaningless, with fear stalking from every trinket, photo, thought... the beautiful wall-mounted chess board she gave me stares at me, in the midst of our last game, daring me to consider what it means that the "Last Move" token hovers over my own silver knight.*

*Shannon Massman - friend and former boyfriend*

My daughter Stephanie and her husband Steve stayed at our house the night we arrived home from Kaitlyn's apartment.

On the way home, I broke the tragic news to Kaitlyn's boyfriend and all of her friends for whom she had left notes, but I had no way to reach the rest of the people that knew her. I decided that I would announce her death on Facebook for the world to see, since all of her friends had accounts.

It was very important for me to announce that her death was by suicide and the reasons she gave. I did this to make sure that no rumors would start about why she did it. I didn't want anyone to think it was because she was not doing well in school, or that some horrible event had taken place in her life. I wanted it all out there so there would be no questions about it.

Somehow, I was strong enough to do this. I was still running on numbness and shock. It was strange that I could barely function in any other way, but I could do that.

Here is what I posted on Facebook that very night:

*Somehow I am able to post this message to all of Kaitlyn's friends so they will know. Kaitlyn took her own life and is no longer with us. This happened at her apartment yesterday and was only today that the message she sent the office manager was seen by him. It turns out, in the letter she wrote to us, that she had been depressed for a very long time. We had no earthly idea, as she was always happy around us, loving medical school, her running and everything she did. She was so looking forward to her upcoming last 2 years of medical school in clinical. I know she would want all of you to know this. Our hearts are broken for our sweet girl that we didn't know was in such pain. To all her friends, thank you for being a part of her life. If anyone would like to know about her funeral arrangements, we will know by tomorrow at 11:00. But we do know it will be here near her hometown in Clarkton. Please call us if you would like to know. Kaitlyn was the sweetest person that could ever be and our joy. We will never be the same. She made very good grades in medical school......we just don't understand......*

After Stephanie and Steve went to bed, my husband and I spent the night talking into the wee hours, still unable to grasp the reality of Kaitlyn's death. Our beautiful daughter who had it all was dead. We never went to bed that night; Allyn dozed a couple of times I believe, but I did not sleep. Knowing that I would wake up and temporarily forget about Kaitlyn's death before the subsequent slam in the

chest of the reality that my baby was dead was too horrible.
I couldn't let that happen. Therefore, there was no sleep for
me.

The next day we went to the funeral home at the
scheduled time of 11:00 am to arrange her funeral. Her
body, they told us, had still not arrived from Winston-
Salem and the medical examiner had still not called them to
release her body as she had promised to do early that
morning. We were concerned, but the people at the funeral
home began interviewing us for information to put on her
obituary and formalities like that. I gave them a picture of
her and told them how she liked her hair, as it was short
then. I told her not to put too much makeup on her because
she wore very light makeup unless she was going to a
special occasion. Yes, a funeral would be considered a
special occasion I guess, but I wanted her to look as she
naturally had in life.

We were then faced with the horrible task of picking out
a casket; a casket for my baby. The thought went
repeatedly through my mind. No mother should have to
pick out a casket for her child.

They showed us all the samples they had and after much
thought we picked out a brownish one with pretty brass
ornamental decorations because she had painted some of
her walls brown and I knew she liked that color. The
funeral home staff told us we would have to pick out a
spray of flowers for her casket if we would like. A spray?
I had never been involved in planning a funeral in my life
and I did not think of this. The only place still open at that
time on Saturday was closing at 12pm, but they agreed to
stay until we got there. We picked out some beautiful
flowers; roses I think. My memory is still fuzzy about that
because I felt like a walking zombie.

During this time, many of her friends were calling to ask
when her funeral was and I couldn't remember to whom I
had spoken because I didn't know all of them. I was so

confused, but I knew they understood. Later in the day, I found out that Kaitlyn's body (Kaitlyn's "body"; I could barely even think of that term) had arrived at the funeral home.

At home, the people started arriving to offer their condolences; my family, my parents and sisters, her friends new and old, my coworkers, friends, neighbors and so many other people. They were so kind, bringing food and drink and talking to me. Somehow I did not go to my bed and die like I wanted to, but I stayed up to talk to them, holding on for dear life to Kaitlyn's Afghan and smelling it often to breathe in her lingering scent.

The first day I saw Kaitlyn was at the funeral home a few hours before her visitation on Sunday. I didn't want to see her. The thought of seeing her laying there lifeless was horrible. When I walked up to her casket with her in it, I almost passed out, so they got me a chair. I looked at her, but it wasn't her; she was not there. I could not bear staying long, so we left shortly afterwards.

When we came back for visitation that night, I stood at her casket. Many mothers touch their loved ones, kiss them and talk to them. I could not do this. I just could not touch her lifeless body that only a few days ago had had so much life in it. Once I accidentally touched her hand; it was cold and hard and it sent chills of despair through my body that I cannot explain. This was not her warm, soft skin that I so often touched and hugged.

Her sister Stephanie drew up a chair right next to her and sat there during the entire visitation talking to everyone that came to view Kaitlyn and never left her side. I don't know how she did this, but she could not leave her. And I could not be with her. I just couldn't do it.

When it was all over and everyone was leaving, I stopped by her casket to look at her body once more. I looked at her, visualizing our wonderful, loving past and all her potential and future dreams. I have her past, but her future here will never be. I kissed the top of her hair like I always did when she was alive and I smelled it. It did not smell like Kaitlyn. It smelled like someone else's hairspray. Her hair did not feel like her hair, but this did not really surprise me because who she was - and is - was no longer there. She had long gone. She was not there at all. I said goodbye to her and told her that I loved her, but she was not there to hear it.

To me, that last time I saw Kaitlyn at visitation was not the last time I saw her. The last time I saw her was when she had left our house about a week earlier to go back to her apartment; the time when she looked at me with those beautiful, sweet eyes and held me close; when I felt her warm, soft body that smelled so good. I smelled and kissed her hair like I always did. That is the last time I saw her. That was when Kaitlyn was Kaitlyn.

I'm sorry I could not hug, touch and talk to her at visitation like so many people can do. I don't know how they do it. I loved her so much; I could not bear to see her in death, to feel her body that she no longer inhabited. If I had, I would have surely died there and then.

Kaitlyn's funeral was a surreal event for me. I didn't even feel like I was in my own body, or maybe I was in a dream. I remember all the kind words and the faces that voiced their sorrow to us, but it seems as though I was in some fog; a horrible, acid fog. To be honest, I don't remember much of what was said during her gravesite service. All I remember is sitting there while it was going on staring at her casket. It seemed to me that the lid was ever so slightly open and I kept looking to see if I could see her in there, really hoping I wouldn't.

I didn't have the presence of mind to write a eulogy for her, or even ask someone if they could do it. But her sister Stephanie did write a poem for her one hour after she found out about her death and she asked the preacher to read it at her funeral:

*I miss you already*
*It's barely been an hour*
*Since I got the news*
*My heart is shattered*
*Ripped only in fragments*
*I am angry*
*And sad*
*Not yet numb*
*But I weep nonetheless*
*Because I'll never see you again*
*And I don't know how to deal with that*
*I wish I could have helped*
*I would have listened*
*But I know it's too late*
*I just want you to know*
*That I love you*
*Now and forever*

*Stephanie Alford*

When the service was over, all of the people that were there came up to talk to us; Kaitlyn's former employer Dr. Jon Won who drove the two and a half hours from his practice, many of her fellow medical students that represented her whole class who drove for three and a half hours, one of her best friends Ian who dropped everything to drive many miles from up north where he attended school, which caused him to postpone his graduation, her good friend and running partner Neal, her ex-boyfriend and continued friend Shannon, both of whom had driven many miles to come. Her ex-boyfriend Jonathan was there and another friend who drove across the country to be there. Many of her old friends from school attended, together with my friends and co-workers - past and present - and my employer. There were so many people there.

After the funeral we came back home, as did many of the people who attended. I had not been eating much, but my sister Judy had cooked something that tasted so delicious that it felt good eating it. I wondered how I could be eating and drinking at all. Why was I not in the bed unable to do anything at all? I could not understand this. It's what I wanted to do, but I felt comfort in being around people who knew me and knew Kaitlyn, and from the moment I learned of Kaitlyn's death, I could not stop talking about her. I was keeping her alive. I had to keep her alive.

Some of her close friends came back after the funeral including Neal, Nathaniel and Shannon. Kaitlyn had always had a talent for retaining friends.

Shannon sat beside me most of the time that night, in utter despair. He had continued to love Kaitlyn deeply and he was intensely distraught by her death.

Kaitlyn's pocketbook that I had taken from her home was beside me. I talked about that to Shannon and of the matching billfold that was in it and he said that he had bought that for her.

I got to know her good friends Neal and Nathaniel, whom I had never met before.

After the sun went down, we all had supper that my employer Ms. Campbell had brought. We talked throughout the night and eventually everyone went home. My daughter Stephanie and her husband Steve stayed the night.

The next day after it was all over, everyone left. Allyn and I were left alone to continue to try to make sense of it all and cry. That was all that was left to do then, but that would not be all I would do as the days, weeks and months went on. I had to do more. There were too many questions still.

41

## Blog Entry: And You Are Gone

*I see your smiling sweet face and eyes that I have known and loved for 23 years, sitting across the table from me at the Chinese restaurant we took you to the last day I saw you when you left to go back to medical school. I reach out to touch your hands and your image crumbles like a pile of ash and there is nothing there.*

*I feel you in my arms as I give you that last hug and smell your hair, wish you a safe trip back to your apartment many miles away, telling you to call when you get there. I see your black Honda Civic pulling out of the drive and see you waving bye to us and the image fades away before your car rolls a foot down the road. Vanished.*

*I see your image in my mind that spans the 23 years of your short life. I feel the hugs you gave me as you lingered in my arms. I feel the love you gave so freely to me even during times when most teenagers push away. You never did. I hold you tightly in my arms and then, all of a sudden, my arms are empty.*

*I see you standing before me in your cap and gown with the gold tassel and medal that indicated you were valedictorian of your High School Class. I hear the words you said during your speech, so full of hope and happiness. I see you in your cap and gown when you graduated undergrad summa cum laude. I turn away for a second and you are gone. Caps and gowns lying on the ground.*

*I listen to all your hopes for the future, your love of medical school. I sit there amazed at all the things you've learned and I wonder how in the world anyone can contain all that knowledge in one's head. I see you so excited and so happy telling me you were going to be a doctor and be the best at what you became; how doing this was what you were born to do. I see the light and happiness in your eyes. I still see you telling me these things at my kitchen table, or at the restaurant we would often take you to when we visited you. I pause for a second to take it all in, and your words are silenced and you disappear. Where did you go? What happened to the words?*

*I sit and I wonder what you are doing today, if you are in class or are able to listen to your lectures online at your apartment. I wonder if you have had your run today, or whether you went the gym. I wonder if you will you answer if I try to call you, or whether I would get your voicemail. I wonder if I post something on your Facebook, whether you would comment back. I wonder if you are getting out and having fun in the midst of all your hard work. I pause during these wonderings and the need to wonder blows up like the eruption of Mt. St. Helens. Nothing but ash and smoke.*

*I see you standing before me Kaitlyn. I see how pretty you are; your pretty blonde hair, your fair skin, your delicate features, the way you held yourself, the way that anyone who looked at you knew without talking to you that you had a great depth and maturity in you. I see the extremely fit body you had developed within the past year and see the results of your hard work, though I always thought you perfect before. I see you before me, one of the most wonderful people I've ever known, feeling so blessed to have you for my daughter; feeling everything important to you, was important to me. I see you standing there Kaitlyn, with an intelligence and wisdom I have always admired, knowing without a shadow of a doubt that you would conquer this world on your terms, become a great physician, continue all your wonderful pursuits. One day when your life settled, you would have time for your other talents; sewing, crocheting, drawing, writing.*

*I see you; there you are. All the years of seeing you evolve and grow into the amazing woman that you have become. You are standing there in your jeans, your blouse and those beautiful black boots. Your pretty blonde hair starting to grow out now like you said you wanted it to do.*

*You wanted your long hair back. I see your eyes, so full of life, light and happiness. I see you looking into my eyes, into my soul, knowing how much I cherish you. I see you Kaitlyn, and then piece by piece, small blocks, like a digital TV losing its signal, pieces of you disappear until there is nothing left. Where you stood just a moment ago is an empty space. Before the last bit of you has disappeared, I reach for you to try to bring you back, but my hands go through you; there is nothing left to grab hold of, and you are gone.*

*I go to your grave Kaitlyn and I feel the stone that is at its head. I touch it; it is hard, it is final, it will never disappear. Oh, if I could only see it disappear and not even leave ash behind like it's never been there, I would give my life. But it remains, hard stone and final.*

*I keep reaching for you Kaitlyn; I see your delicate hands reaching out for me to grab you, and at the last minute before I can touch you, you pull away and you are gone. And you are gone. Gone.*

Kaitlyn standing proudly in front of her beautiful Christmas tree during her last Christmas before she died, December 2012. She named it "Charlie"

Kaitlyn and I in Washington, DC 2008; the last vacation we took together when she was 18. This was one of the pictures hanging on her wall in a beautiful picture frame. It now hangs on the wall beside my bed. I trace her image often with my fingers

# Chapter 4

## The Aftermath and the Pain of Reality

*And can it be that in a world so full and busy, the loss of
one creature makes a void in my heart, so wide and deep
that nothing but the width and depth of eternity can fill it
up.*

*Charles Dickens*

After Kaitlyn's funeral, though I still had some element
of numbness, I was in a terrible state. All this pain! It felt
as if my insides were going to explode and I had no way to
ease the feeling. It was at that time I started reaping the
benefits of Facebook.

I had a Facebook account before Kaitlyn died, but it had
started as a means to keep in touch with my daughters'
lives. Gradually, I began posting a few more things like
cute cat videos and just silly, superficial things. I had
always been very private about my personal life and only a
minimal part of it was shared publicly.

I really began to notice the outpouring of affection and
condolences from people whom Kaitlyn and I knew. Many
of her friends were posting on her Facebook page. The
messages, the private messages and the emails came
pouring in.

Then I began writing about Kaitlyn, about my staggering
disbelief that this could have happened and about my grief
and my unbearable pain. It all just came pouring out of my
mind and onto the screen via my keyboard. This is the only
way I could continue to live; the only way I could cope
with such a devastating loss. It was to be the beginning of
my insatiable desire to write, to question, to research. My
brain could not be still. I needed to vent; I needed to find
reasons for my daughter's suicide. She said she died due to

depression, but I had never in my life heard of anyone being so brilliant with everything going right in her life, who showed no signs of depression, taking their own life.

A few days after her funeral, my husband and I were faced with the daunting task of going back to the town in which my daughter had lived and attended medical school to clean out her apartment. On the first day, Allyn and I went there by ourselves, gathered up Kaitlyn's belongings and put them in containers. Then we went to a motel for the night.

The following day, Allyn's two brothers Ande and Ashley came to help us load the containers up and lift out the heavy furniture.

Allyn said his mother wanted to go with us on the first day, but we wanted to go by ourselves. I wanted my baby's things to be sorted through and packed up by us and no one else. This was very important to me.

When we got back home from her apartment, I wrote the following for Kaitlyn, which portrays so many of the feelings I had in doing this most painful process.

**Blog Entry 4-13: Cleaning Out Your Apartment**

*Kaitlyn, we went to your apartment today to clean out your things. When I opened the door, the scent of you still lingered. In every room, every piece that you had there, your spirit was there. My hands have touched and gone over every one of your possessions in there because I felt you in every one. The living room suite, the bedroom suite, the lamps and tables; all the things we had such fun buying on that special day in Wilmington. Oh Kaitlyn, why would anyone who was contemplating ending their life have a refrigerator and pantry full of food ready for the many upcoming weeks? Why would you have clothes that you bought only days before for your clinical rotations, if you were never to wear them? Some of the clothes still had price tags on them.*

*In handling your many books to store away, I felt inside every single one. I felt the blood, sweat and tears you invested into studying for the Step 1 Medical Board's exam, which would determine which residency you could apply for. You felt so good about the test, yet never knew the results. Your white coat for clinical hung in your closet, never to be worn again, complete with your stethoscope in one of the pockets; your nametag hanging on the front.*

*I sat on your couch, which I knew was your favorite place to sit. You were there. I lay on the bed where you took your last breath and I cried, recreating in my mind your final moments of life. Even after they took your bed out, I lay on the floor in the exact same place. I could feel you there. I wanted to die there too; my pain was so awful. We had not long before helped you move into this place Kaitlyn; now we were moving you out, but not in any way I would have ever guessed.*

*In your bathroom Kaitlyn where you once so proudly showed me how beautifully you decorated it with the wall hangings and the cabinets, rugs and shower curtains you bought for it, your towel was still on your towel holder, your bath sponge you recently used and your shampoo, conditioner and razor were still there, as if you had just stepped out of the shower. Your cabinet held the special case that contained your makeup. The pain I experienced in having to remove these things because you would never be able to use them again is beyond description.*

*There were memories on your wall; your trip to Africa, sitting with African children, pictures of your dad and me, you and me and some of your friends - all telling a story. But no story is good enough my sweetness, in telling of the truly special person I had the honor to have in my life for 23 years. You were so intelligent, wise beyond your years, deeply thoughtful, artistic and talented in so many ways. I*

49

*feel though, that you were lonely in your soul, yet I didn't know it. We introverts go into ourselves so much and nobody knows the depths of our pain and loneliness, even those closest to us. I just hope in your heart that you knew just how many people loved you and how many lives you touched.*

*I died inside with each and every thing of yours I touched a million times over today. And as I looked back before walking out of your apartment for the last time, your scent and spirit was still there, but then I took you with me, where you will be in my heart forever. My love for you is bigger than the universe.*

Having to clean out and pack up all Kaitlyn's belongings was undoubtedly one of the hardest things that I have done since her death. It was even more horrible than her funeral. At least during her funeral I had the luxury of being numb and in shock. But with this, I was all there. Pain seemed to be shooting into every cell of my body. Each and every thing I touched of hers screamed out to me of memories. My daughter's life was there. All the things she had painstakingly picked out and bought with her wonderful taste, all packed up in boxes; just packed up in boxes.

I never could find all the new clothes that she bought on our shopping day together during Easter break. However, I did find many items of clothing that still had price tags on them that she had recently bought during her trip to see her boyfriend. I knew this because they had the name of the city on their price tags. "Oh why Kaitlyn? Why would you buy new clothes only to go back home to kill yourself? Suicidal people don't do this. If anything, they give some of their things away," I thought. Why would she have a refrigerator full of recently bought groceries, never to eat them? The more I learned, the less I understood any of this.

In the middle of all my packing up and working and wondering, I was plunged so far into despair about my youngest daughter killing herself; someone whom I believed was the happiest person in this world.

I was extremely surprised that I did not die the moment I learned of her death. I had always thought that if either of my children were to die, I would die right along with them. I wouldn't kill myself, but I would mercifully die by a heart attack or something, for surely there would be no way I could live through this horrendous pain. But I didn't die. I lived to endure the perpetual hell into which I was thrust.

Once we got home, we put all her possessions in our garage. I felt a great drive to do something with her things so they would not develop mildew out there, so I decided to categorize everything, trying to decide what to keep, what to give to some of her friends, what to give to her sister and what would go to goodwill.

In hindsight, I wish I had just put everything I could in my house and let it stay there until I had the presence of mind to handle her belongings in a way that I would not regret later. But I felt the urgency to do it. Perhaps I just had the urgency to keep busy, to have some purpose.

I went through her clothes, which was the hardest of all to do, pausing frequently to bury my head into them and cry. Her scent permeated everything, which brought me to my knees in grief. She would never wear those clothes again. For some reason, I thought I had to be practical, so I went through them and placed practically everything in a container to give to my mother-in-law to give to goodwill. Isn't that what people do with their deceased loved one's clothes? That's what I always saw in the movies. It proved to be my greatest regret of all regarding her belongings.

I also felt a great mix of emotions. How dare I? How dare I go through all the beautiful things that she so carefully, excitedly, happily and painstakingly bought? She never bought anything lightly; everything was for a purpose, whether it was for leisure, functional purposes, or for beautifying her apartment, which she decorated so expertly. She had the most wonderful taste in everything and bought the most high quality items. How could I go through those things, deciding where they would go? Those things were HERS!! Pieces of her life that told so much of her story and the unique person that she was. How dare I pass them on as though they were only things? Her soul was in them. Oh God, what torture it was!

I kept a few of her clothes however; some select blouses and her new blazer that she bought on our last shopping trip. I also kept her white coat that she wore in medical school and the things that were left in their pockets; a high quality stethoscope, a notepad and a little chart of medical information. Hanging on the outside of the coat was her nametag with "Kaitlyn Elkins, Medical Student. Wake Forest Baptist Health", complete with her beautiful picture. Underneath this tag was another tag that said "I Care". And she did.

In hindsight, I wish I had kept every single item of her clothing. I did not begrudge goodwill getting them or St. Jude's, but now that so many of them are gone, I so wished I had them back. All the time she spent in those clothes, her spirit still inhabited them I felt.

I gave all her jeans away and it tears my heart to pieces not keeping at least one pair. What was I thinking? I gave away all her pretty dresses that she wore to operas, the symphony and to plays. All her coats and other possessions were placed in containers to give away.

I decided to keep what was in her dirty laundry basket and started to wash it all. I stopped after I had only put a couple of items in there. No, I would not wash them, ever. They still sit in my spare room to this day just as I had found them and are still in the laundry basket. Her pleasant scent is still infused into them.

I kept most of her furniture and kitchen supplies and gave the things that I could not use to her sister Stephanie, such as her nice bedroom suite, kitchen table, etc. I kept everything that was in her living room and gave my old living room furniture away.

I gave all of her medical books back to her med school so they could give them to someone else who needed them. The only one I kept is the book she used when studying for her Step One Medical Board exam.

I gave all her running equipment, clothes and shoes to her good friend and running partner Neal, so that maybe he could find a worthy recipient for some items and keep what he wanted. As it turns out, he kept them all as memories, which I think is a very good use. He did, however, send her running shoes back to me because he knew I regretted giving all her shoes away. This is the kind of person Kaitlyn kept as a friend. Wonderful.

I gave her climbing gear to a friend of hers whose hobby was rock climbing. Kaitlyn had a brief love affair with rock climbing, which she found exhilarating. I, however, found this nerve-racking, but Kaitlyn was fearless. She did not pursue it because I think she simply did not have time, but of course, she had some nice rock climbing gear.

I sent her skiing boots off to goodwill. Looking back, I wondered who would find skiing boots of any use at all. I feel that was a wrong choice, but I knew of no one who skied or would have worn her size. I should have kept them.

I did not regret giving the books way, the running and climbing equipment and all I gave to Stephanie. I felt in my heart that Kaitlyn would not want these things sitting dormant somewhere collecting dust, but would want them used by someone who needed them and would appreciate them.

In dividing up and giving away all the equipment that she used in the many exciting things she did in her life, I winced at the irony that someone who seemed to enjoy life so much, that had so many adventures in life, had so many things left she wanted to do, would take her own life.

I kept many sentimental items of hers like her running tags that hung on her during marathons, her medals, her Wake Forest School of Medicine backpack and her jewelry. So many things like that I put away in boxes to keep forever; pieces of her life just thrust in boxes and hidden away.

One of her many adventures in her life was her trip to Africa. I want to include her experience to demonstrate her love for life and the beauty of this world.

## Kaitlyn's Trip to Africa

Back in May of 2010 when she was 20, Kaitlyn was in undergrad at Campbell University and went on a trip to Tanzania in Africa with members of some of the faculty and students to assist a medical facility and orphanage there. This was an exciting experience for her, going into the medical field as well as wonderful trip to a vastly different country.

There was much planning for this trip. She had to have vaccines and a passport had to be obtained. She spent many hours in class learning about the local culture and what they would be doing there. She so looked forward to this trip and I was extremely excited for her.

When they first arrived, they were able to experience the best of Africa, such as a safari and staying in a fine hotel. But after that, it was on to the orphanage to help in a clinic. From then on, Kaitlyn was not able to email and lived a very sparse existence, like they all do in that area.

I listen to a radio station that plays a variety of music from the past and present and they often play the song "Africa" on there. While Kaitlyn was away, I heard that song many times and thought of what she was doing there. After she came home, I still heard it many times. Now that she has gone forever, I still hear it and it takes me back to that time.

This was to be the first of many trips around the world that she would take in her lifetime. Now her passport lies dormant in a box that looks like a book on her table in my living room. I also have memories of what she told me about the trip, items that she bought there, pictures that she had on the walls of her apartment and the emails she wrote.

Below are excerpts from two emails that she wrote when she first arrived in Africa and had internet access.

## 5-24-10

*We are here in the Ngorongoro Crater, and it is breathtakingly beautiful. Today we went on safari through Lake Manyara, and it was absolutely gorgeous. We saw baboons, impalas, warthogs, lions, buffalo, hippos, egrets, and so many more that I'm forgetting about already. It was absolutely amazing. We are staying at the Ngorongoro Sopa Lodge, which is probably one of the finest hotels I have ever stayed in. I had lamb stew tonight, and we were serenaded by traditional African folk music. I watched the sunset over Ngorongoro, and I cannot describe how beautiful it was. I never expected it to be this gorgeous. It is just something you have to see to believe. Tomorrow we go into the crater, and then we set out through the Serengeti. After that, we head out to Ntagatcha village, then to Shirati.*

**5-25-10**

*Today we safaried down into the Ngorongoro Crater, and I must tell you that is the most breathtaking place I have ever seen in my life. It is absolutely gorgeous. We saw a lioness with three cubs, and it was almost reverent. We also saw two black rhinos, another pride of lions, a herd of elephants, along with zebras, impalas, gazelles, wildebeest, hyenas, dozens of exotic birds, and many more. After the crater, we journeyed into the Serengeti, and that is where we are staying tonight. My room overlooks the plain, and I watched the sun set tonight. It was absolutely beautiful. I cannot wait to tell you all about it .Tomorrow is the last day of our safari, and we are heading to Ntagatcha village to the orphanage.*

# Chapter 5

## A World of Devastation and Questions

*Unable are the loved to die. For love is immortality.*

*Emily Dickinson*

There is no way that I can articulate exactly the depth of my horrendous pain and sorrow at Kaitlyn's death. Her loss thrust me into the pits of a living hell on this earth that I didn't know could exist.

There were times before her death when the ghastly thought would slip into my head, "What if one of my children ever died?" At those times, I would shove the thought to the back of my mind as quickly as I could, because it was just too horrendous to contemplate. Now I'm living with the reality that what was previously too awful to imagine, has come to pass. If I could not bear thinking about it then, how in the world would I be able to live with it now? I had no idea, but I was still waiting for death to take me. Surely there would be no way my body, mind and soul could survive this horrific assault; this amputation of an essential part of me. No one could live through this. My daughter was dead.

I have never before lost anyone with whom I have had a close relationship. I lost my father-in-law, which although very sad could not compare - and certainly could never prepare me for losing my daughter. My days consisted of waking up and remembering that Kaitlyn was dead; that she killed herself; that she had everything to live for, but she ended her life. My days were filled with excruciating pain that originated deep within my soul and I cried for hours, several times a day. Videos in my mind played repeatedly from the time she was born on up until the last day I saw her. They would not stop. My mind would not stop. My tears would not stop. Intermingled with this pain was my intense desire to write about her, about losing her, about my disbelief and my pain. If I didn't write, I would die.

Along with my intense grief and deep need to write, was my need to ask questions; to find out how something this horrible should ever come to pass. Yes, Kaitlyn wrote that she was sad and how she could no longer stand the weight of it, but WHY was she sad? Why, why, why?? I simply had to root out the answers to these questions. My daughter was too happy to have been sad, much less sad enough to end her beautiful life. Something like this simply did not happen to people like my daughter who had such a bright future. They just didn't. So, the questions and my search began.

I had to start with the situation that I thought could very well be the source of her sadness; romance. Many times that is the origin of so much sadness, so this is where I started my search. She had been in a relationship for four months with a man who lived several states away. She had visited him for a week before she returned home and killed herself, just a few days later. Seeing him so recently, then coming home and ending her life seemed too suspicious. I had not met him, but that was not going to prevent me from asking him questions.

Kaitlyn would sometimes meet people through online dating sites after she went away to college. This thought made me cringe, because I was of the old-fashioned mindset that this could be so dangerous. People can pretend they are anybody online and fool others. Once you meet them, they could be nothing like you thought or, at the very worst, have a sinister ulterior motive. I just had to accept the fact that this was the way it was done these days. I'm online so much myself and have formed many friendships through forums and Facebook, so I really had no ammunition to prove my point other than the horror stories I've seen on TV, which I would relay to Kaitlyn.

She always assured me that she was very careful and would only meet someone for the first time in a public place, like a restaurant.

What would bother me the most though, is when her online dating searches led her to people who lived so far away. I tried to tell Kaitlyn that a long distance romance was nothing but a recipe for loneliness. Yes, you can communicate by phone, text, Skype, Facebook and sometimes go on visits (which would involve plane fares, etc.), but the vast majority of the time you would be at home lonely, only living for those communications and limited visits. At first she told me she would never have another long distance relationship, but eventually she fell in love with someone she met who did live many states away. She told me about him before she came home the previous Easter.

Kaitlyn was a pretty girl and had no trouble attracting attention from men, but she was very particular about the kind of person she dated or spent time with. I feel that she had trouble meeting people that she could relate to and that is why she chose online dating.

Her boyfriend's name was Shai, a professor of electrical engineering at the University of Michigan. The only time I had ever talked with him was to inform him of Kaitlyn's death. He told me that he had been trying to get in touch with Kaitlyn since the Wednesday night and was just about to call us when I called him. He said it was unlike Kaitlyn to go so long without contacting him by text message, phone, or Skype. He said he had been very concerned.

I came flat out and asked him, "Shai, you must tell me, did you and Kaitlyn fight or break up during her visit? If you did, I understand, because sometimes it just happens and I would in no way blame you. I just have to know." He told me it was quite the contrary. They had had a wonderful visit. They were talking about a life together when she graduated medical school and she was already looking into hospitals there where she might obtain a residency. He said there was nothing to indicate she would go home and do what she did. He said they were very much in love. He was devastated by her death and, like everyone else who knew her, in a state of disbelief.

I had even asked Kaitlyn when we picked her up from the airport after seeing him if now that she had spent more time with him, did she think more of him or less. She smiled very sweetly and said "more" and said she had had a wonderful time.

We had drawn a blank there, so what next?

I then went on to question her ex-boyfriend Shannon. They had dated for two years and had broken up the previous December, but had remained friends. However, they had not been communicating much for a number of weeks since Shannon's new girlfriend did not like the idea of Kaitlyn remaining friends with him. Did missing him and losing him in some way devastate Kaitlyn so much that she didn't want to live? Their separation was a mutual decision, but still sometimes these things have intense emotions attached to them. Nevertheless, they had both found someone else, so that theory made no sense. However, Shannon felt terribly guilty about not being able to talk with Kaitlyn before her death and felt that if they had still been communicating, Kaitlyn may have reached out to him. He should not feel guilty, but he does. In no way do I blame him. They had both moved on.

I asked him if Kaitlyn ever seemed depressed when he was with her. He told me that she had been down at times about regular things in life, but never anything to indicate she was depressed. He said that most of the time when they talked about things, she would feel better and bounce right back as if she had not been down at all.

So nothing there either. I continued my questioning.

I asked her running partner and close friend Neal if she ever seemed depressed to him. He said she never did. He said she seemed to have her life well under control and was always cheerful around him. They were in daily contact, at least by text. He said she would always text him early in the morning and ask how his day was and wish him well. They would also sometimes go out to eat, cook for each other and go to events. He said Kaitlyn always seemed so happy.

Nothing wrong in that situation either.

I continued to receive floods of emails from Kaitlyn's old friends, newer friends, acquaintances from near and far, teachers from school and just so many people who all said what a special and wonderful person Kaitlyn was. All stated that though Kaitlyn was quiet, each and every one of them was struck by what a beautiful person she was. Many said that she helped them by talking to them when they were depressed, never once letting on that she was depressed herself. No one knew.

I went on to ask Kaitlyn's friends from childhood, high school and college whether she ever appeared depressed. No one said she did.

I asked Ian, who was her best friend through high school and college, about Kaitlyn. He said that she and he were very similar in their beliefs and intellect. He said that sometimes they would both be somewhat depressed and lonely, but they always talked about it and made each other feel better. He loved Kaitlyn very much as a friend, but once they graduated undergrad, he went up north for his graduate studies and Kaitlyn went on to medical school. They were no longer in touch in person, but kept in contact by text, email and calls. However, their contact became less frequent due to the distance and demanding nature of their class work.

I looked through her phone messages, her email messages, her Facebook and her computer files to try to find some kind of sign that would indicate the source of her sadness, or any writing about it. Again I found nothing. In life, I respected her privacy and would never dream of reading her private things, but in death I just had to look at what she left available to me to try to find answers. I found none.

Kaitlyn was a very thorough person in everything she did. She thought out her suicide very carefully and prepared for it as though it were one of her many school projects. I don't know how many years she had thought about reaching the point of no hope and what she would do, but I'm almost positive that she thought about this for a long time. I believe this in hindsight, but never dreamed of this before she died. She left all her email from 2008 on her computer, yet her history had been erased, although I don't know whether she had amended her settings to delete it automatically each day. All her outgoing mail was also erased, but she left me with five years' worth of incoming email. Again, I found nothing sinister that would make her want to take her own life. I found no gradual downhill spiral into depression; I only found hope, joy and excitement.

Though I did all this snooping, and tried to justify my actions, I felt very much like a voyeur; invading her privacy, reading things she never intended her mother to read. I felt guilty. I still do. But I just had to read it. I had to see if there was something there to answer my questions. There was not. But I wondered if she left these messages there for a reason. It was unlike Kaitlyn to forget to do something, even in the frame of mind she was in when she ended her life. She did so much planning in that state of mind, so why would she forget this?

The only thing I found was a book of writings and poetry that she started when she was 17 and ended when she went away to college. Many of these were love poems; some of them sounded sad, others were happy, some were religious. I had never seen them before. I found one piece of writing in her diary that reflected so much of how

Kaitlyn felt about life and lived her life. How could anyone believe that she was hiding severe depression?

At times I wonder why she kept this little diary in her current things that she had not written in for five years. I will never know the answer to that.

**A Letter to my Younger Self by Kaitlyn Elkins 8-24-07, age 17**

*First this: love and love often. Love like yesterday never happened and today is all you have, all you'll ever have. Love like it's the only thing that matters because you'll soon find that it truly is. Say I love you, but show it more than that. Let your love be strong, and let it be for all: the undeserving, the unworthy. Let it be willing to be unrequited, but let it be willing to be returned as well. Let yourself be loved, even when you don't deserve it. Open yourself up to the power of love: how it can make the ugly beautiful, the weak strong, the fearful courageous. Make your life a love song, real and unromantic.*

*Learn to pursue. Pursue people, relationships, knowledge, wisdom, and truth, but most of all truth. Saturate yourself with what is true when you find it and fight fiercely to keep it close; build your life on its foundations. Know that you will have to fight to keep what is precious to you; be willing to. Don't be passive, don't be complacent, don't be content where you are. Know that you could be better; know that uphill battles are the only ones worth winning.*

*Give of yourself. Don't be selfish, don't seal up your heart. Know that you are a treasure, that you are precious and beautiful. Know that every single person you meet is just as valuable. Try to realize how important people are and conclude that you will never fully know. Invest in people, in relationships. Challenge your friends and be challenged by them. Grow with people, alongside them.*

*Keep your promises. Sacrifice yourself; your comfort, your fear, your laziness, your apathy, for those who need you. Learn to need as well. Be willing to lean on a friend, be willing to trust. Bare your soul. Let others be changed by you, and change for them also. Cherish everyone.*

*Discover who you are. Learn why you are here, discover what your purpose is, find out where it is you should be going. Cherish the journey, but always face your destination. Don't betray yourself, follow your heart and never stop searching. Be willing to take chances, to risk. Know that living your life means you won't always be safe. Don't long for what is comfortable or easy, but for what is true and good and pure. Know that you will probably get hurt along the way. Know that the victors carry heavy scars. But know that you will find what your heart cries out to.*

*Know that you are imperfect, that you will make mistakes. Don't put yourself on a pedestal, or in a hole in the ground. Discover that you are missing something, that you need something outside yourself. Begin to know that you're not in this alone nor could you survive it alone. Learn to forgive yourself and others; constantly. Never give up on yourself or on others. Don't veil yourself, the mistakes you've made, the flawed person you are. Don't put on pretense, don't be ashamed of yourself. Know that you are human, but learn from your failures and become stronger because of them.*

*Express yourself. Dance, sing, laugh and cry and smile when you are moved to. Do not live under fear. Do not do what is appropriate, do not conform, do not fit a stereotype; be true to yourself. Be passionate; keep your flame burning brightly. Appreciate others who do the same.*

*Learn to hope. Know that where you will end up is better than where you started. Have confidence that you will get there, that you will get there not entirely by your own hands. Have faith that promises made to you will be*

*fulfilled. Learn to trust. Be willing to go through the valley*
*before you can reach the mountain top. Know that you*
*won't get there alone, that you'll be able to share your joy*
*with others. Be patient, hold out for things you cannot see,*
*but you know are there waiting. Know that you will get*
*where you're going.*

My daughter lived these words. She was absolutely
amazing. What happened to her to make her forget the
words "learn to hope and to know that where you end up is
better than where you started?"

Since it didn't appear that anything in her personal life
had caused her depression, I thought maybe it had
something to do with school. As I had mentioned
previously, before she came home for Easter the last time,
she had spent the previous six weeks studying intensely for
the Step One Medical Board Exam. This was, she told me,
the most important exam in medical school, as it can
influence the type of residency you are offered when you
graduate medical school.

After Kaitlyn began medical school, I learned many
things I didn't previously know. I had assumed that when
you went to medical school, you would eventually study
the field in which you aimed to specialize. Then, once you
graduated, you would take up residency to gain further
experience in your chosen field under the guidance of other
MDs. What I learned is that you go through medical school
studying generically with the other students until
graduation. However, before graduation you undergo
"matching" where a student applies to residencies that they
are interested in and subsequently qualify for by test scores.
The most important test scores are those achieved in the
Step One Medical Board Exam at the end of 2nd year and
then the Step Two Medical Board Exam toward the end of
the 4 years. The higher you score in these exams, the
greater chance you have of obtaining one of the highly

competitive residency places. I thought you just picked out your specialty and applied for it. It does not work that way. You only apply to the residencies for which you qualify with these scores and through your performance in medical school. These residencies pick you, not the other way around.

Kaitlyn had been studying for the Step One exam on and off since she started medical school, but toward the end of her 2nd year, and during the six weeks off to study for it, she studied intensely. I found that during those six weeks, she studied 10 hours a day, taking a 10 minute break each hour and, I hope, more for lunch. She was absolutely driven to do well on this test.

When it was over, she had told me she felt very good about it and did not seem to worry about it at all.

After Kaitlyn died the thought hit me, "What if she found out her test score was not good at all and that drove her to kill herself?"

Of course, I then contacted one of the deans from the school to find out if she knew about her test score before she died. He assured me that she did not know the score because they had been released to no one at the point when she took her life.

I know how very determined Kaitlyn was to perform well in everything and although she did not expect to make the top grades in her classes in medical school, it was extremely important for her to do well on this particular test. I had feared if it was not good it could have been the last straw, but that was clearly not the case.

I later learned that Kaitlyn did very well on the test and she would have been well positioned to obtain the residency that had looked appealing to her; anesthesiology.

All Kaitlyn's life, even as a little girl, she had always wanted to become a doctor. Every time anyone ever asked her what kind of doctor, she would always say, "Cardiac surgeon!" As the years passed, just the word "surgeon" would come out of her mouth when asked what she wanted to be. However, once she entered medical school she realized that most of those residencies last 7 years and they work horribly long hours and are on call a great deal. She decided against becoming a surgeon because, as she told me, (and she also told me this the last time I saw her), she wanted time to get married, have children and enjoy a family life one day. Anesthesiology appealed to her and she felt by doing it she would have more time to devote to a family. It's so sad that her dreams will never be realized. So unlike my daughter to leave anything unfinished. But she left the rest of her life incomplete and I still don't understand.

I know that she must have been in severe emotional pain to do something that she knew would devastate me. However, I do not have any anger toward her. I too have struggled with depression for a long time and I know the depths to which you can sink. The difference is that I asked for help and I wish she could have done the same, or at least have given us even a hint that she felt this way. My heart and my soul went into that grave with her and my life will never, ever be the same. No matter how bad the world was outside, and it is a hard world, there was Kaitlyn and my connection to the few good things that are in this world. I only hope that she is at peace. My grief and my pain are beyond anything I could have ever have imagined. I would live in horrible pain for the rest of my life if only she could still be here and in peace.

**Blog entry 5-13: I Do Them No Justice**

*Kaitlyn, I walk around my house that is filled now with the things that inhabited your apartment. I will always cherish them, but I do them no justice. I have the nice spice rack, the blender and the multiple knives' set in the wooden block, the chopping block. Kaitlyn, you know I'm no great*

67

*cook and didn't think of it as an art like you did, so I can't do them justice. You were a wonderful, self-taught gourmet cook.*

*I have the nice wine rack with 3 bottles of unopened wine, complete with an array of wine bottle stoppers. I don't drink wine and wouldn't know the difference between a bottle from Walmart and one from a vineyard in Italy. But I cherish them.*

*I did have all of your running clothes and running equipment, so I just had to do them justice and find another home for them. I don't run.*

*I very mercifully sent your ski shoes and your climbing equipment to a new home. I would break my neck if I tried to ski and when you rock climbed I had visions of you falling down the thing, so I would never climb rocks or mountains.*

*I kept some of your symphony and opera magazines, but I've never been to one, even though I always wanted to go with you. We never took the time, always saying we would do it soon. You knew I was very interested in going and we looked forward to it.*

*I still have many of your books that you left here when you went away to college, but strangely, you didn't have as many in your apartment as I thought you would have, other than your medical books. I never could find White Oleander that I let you borrow once, but that's ok. There were just a few, some of them being C.S. Lewis and Pablo Neruda. I even kept those hauntingly prophetic books by Sylvia Plath that you had bought just before your death (I saw the receipts inside). She was a depressed woman and I wonder whether or not it plunged you further into despair, or whether you just wanted to relate to another very intelligent, successful woman who was also very depressed and ultimately killed herself. I don't know. You left the vast majority of your books here before you went away to college. I can relate to you very well in reading because we are a family of readers and you and I shared many of the same interests in that area. I can do the books justice.*

*Your furniture now fills my living room where it displays your good taste. My living room never looked so good because you had as much taste in your little finger as I have in my entire body.*

*I have your pictures from your trip to Africa where you went to help children. I've never been so selfless to do something like that, but you did.*

*You had a professional camera with all the fancy lenses. I know no more about picture taking other than pointing my simple camera at something and shooting. But I will keep it.*

*Kaitlyn, my gift that I have is being able to do something if I really, really put my mind to it and have an interest in it. Your gifts were many and came easily for you. And oh how I admired you for them all. I was so proud of you! So I keep all these things, though they were far beyond my capabilities and abilities to use them well. I will keep them in your memory, and who knows, maybe I can learn, but I did not have your innate ability to be cultured and refined and so I'll just stumble along. Where did you come from Kaitlyn?*

*One would think that with all our differences we would not be close, but we were. We had many other interests that we shared like science, astronomy, books, and just the great interest in the meaning of life and so many other things. We had a special bond. Sometimes you could read my thoughts. Sometimes you would finish my sentences. I asked you one day if I was just so predictable and I said the same things all the time, or did you just know me that well. You always said you just knew me that well. How nice it felt to have someone really know me.*

*I guess what I'm trying to say is that Kaitlyn, I admired you so much for the person you were. You were wise beyond your years, possessed a keen sense of understanding that not many people have, an intellect along with common sense, and I have never seen one thing that you could not conquer when you had an interest in it. Heck, you even mastered things in school you didn't necessarily like, but did anyway. Unfortunately, you were a good actress too. I didn't know this ability in you until after you were gone, because you always acted so happy. But Kaitlyn, there was just one thing you could not conquer and that was depression. And for reasons I'll never understand, you never sought help. Unfortunately, you succeeded in one last thing, because you never did anything half way; you succeeded in ending your life.*

*I cry every day, several times a day, and your departure from this earth and its circumstances is beyond anything that can ever be eased. I will never forget any single thing about you; your smile, your kindness, your affectionate ways even when you were little that continued on until the last day I hugged you goodbye.*

*I always thought you were sent to me to take care of, to love, to raise and then to release you into the world where you belonged, doing great things with the intellect that you had; mine to have until I had to let you fly away. Kaitlyn, I had no idea you would go this far.*

Kaitlyn and Stephanie

Kaitlyn in 2011

# Chapter 6

## My Own Personal Experience with Depression

*Depression is a disorder of mood, so mysteriously painful and elusive in the way it becomes known to the self - to the mediating intellect - as to verge close to being beyond description. It thus remains nearly incomprehensible to those who have not experienced it in its extreme mode."*
*"[However], the sufferer from depression has no option, and therefore finds himself, like a walking casualty of war, thrust into the most intolerable social and family situations. There he must ... present a face approximating the one associated with ordinary events and companionship. He must try to utter small talk and be responsive to questions, and knowingly nod, and frown and, God help him, even smile.*

*William Styron (Darkness Visible)*

Though Kaitlyn and I were very close, she obviously hid a major part of her life from me; her depression. Though we also shared similar interests and spent wonderful times talking and being together, we were still very different people. Her experience in school was vastly dissimilar to mine. She was motivated, goal oriented and a super achiever. I was anything but that, though I did change later in life. I'm not stupid by any means, but my intelligence did not touch hers. I admired and loved her so much.

I suffer from depression myself. However, I never hid mine from those I loved as Kaitlyn did.

Let me tell you how I feel when I am depressed. I can tell when I am becoming depressed because I start feeling very disillusioned with the world and most of the people in it. Instead of trying to see the good in things and people, I see all the worst, and start thinking that the majority of what goes on in this world is evil. There is evil in the world of course, but seeing it becomes intense for me. Normally, I see the best in people and I'm enthusiastic about travel, the world, scenery, doing things, etc. When I'm becoming depressed, I, who always loved looking at scenery as I travel because everything looks beautiful to me, start thinking the world is ugly because everything that is actually ugly, is what I focus on. All of this makes me very sad. For example, on a motorcycle trip to Key West once with my husband (a very long trip), we took the back roads and I saw so many dilapidated buildings, nice places that were simply abandoned and falling apart - just ugliness. I could tell on that trip that I was descending into depression. When I'm depressed, I start seeing the world in black, white, and gray; no color. I know my eyes see the color, but my mind does not. It's like perpetual winter and everything looks dead.

Then I start wondering just what I have given to the world, which I think is not much (except being a good wife and mother which I have always prided myself on. At least I love them and am good to them). I don't do enough for people; I don't go out of my way to help people and I'm selfish and ungiving. I don't have close friends because I don't take the time to cultivate friendships, so it's my fault. I think that when I die there will be no one but my family at my funeral. This thought always runs through my head when I'm depressed, which caused me to tell my children once that when I die, I want no church service, just a few words, cremate me and throw my ashes into the mountains of NC off the Blueridge Parkway somewhere. No visitation because I'm sure hardly anyone would be there except my family and I didn't want my family embarrassed by this. These are very selfish, bleak and hopeless feelings I experience when I'm depressed and I'm ashamed of them. But when I'm depressed, this is how I feel. I guess I feel worthless.

I have since changed my mind about cremation, but don't want a visitation except at my house and a graveside burial right beside Kaitlyn. Once before Kaitlyn died, my daughter Stephanie asked me if I still wanted to be cremated. I said, "Oh no, I've changed my mind. I forgot to tell you." She said, "Well mom, I'm glad I found out because there's a big difference between being buried and being thrown off the side of a mountain." I agreed.

Kaitlyn never spoke of feeling the way I described above and I don't believe her feelings of depression were the same for her. I just think she was endlessly sad, but at no particular thing or people. I don't know for sure. It's just a feeling I have.

I have had suicidal ideation many times in my life. I started having depression when I was 39 (1999) and I took medication for a while. I felt better and depression left me alone for 10 years. Then I started a very stressful job, I went through menopause and I had an empty nest (all at the same time). In 2009, the depression returned and has never left. I have struggled horribly since then and have experienced personal situations that made it even worse. I have admitted myself into mental hospitals voluntarily a few times due to suicidal thoughts, because I did not want to hurt the people that loved me. That made the difference, but the two I thought about most of all were my children. I could not leave them with the legacy of a mother who killed herself following them around the rest of their lives. I envisaged Kaitlyn having to put her medical studies on hold due to being so devastated and forever wondering whether this would end up happening to her. I saw my daughter Stephanie being equally distraught, affecting her future and causing her to be depressed. So when I found myself at the edge, I would seek help. Not everyone can do that, because the pain is so horrible, but for some reason I was able to reach out.

During this time, believe it or not, we had a stable home life. There was never any drinking, drugs, smoking or anything in our home. I worked regularly except when I was in the hospital and then once stabilized I would go back to work, functioning quite well. My children never had a disruptive, dysfunctional home. We were very involved in their lives. We went to church every Sunday, which they seemed to enjoy. The only thing was that I was depressed, and the worst of it happened after they had both moved away to build their own lives. They always knew what was going on with me, but I never really told them how horrible it was, or the things that I went through in trying to obtain the right medication. It felt as though I tried a million before I was finally prescribed something that worked. I went through many mental health care professionals for various reasons; either I was not pleased with them, or they were too far away etc.

To be even more honest, I was not a happy child or teenager either. I was cripplingly shy and introverted, which caused me to be scared to death to do anything at all where people would actually have to look at me. I didn't fit in anywhere because of this. I was terrible in school because I felt mentally paralyzed by my shyness. I didn't know what was wrong with me, but I felt so ashamed. Looking back I know I was depressed, but I didn't even know what that was then. I thought I was just an awful person who didn't fit in anywhere. I never told anyone, especially my parents. My mom just thought I was shy and that she didn't have anything to worry about. I never told her. There was no reason for her to think something was wrong with me. I was shy and a poor student; that is all I let her know. It was no one's fault that no one knew.

Miraculously, not long after I graduated from high school, my depression disappeared and didn't reappear until I was 39. I enjoyed myself more and took greater pride in myself, though I was still very shy and continue to be so until this day, although it is no longer crippling anymore. Depression has played with me all my life.

The last time I saw Kaitlyn the week before she took her life, she asked me how I was coping with my depression and I told her I had been doing very well for a year and that I had finally found one medication that kept my depression at bay. We talked about the medication, which she knew very well because she had already studied all of this in medical school. She said she was so glad. Then we started talking about other things and she never even hinted at her depression. One week later she had taken her own life and I was left devastated and clueless.

So, I have this horrible guilt. Though I know it was not my fault, she inherited her depression from me. I always thought severe depression was noticeable. If I had thought it could be hidden so well, I would have worried about the possibility of her having it. But she was SO far away from being a person that I would think would suffer from mental illness that I never had a clue.

However, no one knew I was depressed in my youth, but even so, I did not go around conquering the world like Kaitlyn did either.

I know from my own experience that everything can be going so right in one's life, yet one can still be depressed because most of the time it is a chemical imbalance and is not related to any life situation or personal circumstances. I had a wonderful husband, two beautiful children, a comfortable home and a good job, but none of it would fill the hole of emptiness and sadness I felt when my depression became severe.

What makes it so much worse, if you are someone that seems to have it all and people know you are depressed, is that they think, insinuate and even sometimes go so far as to tell you that you have no right to be depressed because there are so many more people worse off than you. Then you believe that, which makes you feel more depressed AND guilty. But that's not how depression works.

I mistakenly thought that all depression was noticeable. I was so horribly and terribly WRONG and I didn't even know it.

That is my experience of depression and how I feel when I'm going through it. I am of no danger to anyone but myself when I'm like this. Depression is horrendous. You feel hopeless, helpless and the world is gray. I know when it's happening to me, I know when it's coming on and I know when I've reached the edge. But I never went around talking about it. In 1999, I kept it as much of a secret as I could. Since 2009, I talked about it with some of my family and co-workers, but I never got up and announced it to the world, because it is simply something you don't want to do; you think people will treat you and look at you differently and often they do. This must change. Depression is an illness, a disease that should be treated and not be stigmatized.

I remember the last time I admitted myself into a mental health hospital for a few days. This was the worst experience of depression I had in my life because it was also accompanied by panic attacks caused from a side effect from a medicine that made my thyroid barely function. It was dreadful. When I went back to work, I talked to someone I confided in a lot and I told her that this was the worst experience I had had so far. I wasn't going to talk about it much, because I never did, but she stopped me short and said, "You know, talking about it usually makes it worse." I got the hint, shut my mouth and never mentioned my depression to her ever again. These are the things you go through with depression. No wonder people do not admit to it. But just remember, treatment is so worth it; not everyone has to know. It would be far preferable than being where my youngest daughter is now, three miles down the road in her grave.

During the depths of my depression, I wrote a poem to Kaitlyn. I don't think I ever showed it to her. I felt like I was on the edge and might not be around to see her reach her goals.

### Beautiful Flower

*I see you there*
*In the misty memories of my mind.*
*Bright new, golden flower,*
*Beautiful flower of mine.*

*I see you there,*
*Sun kissed dew on your leaves,*
*Reaching for the sky*
*Like a gull upon the seas.*

*I see you there;*
*Your flowering will never end,*
*The universe you'll reach without me,*
*Never to descend.*

*I see you there*
*In the misty memories of my mind,*
*Bright, young, strong flower,*
*Beautiful flower of mine.*

*Rhonda Sellers Elkins, June 3, 2011*

Ultimately, she did reach the universe without me, but not in the way that I had expected.

In writing about what I have experienced with my depression, I realize once again that everything I knew about depression, all the signs to watch out for, simply did not apply in Kaitlyn's case. Nothing in my nursing classes, nursing jobs, or my own personal experience gave me any idea that there were people achieving great success and appearing cheerful, yet inside wanted to die.

I knew very well that mental illness is thought to be inherited, so I watched my children carefully. I never once sat down with Kaitlyn and asked outright, "Are you depressed?" I didn't feel the need to ask her. This girl had the world figured out and she knew what she wanted. She was one of the most remarkable people I have ever known. How would seeing this give me the slightest hint that I needed to ask her that question? However, I frequently asked her if she was happy, whether she was spending enough time having fun and whether she had friends. Each and every time I asked, she assured me that she was happy and took time for herself between her studies.

My perception of my youngest daughter was a person who was highly intelligent, goal oriented, creative, full of common sense, sweet and loving and who achieved everything she set her sights on. This is what I saw; what everyone saw. This is how she presented herself and it was so believable. She was also something neither I, nor anyone else, realized; severely depressed.

All the signs I had learned to look for were wrong. Everything I had read about, or had heard spoken about at seminars about depression did not apply in Kaitlyn's case. These signs they speak of are true for many depressed people, yet never in any book or article or lecture have I seen or heard included, "Then there are the people that show no signs and seem very happy…." It's not there; not that I have found anyway.

According to the Mayo Clinic website, possible signs of depression include:

- Feelings of sadness or unhappiness
- Irritability or frustration, even over small matters
- Loss of interest or pleasure in normal activities
- Reduced sex drive
- Insomnia or excessive sleeping
- Changes in appetite - depression often causes decreased appetite and weight loss, but in some people it causes increased cravings for food and weight gain
- Agitation or restlessness - for example, pacing, hand-wringing or an inability to sit still
- Irritability or angry outbursts
- Slowed thinking, speaking or body movements
- Indecisiveness, distractibility and decreased concentration
- Fatigue, tiredness and loss of energy - even small tasks may seem to require a lot of effort
- Feelings of worthlessness or guilt, fixating on past failures or blaming yourself when things aren't going right
- Trouble thinking, concentrating, making decisions and remembering things
- Frequent thoughts of death, dying or suicide
- Crying spells for no apparent reason
- Unexplained physical problems, such as back pain or headaches

Obviously, there are some symptoms of depression that no one can see, but I never once noticed any of the above signs in my daughter; not once in my whole life. She received so much attention too, so it was not that I did not spend enough time with her to notice these signs; they simply weren't there.

Having said that, once she started college, I did not see her as much and when she began medical school, I only saw her about once a month. So much of this could have been happening and I would not have known. However, none of her friends noticed any signs of depression either.

According to The National Foundation for Suicide Prevention's (NFSP) website, these are some warning signs displayed by people who are thinking of suicide:

"Most of the time, people who kill themselves show one or more of these warning signs before they take action:

- Talking about wanting to kill themselves, or saying they wished they were dead
- Looking for a way to kill themselves, such as hoarding medicine or buying a gun
- Talking about a specific suicide plan
- Feeling hopeless or having no reason to live
- Feeling trapped, desperate, or needing to escape from an intolerable situation
- Having the feeling of being a burden to others
- Feeling humiliated
- Having intense anxiety and/or panic attacks
- Losing interest in things, or losing the ability to experience pleasure
- Insomnia
- Becoming socially isolated and withdrawn from friends, family, and others
- Acting irritable or agitated
- Showing rage, or talking about seeking revenge for being victimized or rejected, whether or not the situations the person describes seem real

Individuals who show such behaviors should be evaluated for possible suicide risk by a medical doctor or mental health professional."

Again, I saw none of these signs as obvious in Kaitlyn. Whether she thought these things or not I don't know. It's clear now that she must have, but they were never apparent to anyone.

In many cases, it is possible to spot a depressed person. They actually look depressed; no smiling and an evident disinterest in activities that they once loved. Some people can't even get out of bed, bathe, or change their clothes if it is very severe. None of these applied to my daughter.

My investigations into her life, asking questions of all her friends and inquiring about her grades in medical school, all led me to a dead end regarding any clear reason for her depression. It was not something that happened to cause this. I became absolutely driven and obsessed in finding the answers.

I knew you didn't have to have a circumstantial reason to be depressed if it was caused by a chemical imbalance. This I understood. However, I just could not wrap my head around the fact that my daughter could be depressed all her life, yet act completely to the contrary. It defied explanation.

Shannon expressed his emotions and pain of losing Kaitlyn on her Facebook page frequently after she died. Following is one of those entries:

*When it's late and I fail to sleep, I can still hear you, see you so vividly.*

*The part of me that is reserved for empathy with you, for knowing what you are thinking even when you aren't here, and for predicting how you will feel from day-to-day in response to events, is still calculating in your absence; running, detached from any reality. It is a part of me forever lost, a phantom limb that I still reach for a handle with, opening only grief.*

*And it calls into question what I valued most about myself. It seems I've deceived myself. Tragically deceived you, for you always told me I truly saw you, knew you as no one else did. And I believed you, or you believed me. I cannot say which. But I can say I did not foresee this.*

*You cared so much. You cared about the things that most people with your intellect can't be bothered to invest in. You wanted to make a difference. To promote harmony across all social groups and beliefs. To foster environmental conservation. To improve the poor state of our medical system. To help people.*

*You cared deeply about your family, your friends. About me.*

*When I first posted here about this, I already knew I would be forever altered, but also knew that I couldn't predict in what manner. Unfortunately, it seems the form that change is to take is most akin to an injury.*

*And I've tried so hard to grow from this, as I told you I would. I've tried to leave that voice in my head that is what remains of you to lend me aid. But I'm afraid I'm not doing so well, because instead of the keen insight you brought me, it brings a sadness I haven't felt since I was very young.*

*I'm still here Kaitlyn.*

*Shannon Massman, 5-29-13*

# Chapter 7

## Amazing Discoveries

*When people are suicidal, their thinking is paralyzed, their options appear spare or nonexistent, their mood is despairing, and hopelessness permeates their entire mental domain. The future cannot be separated from the present, and the present is painful beyond solace. "This is my last experiment," wrote a young chemist in his suicide note. "If there is any eternal torment worse than mine I'll have to be shown.*

*Kay Redfield Jamison (Night Falls Fast: Understanding Suicide)*

All my questioning of Kaitlyn's friends - past and present - and looking through anything that she left to which I had access, did not give me any satisfaction as to why she took her own life, or more accurately, how she kept her severe depression so hidden for so long. I felt this very powerful drive to continue on with my quest to find out answers.

I began to read many books about recovering from the suicide of a loved one because I needed all the help I could get. Though they were good, each and every one contained the story of their loved one who committed suicide and all of them showed some sort of sign beforehand. I found one book particularly helpful in helping me know that all the mixed up horrible emotions I was going through were normal. But what I now needed was a book that told of the seemingly successful people that took their own lives, yet showed no signs of depression whatsoever. I never found one. So I started searching for articles of any kind online.

Here is an article I found helpful on Yahoo Voices by Sherri Granato. 12-6-06.

### *The Common Link Between Writers & Mental Illness.*
### *Mental Illness and Brilliance Go Hand in Hand*

*"Many well-known artists, writers and musicians have had a history of mental illness. In fact some of them have become so deeply depressed that they eventually ended their own life in an effort to stop the pain and suffering. So, could there actually be a link between artistic creativity, brilliance, and mental illness? Several studies have suggested that there is indeed a very strong link and that writers or people with strong creative capabilities are more likely than others to suffer from a class of mental illnesses that fall under various categories from mood disorders to major depression, and manic-depressive illness.*

*An examination of writers concluded that poets tend to be the most emotional and introspective among all writers, and had a much higher rate of mental illness than nonfiction writers who tend to be the most rational and analytic. Many researchers that have surveyed people with creative minds speculate that mood disorders allow people to think more creatively. In fact, one of the criteria for diagnosing mania includes sharpened and unusually creative thinking.*

*Does brilliance go hand in hand with mental illness? All of the famous people listed have suffered from some form of mental illness.*

*Patty Duke, Connie Francis, Peter Gabriel, Charles Haley, athlete for the Dallas Cowboys, Kristy McNichols, Spike Milligan, Abigail Padgett, Charley Pride, James Taylor, Mike Wallace, Kurt Cobain, Elton John, Sheryl Crow, Axl Rose, Ted Turner, Robin Williams, Winston Churchill, Princess Diana, Edgar Allan Poe, Hans Christian Andersen, Charles Dickens, Michelangelo,*

*Vincent van Gogh, Sylvia Plath, Anne Sexton, William
Faulkner, F. Scott Fitzgerald, Ernest Hemingway, Margaux
Hemingway, Marilyn Monroe, Audrey Hepburn, Drew
Carey, Judy Garland, Jim Bakker, Abraham Lincoln,
Richard Nixon, and Virginia Woolf."*

Yes, the above does answer the question that I already
really knew; that sometimes many brilliant and creative
people are susceptible to depression and some have even
gone on to commit suicide. But of the ones that I know
about, though they were brilliant, all of them showed signs
of depression before they took their life. Sylvia Plath was
known for her depression and even attempted suicide once
before she eventually succeeded in completing suicide.
Vincent Van Gogh also showed signs as indicated when he
cut off his own ear. Ernest Hemingway was obviously
depressed before he ended his life. Virginia Wolfe showed
severe symptoms before she ultimately walked into that
river with rocks in her coat. Kaitlyn showed no signs. I
continued to be confused.

I found the following article on perfectionism entitled
*Perfectionism and Youth Suicide* by Hilary Thomson from
The University of British Columbia online.

*The headlines are shocking, confusing and all too
familiar. A teen commits suicide without warning, ending a
life full of accomplishment and promise - a seemingly
perfect life. But UBC Psychology Prof. Paul Hewitt
suggests that a seemingly perfect life could signal the risk
of teen suicide.*

*"Most people don't understand the toxicity of
perfectionism," he says. "Perfectionists put enormous
pressure on themselves, making their lives far from
perfect."*

*Hewitt and Gordon Flett of York University are conducting a variety of studies to examine the relationship between the need to appear perfect (perfectionistic self-presentation) and suicide, including studies that include youth. They are also testing a model they developed, called the Social Disconnection Model (SDM) that links social disconnection with perfectionism and suicidal thoughts. One study looks specifically at the social disconnection markers of bullying and feelings of social helplessness or never being able to fit in.*

*"Suicide rates are increasing among youth," says Hewitt, a registered clinical psychologist. "We urgently need to know more about the mechanisms of perfectionism, how it starts and how it develops. If we are to provide better interventions and targeted treatments, we don't need more evidence that perfectionism is a problem, we need to know why it's a problem."*

*Fuelled by fears of rejection and abandonment as well as a strong need to belong, be approved of and cared for, individuals with perfectionism do whatever is required to get the acceptance they need. This difficult path is characterized by severe and routine self-criticism, retreat and disconnection from the world as well as frustration, anger, and depression.*

*Hewitt has been intrigued with perfectionism from the time he was an undergrad at the University of Manitoba in Winnipeg. He has conducted extensive research on perfectionism and its relationship to problems such as suicide, depression, personality disorders, as well as relationship, achievement, and health problems. He also conducts research on the treatment of perfectionism and provides assessment and treatment for individuals with perfectionism problems and trains clinicians in the treatment of perfectionistic behaviour.*

*A recent study involved working with children and adolescents aged 8–20, to complete a variety of questionnaires and scales that measure: perfectionistic behaviors, need to appear perfect, experiences of bullying, social hopelessness and suicidal thoughts and actions. Participants were involved in psychiatric outpatient counseling for anxiety and depression at B.C. Children's Hospital.*

*"The perfectionism and suicide connection among teens is especially relevant because of adolescents' inherent self-consciousness and concerns about social relationships," says Hewitt.*

*Perfectionist children believe if they are perfect others will like them and won't abandon them - they can fit in. However, just the opposite happens. The child is seen to be someone outside the norm of the group and therefore a perfect target for bullying. Worsening the situation is the fact that teens are known to hide their negative feelings, making them especially vulnerable to depression and suicide.*

*There is a real difference between needing to be perfect and needing to be excellent, Hewitt emphasizes. Striving for excellence can motivate individuals. Striving for perfection can hinder individuals. It can lead to procrastination to avoid possible failure or unconscious self-handicapping so the goal of perfection is not tested. For example, an individual may enter a race without having trained sufficiently. When they don't win first place, they can blame the "failure" on the lack of training rather than their own imperfection.*

*People who need to appear perfect are often difficult to be around. They can be hostile, rigid thinkers, and exquisitely sensitive to criticism, earning rejection by others. The phenomenon is called a neurotic paradox - the individual creates the very outcome they so desperately want to avoid.*

*Hewitt has worked with artists, entertainers, physicians, elite athletes and others who can become paralyzed by their perfectionism and suffer from writers' block and other aversion behaviors. Their sense of disconnection and alienation from others, the most feared state of the perfectionist, makes them vulnerable to suicide.*

*"I have worked with extreme perfectionists for many years and I am still surprised by the depth of their pain and the level of their desire to die," says Hewitt.*

*Perfectionism is a basic personality style and treatment is intensive and long-term, made uniquely difficult because patients do not want to disclose any problems.*

*"Perfectionists try to be the perfect patient," says Hewitt. "Our goal is to help them see and accept who they are under the perfect façade."*

*More information about perfectionism may be found on the FAQ section of Hewitt's website at: http://hewittlab.psych.ubc.ca/*

I found the above article very fascinating. Kaitlyn was a perfectionist and I think she put great pressure on herself to be as perfect as possible. She did not display all of the signs above, like being hard to be around or appearing angry, but I can see so much of her in many of the things that were written in this article. Of course, during her life, my thoughts were that striving to be the best she could be at everything was not in any way a character flaw and I thought she thrived on it and it made her happy. If I had only known that it could have possibly been killing her.

Then I started looking up articles on medical school students and doctors and I was shocked to find out the following information about the medical profession. I came across a very informative article on medical student and physician depression and suicide and contacted the author, Louise B. Andrew, MD., J.D., F.A.C.E.P. who graciously agreed to let me include her article (one of many she has written on the subject) in my book. She is an expert in this field. Her website is Black-Bile.com: http://www.black-bile.com/index.html.

Here is the article that sheds so much light on the difficulties that medical students and physicians face with depression:

**Physician Suicide**

**Overview**

*It has been reliably estimated that on average the United States loses as many as 400 physicians to suicide each year (the equivalent of at least 1 entire medical school class).*

*Sadly, although physicians globally have a lower mortality risk from cancer and heart disease relative to the general population (presumably related to self care and early diagnosis), they have a significantly higher risk of dying from suicide, the end stage of an eminently treatable disease process. Perhaps even more alarming is that, after accidents, suicide is the most common cause of death among medical students.*

*In all populations, suicide is usually the result of untreated or inadequately treated depression, coupled with knowledge of and access to lethal means.[1] Depression is at least as common in the medical profession as in the general population, affecting an estimated 12% of males and 18% of females. Depression is even more common in medical students and residents, with 15-30% of them screening positive for depressive symptoms.*

*However, because of the stigma often associated with depression, self reporting likely underestimates the prevalence of the disease in both of the above populations. Indeed, although physicians seem to have generally heeded their own advice about avoiding smoking and other common risk factors for early mortality, they are decidedly*

91

*reluctant to address depression, a significant cause of morbidity and mortality that disproportionately affects them. Depression is also a leading risk factor for myocardial infarction in male physicians.*

*Perhaps in part because of their greater knowledge of and better access to lethal means, physicians have a far higher suicide completion rate than the general public; the most reliable estimates range from 1.4-2.3 times the rate in the general population. Although female physicians attempt suicide far less often than their counterparts in the general population, their completion rate equals that of male physicians and, thus, far exceeds that of the general population (2.5-4 times the rate by some estimates).*

*A reasonable assumption is that underreporting of suicide as the cause of death by sympathetic colleagues may well skew these statistics; consequently, the real incidence of physician suicide is probably somewhat higher.*

*The most common psychiatric diagnoses among physicians who complete suicide are affective disorders (e.g. depression and bipolar disease), alcoholism, and substance abuse. The most common means of suicide by physicians are lethal medication overdoses and firearms.*

## Depression in Medical Trainees

*Prospective medical students and residents are extremely unlikely to report a history of depression during highly competitive selection interviews. The prevalence of depression in these populations and in medical student and postgraduate trainees is unknown, but it is estimated to range from 15-30%. [28] After accidents, suicide is the most common cause of death among medical students.*

*One report has suggested that depression is not uncommon in pediatric residents (up to 20% self reported in 3 programs). This preliminary study found that residents*

92

*who experienced depression may be as much as 6 times more likely than nonaffected controls to make medication errors. Other studies have confirmed the association of depression with self-perceived medication and other errors. Stressful aspects of physician training - such as long hours, having to make difficult decisions while being at risk for errors due to inexperience, learning to deal with death and dying, frequent shifts in workplace, and estrangement from supportive networks, such as family - could add to the tendency toward depressive symptoms in trainees.*

*Harassment and belittlement by professors, higher-level trainees, and even nurses contribute to mental distress of students and development of depression in some. Even positive workplace changes, such as translocations to secure further training or job advancement, can contribute to job-related stress.*

*A few schools are implementing programs to recognize and deal with depression and other stresses in medical trainees. The American Foundation for Suicide Prevention has created a video on the topic for physicians and other medical trainees.*

Now some things are starting to make a little more sense. I had no idea that the suicide rate among MDs was so high, nor was I aware of the prevalence of depressive symptoms among medical students. Of course, I knew that medical school and being a physician had to be extremely stressful, but I had no idea of the above figures.

I have been in contact with some medical students since Kaitlyn died. Some say that there would be no harm to a medical student's education and career if they admitted to any form of mental illness and that they should seek help if they have problems in that area. However, there are others that say a mental health diagnosis is the death knell to a medical career. What is one to believe?

If it's true that a mental health diagnosis will harm a medical school student's education and chances at a career, then no wonder so many students do not seek help for their depression. But it needs to be stressed that one's life is so much more important than not being able to continue in medical school. Of course you would have a hard time telling a perfectionist that this is true. Some would rather make it "on their own" than potentially risk ruining their dreams of a medical career by admitting they suffer from depression. However, again, I have no idea if this had anything to do with Kaitlyn's depression. Obviously from her note, she was depressed for many, many years prior to medical school and she never sought help then either.

I wish to emphasise that if someone is severely depressed or has severe mental illness and is unable to function, it is unlikely they would be able to practice as a physician. However, it is also important to know that a student should not fear reporting their problem, so that they can receive help for it without jeopardizing their career. Many medical students, doctors, PhDs and other successful people who have had mental illness, were treated and went on to pursue successful careers. But one must have a chance first. If these professionals had not sought help, they may not have lived to be successful.

I remember when Kaitlyn was at the verge of applying for undergrad colleges and choosing her major. I talked to her many times about making sure that being a doctor was what she really wanted because I knew that it would be such hard work in school and extremely stressful. In addition, it took so many years to become an MD, following which the lengthy hours of work and pressures of the occupation could also take their toll. I told her to make sure. She said that she was sure this was what she wanted to do.

I discovered again what I already knew; that creative, brilliant people are prone to depression. I also found out some things I didn't know; that perfectionists have a high rate of depression and suicide and that there is a high rate of depression amongst medical students. I also found out that a mental health diagnosis may or may not be detrimental to a medical school student's education and career. But it still didn't satisfy me. It still didn't explain how someone like Kaitlyn could be highly functional until the day they died. This was nowhere to be found no matter how hard I searched on the internet or in books. Somewhere there has to be answers. I just could not quit until I found out.

## Blog Entry 8-13: Field of Stones

*"Kaitlyn, your tombstone has finally arrived. It came from across the ocean from India and is now at the monument place I bought it from. It's been there a few weeks now, but I had to wait for the sketcher to come to do the scene I want on it. He came today and I had to make sure everything would look good with placing of the sketch, picture and lettering before they proceed.*

*Oh it's a beautiful tombstone Kaitlyn. Worthy of the beautiful person you were and the beautiful spirit you are. It's a shiny, smooth black granite stone in the shape of a teardrop. Your picture that has been somehow transferred onto an oval smooth stone is beautiful, crisp and clear, showing how beautiful you are. This will go near the top near the curve of the upper part of the teardrop. Below that will be the inscription, "I Love You Bigger Than The Universe"; something I've told you almost every time I saw you, or emailed you or called you your entire life. Because I do. I love you bigger than what the universe can contain. My love transcends all that is above us; our universe, our galaxy that holds billions of stars, to the other billions of galaxies that also hold billions of stars, which is more than our mere human minds can comprehend. The light-years of space; my love fills that up and spills over. It has and always will.*

*Below this inscription will be the beautiful sketching that the man that came all the way from Georgia will be inscribing onto your stone. It will be the scene of a beautiful beach with the sun setting into the ocean. It will be intricate and beautiful. Below this will be your name, Kaitlyn Nicole Elkins. Below that will be 1-19-90 to 4-11-13. As beautiful as it will be, it can never come close to being as beautiful as you.*

*As I stood there next to the stone as it was sitting on the platform and the sketcher was marking the areas all of this would go for my approval, I ran my hands over the smooth, slick, shiny black stone. I thought about what it would represent; the beautiful person that it will honor. But nothing any human could ever come up with could fully represent your magnificence in all things, but I did my best. I thought about the engraving; how this in no way was any engraving I would ever want to see associated with you....an engraving on a headstone. The engraving I was so looking forward to was a plaque at your medical practice that read, "Kaitlyn Elkins MD". That plaque will never be so I'm enduring what no mother should ever have to do; the supervision of the words that will go on this stone in a field of other stones that will let people know for years that you once graced this Earth. But they will never know the whole truth; the whole truth of what a remarkable person you were and how very much I love you; how much so many people loved you.*

*It will soon be placed at the head of your grave in a graveyard that is very old. One day your grave will be very old and I will be gone, but your stone will still shine like glory, just as your presence illuminated this world. I love you Kaitlyn.*

Kaitlyn's headstone

Shannon and Kaitlyn

# Chapter 8

## I'm Lost, We're All Lost

*When someone you love dies, and you're not expecting it,
you don't lose her all at once; you lose her in pieces over a
long time - the way the mail stops coming, and her scent
fades from the pillows and even from the clothes in her
closet and drawers. Gradually, you accumulate the parts of
her that are gone. Just when the day comes - when there's a
particular missing part that overwhelms you with the
feeling that she's gone, forever - there comes another day,
and another specifically missing part.*

*John Irving, A Prayer for Owen Meany*

In addition to my hurt, my sadness and my quest to find
answers, my husband described the feeling of me "sliding
down a slick well with everyone's hands trying to bring
you out, yet you keep sliding down." I just looked at him,
knowing he was telling the truth. As a matter of fact, I
described this feeling during my phases of deep depression.
I would say he was accurate in his assessment of what was
going on with me.

What really confused me is that even though my
husband loved Kaitlyn just as much as I did, he didn't show
his grief in the same way. Everyone has their own way to
grieve. When Kaitlyn died, he took two weeks off from
work and then he had to go back. He had no choice. He
could not stay home immersed in grief because someone
had to make money to pay the bills. However, one week
after Kaitlyn died, I realized it would be a long time before
I could even bear the thought of going back to work. I
called my boss and resigned, knowing that they would have
to hire another nurse, because I was the only one there, and
realizing I would not have a chance at that same job again.

I have not mentioned Allyn's pain and the pain of my eldest daughter Stephanie much in this book. They both handle their grief differently. As I had mentioned before, Allyn does not like to write about anything; he does not particularly like to read books and he doesn't spend hours researching suicide and mental illness the way I do. He does not post on Facebook, he does not have a blog and he does not make video slides of our daughter. He is a very intelligent man, but these coping strategies do not resonate with him and that is not wrong at all. He may think that delving into it makes things worse and perhaps it would for him. We talk about how much we love Kaitlyn and how very sad and devastated we are without her. Sometimes he cries. If he talks to other people about her, he will occasionally break down and cry. I think he tries to be strong for all of us. His feelings are deep and private, but he feels her loss greatly and is as hurt as I am. We all have our own ways of grieving and as long as they are not destructive, it is OK.

My eldest daughter Stephanie, who is 28 at the time of this writing, is devastated by the loss of her little sister. She is married, going to school full time to obtain her bachelor of nursing degree, and works. After Kaitlyn died, Stephanie made a great effort to stay in contact with me more often and devised ways to get me out of the house to do things that we both love. Stephanie and I have different interests to those which Kaitlyn and I had. For instance, Stephanie and I love ghost stories, ghost tours, history and touring old, historic houses, shopping in quaint little shops, browsing through old book stores and, if you can believe this, going to the Oakdale Cemetery in Wilmington, NC. We love to go there because it is VERY old and some well-known people are buried there. For instance, Rose Greenhow is buried there; she was a civil war spy for the south and drowned off the coast of Wilmington. Unlike the modern cemeteries of today, back then tombstones were very ornate and all were unique. So, we do these things and then go out to eat.

Stephanie now calls me almost every day. I don't know whether she is trying to make me feel better, or make us both feel better, but being with her does lift my spirits. She has days when she is strong, and then days when she can barely study because she is so sad at the loss of her sister. She sometimes calls me crying, but she is coping as best she can. She's sad that her children to be will never have an aunt and that Kaitlyn's children that she would have had and her children will never get to play together as she had dreamed.

My parents and my mother-in-law are deeply saddened by the loss of Kaitlyn. All the years of being with her as a child, teaching her things, loving her, watching her grow into a wonderful young woman and then having to suffer the loss of her is so hard on them all; not to mention all of her cousins and other family members. Our entire family has been tragically altered.

My days at home were filled with being on the internet and writing about Kaitlyn, her life, my grief, and anything I could about her because it gave me relief. When I was not doing that, I was making video slides set to music about her. I talked about her to anyone who would listen. And I cried. Oh how I cried. I do believe my tears could fill an ocean. There were times when it was so bad I would be on the floor of the spare bedroom - where I have so many of her things - crying and feeling like I would die at any moment. I would often pick up the clothes in her clothes' basket, look at them and smell each item one by one, remembering her wearing every piece. At other times, I would just grab an armful, hug them tightly and pretend that it was Kaitlyn.

I often pick up her running shoes, cling to them, and almost feel the pounding of each foot on pavement, grass or dirt on which she ran. I'd sometimes go through her billfold looking at her driver's license and the old expired ones she kept in there, seeing the way had she matured over the years.

I sometimes take out and look at each card in her card folder, the credit card that she paid off each month, the Victoria's Secret card and shopping cards that I have no idea if she ever used or not. I look at the change in her change compartment and the bills in the bill section; one dollar bill and a five dollar bill. I take out the one money bill that came from Tanzania that she always kept in there. I run my hands over the billfold itself and over the matching pocketbook in the hope that maybe some of her skin cells would rub off on me and would therefore allow me to have a piece of her still. I thought of her every single second of every single day, except when I was asleep. And that is no exaggeration at all. My dying would have been more humane. As of this writing, I still do all of these things. I probably always will.

My husband continued to bury his emotions deep inside so he could function. I continued to let them out because it was the only way I could survive. Keeping them inside would have killed me. It was difficult for us grieving in such different ways, but often that is the way it is; both parents dying of grief, but showing it in diverse ways, or not showing it at all.

My life was irrevocably changed. Not only was I horribly sad, but I was totally adrift in my life. There was no job I thought I could handle, yet people told me if I kept busy, it would get better. But I did not feel I could handle the stress of my occupation. I did not feel capable of applying for a different role at that time because it would have been too stressful to learn anything new. So I stayed at home.

I no longer went to church, not since the Sunday prior to the news of Kaitlyn's death. As of this writing, I have still not gone back, yet we were regular church attendees. I was mad at God. I know this may horrify some of you that I can say such a thing, but I think God understands these things and is patient. I was mad at him for taking my bright shining star away from me. I was mad that he allowed her to sink into such a depression that all that she had going for her and all those who loved her did not seem to matter as much as the pain she was enduring. I was mad at him because every single day since I gave birth to my girls - sometimes many times a day - I would pray, and my prayer would be for him to take care of my girls. I prayed for them to make good decisions in their lives and for them to live long, happy lives. I don't pray at all anymore for fear that I may get the opposite, the way I did on 4-11-13.

My faith has fallen by the wayside at a time where most people draw near to their faith and are comforted by it. I am not proud of this and I hope that in time I may find my way back. But at this time, I am changed. I hope those of you to whom this applies, find that your faith sustains you. I've heard many times it is what the made the difference in how people survive such a horrible tragedy and in no way do I intend to say otherwise.

I do, however, remain a spiritual person. I believe in life after death and that in some form, some way, somewhere, that Kaitlyn is in the paradise that she deserves. I believe this with all my heart and if I didn't, I don't think I could live through this at all.

My life has always been full with work and family. But the thought of Kaitlyn fulfilling her dreams, being happy and reaching her potential was such a HUGE part of my life. I can't think those thoughts anymore. She is gone and will never fully reach her potential. A person I found such a strong connection to is now gone and I just didn't know how to handle this.

Other agonizing thoughts that simply would not leave me alone were the questions that if Kaitlyn and I were so very close, why did she not come to me and talk to me

103

about it? Why didn't she confide in me? I, of all people, would have understood depression from my own experience. If we were so close how could I not just FEEL that she was in trouble? But most horrifying of all is the question, "How could you leave me? How could you tear away from the strong bond and love that we had? HOW could you LEAVE ME?" Of course, then my rational mind would kick in and I would know the answer; depression. It does not care who you love, what you have. If left unattended it will only make you think about dying, no matter what. But even knowing that, the questions above persisted.

During the first few months I seldom left my house, despite many invitations to dinner with my mother or mother-in-law. I just didn't want to be around people. If they wanted to see me, they had to come to my house. Once I went to my mother's house when my sisters were there and after a few minutes I left in tears. I just couldn't stand it. They were all being so sweet and understanding as they always have been, but I just became overwhelmed with sadness and I could not cope.

Before Kaitlyn died, my husband and I had planned a two week vacation in June 2013. We had made reservations the previous December for a campground and everything was set. We were to take our motorhome and haul our trailer with our motorcycle in it from North Carolina where we live to South Dakota. It was something we had planned five years previously, but circumstances at that time caused us to have to cancel. My husband and I bought a motorcycle back in 2001 and had been avid riders since. We had always wanted to go to South Dakota (not during Sturgis bike week time) and see The Badlands, Mt. Rushmore, Custer State Park to see the buffalo and to Crazy Horse monument and the beautiful scenery.

After Kaitlyn's death, we cancelled our trip. However, two months later I decided that I would be in the depths of grief no matter where I was, so we decided to go anyway since it would probably be our last chance.

Our trip would have been the trip of a lifetime had I not been in the depths of pure hell. All I can say is that I'm glad I went, but it just provided a beautiful backdrop for my tears. I cried all the way there, all the time we were there and all the way back home. Once in a while, I would stop to look at something wonderful, and then back into the pits I would go.

Kaitlyn never went to this part of the country, but I swear she went when we did, for her spirit was everywhere we went. I saw multiple purple flowers growing throughout the region (purple was her favorite color). I saw symbols and jewelry of dragonflies all over the place (dragonflies represent her spirit to me).

I kept up my writing on my computer during our entire stay. I chronicled everything we did each day and all the awful emotions I felt. Here is a particularly painful experience I wrote about:

**6-24-13 7:15 pm Mountain time**

*We took an hour's ride to Deadwood today. I have looked forward to going there, because of its historical significance. I wanted to take a tour of Deadwood, a tour of Mt. Moriah where Wild Bill Hickok and Calamity Jane are buried. Maybe go into Saloon number 10 where Wild Bill Hickok was shot in the back and killed. Maybe see some gun fight demonstrations. I love old west history; I love all history.*

*However, once we got there, the traffic was so congested and it wasn't laid out as simply as the other towns we had been to and it was confusing to know where to go to do what. I could tell Allyn didn't like it and it's nerve racking driving a motorcycle in tight, congested traffic, so I told him to just get me to that graveyard so I could see Wild Bill Hickok and Calamity Jane's grave and I'd just be satisfied with that. So we found it finally. It's called Mt. Moriah and a mount and a hill it is! By the time we walked to the top where the graveyard is, I was reminded of my age and my lack of stamina. But we got up there and went right to their graves. (There were many more and I would have loved to have stayed longer, but I was hot and tired and a little miffed, knowing if we had taken the tour bus, we would not have had to walk all that way and everything would have been explained to us).*

*But anyway, I saw the graves and we walked towards the motorcycle to leave, but before we did, we visited the restrooms. When I was standing there washing my hands I looked in the mirror and noticed all the freckles that had popped out from riding in the sun. I'm very fair skinned. And suddenly, just like a smack in the face, I saw in my mind Kaitlyn's freckles on her face as she lay in her coffin. I remembered her laying there and I was thinking that she must have been in the sun frequently because there weren't usually so many, but they were just a speckling from being out running in the sun. She was fair skinned like me. With that vision in my mind, Kaitlyn lying in her coffin, those pretty, sweet freckles, I felt a stab in my heart with the severity of none I've ever known. I started crying. Then I finally managed to stop long enough to get back to Allyn and the motorcycle. He saw that I was crying so he put his arm around me and we sat down on the curb, saying all the things I always say; "How could this have happened? She was my everything; I'm lost without her. She was a beautiful person..."and on and on and on. Finally, I just wiped my face and told him we should go.*

*As we headed out of town, he said if I wanted to we
would go back and do those tours I had wanted to do, but
by that time I no longer felt I could. I cried all the way to
Wyoming.*

We finally made the ride back home to NC after we had
done and seen everything we wanted to. During the time of
our trip, I thought I would go there and die somehow. I
would be in the most peaceful and beautiful place I could
imagine and God would have mercy on me and just let me
go. It didn't happen.

Then I had this other thought once I got home. I would
simply stop eating and drinking from the grief and then just
whittle away to nothing and be gone. This didn't happen
either and I continued to eat because nothing else felt good
at all and I gained 20 pounds. So much for the starving
idea.

I don't mean to say that I was suicidal. Wanting to die
by suicide and causing your death is something different
than hoping that you will die in some peaceful way. But I
knew my thoughts were not something I should be
thinking. I still had my husband, my other daughter
Stephanie and my family to live for and I loved them
deeply. But I hurt SO badly, I just could not stand it and
didn't know how long I could endure it.

I continued my regular monthly visits to my psychiatrist,
continued the antidepressant I was taking before Kaitlyn's
death and continued with a little stronger anti-anxiety
medication I had been prescribed since the tragedy. I was
depressed. But I always told them that changing my
medicine wasn't going to help what I was going through. I
went briefly to a grief counselor but she told me I was
doing wonderfully; at least I could write about Kaitlyn, talk
about her, and get out of bed in the morning. I told her I
was not alright. She said I was. I never learned anything
else from her to help me cope, so I quit going. She was

very kind and compassionate and I could talk to her, but I just did not find it helpful. However, although it was not for me, counseling is of great help to many people.

I thought about going to a group meeting that is attended by people who have lost children by any means, but I just felt as though I wanted to go to one where loved ones had been lost by suicide. I needed to be around people that understood what someone was going through in that respect; not just death, but a suicide death. To me, I think it would make a difference. Unfortunately there were no such organized meetings like that anywhere near where I lived.

So I was lost. Lost in a sea of grief, lost in a sea of uncertainty of where my life would go, lost in a world I had no interest in anymore and wondering whether I could even go on at all.

In order to live, I continued to write and try to find answers as to why my beautiful girl no longer wanted to live. It's what I lived for. So the search continued.

**Blog post 5-13: You're Supposed to be There**

*Kaitlyn, you're supposed to be in Winston-Salem having finished up a run or workout at the gym early this morning, then on to your clinical rotation in pediatrics at medical school. Instead, you're in a field not far from here and your belongings are either here or scattered about the US by now (your clothes were sent to St. Jude's Hospital). You'll never graduate, you'll never get married and you'll never have children. You'll never be able to practice in some exciting city like you talked about with me so many times.*

*Who am I supposed to talk to about the things that only we loved to talk about; science, astronomy, books and good movies? I'll never be able to call you up and tell you we were coming to take you out to eat and hear you say "Yay!" like you always did. It would take a book to list the things that we shared and enjoyed together, things that were unique only to us. So I won't write that book here. You know them, we shared them.*

*Kaitlyn, I know you would not want me to hurt the way I do and probably would not even want me blubbering about it everywhere, unless it really did help someone. I'm so sorry but it just hurts so terribly. This loss of someone I loved so fiercely is something almost impossible to endure. If someone could die of a broken heart alone, I wouldn't be here either. But here I am, in this horrific state of grief. In a minute, or an hour, or even a day when I feel slightly better, my heart and mind make up for it a million times over with even more torment.*

*It will soon be a month since you've been gone, and it seems like it happened yesterday. I can't work; I can't go out unless it's something I absolutely have to do because I will start crying. I can't eat at a nice restaurant because you can't have it. I can't enjoy anything because you can't enjoy it and apparently never really could. Besides, I can't enjoy anything right now anyway. How can I eat Chinese food again? It was the last meal we ate together. My life seems destroyed.*

*Kaitlyn, I know you didn't mean to hurt me like this. You must have been in pain beyond belief to have done what you did, that thing that is so permanent and a line you passed you can never cross back over again. I know depression, (I'm sorry; you must have gotten it from me). You've seen my struggles and were silent with your own. I never saw yours. I'm so sorry. I know that deep dark place you were in because I've been there myself, but I reached out and was pulled from the edge of that line you crossed.*

*As much as I hurt from losing you Kaitlyn, I hope with all my heart that you now know nothing about it.*

Kaitlyn at a marathon

# Chapter 9

## The Voices Come Forth

### *Costume*

*Every morning I wake up*
*And get ready for the costume ball*
*I put on my mask*
*And dress that is not my own*
*This outfit I don*
*Is not my true style*
*But I wear it anyway*
*Because it is less daring*
*And I don't take risks*
*Because I am afraid my true*
*Expressions*
*Feelings*
*Reactions*
*Thoughts*
*Beauty*
*Will not be appreciated*
*Will be laughed at*
*Because I am different*
*Like no other*
*Unlike the majority of others*
*But then again -*
*Maybe, they have costumes too.*
*Maybe, I am comparing my true self*
*To their fake appearances*
*Maybe we all have disguises*
*Because we care what others think*
*Even if you can see through your mask*
*If you try*
*And even if it's not so transparent*
*As others*

*Maybe, everyone wears one*
*But maybe, there is nothing to worry about*
*Because everyone is unique*
*In their own way*
*Maybe, I'll shed my costume*
*And put on one that is more*
*Me.*

*Kaitlyn Elkins (age 14)*

I found this poem that Kaitlyn wrote so long ago among many of her things that I kept over the years from her childhood. It won honorable mention in a poetry contest when she was 14. When I saw it again after her death, this poem horrified me. It shouted out to me that, yes, there were signs; she wrote them in her poetry! This poem, in hindsight, clearly indicates someone who felt they could not be themselves around other people because they felt so different. The realization of this thrust me into a horrible state of guilt, because I had failed to see the signs of her depression.

I remember reading this poem after she wrote it. I vaguely remember being just a little alarmed by it and I think I even asked her if that's the way she felt. I don't even remember what she said, but feel that she probably shrugged it off as just feeling the way everyone does. The end of this poem made me feel as though everyone else felt the same way, so I did not take it as seriously as I do now she is no longer with us.

Could this child with the wonderful friends that she had, who were so similar to her, still have felt alone, even with them? That's why I never worried; I didn't feel like she could have.

As time passed and my quest to make sense out of something senseless continued, I began to receive emails and messages from people who had read about Kaitlyn's story. These people had also been successful their entire lives. Letter by letter, I began to understand that my daughter was not the only one who hid severe depression while continuing to achieve highly and presenting a facade of happiness. Here is one such letter sent to me, included with the author's permission:

*Dear Rhonda,*

*I wanted to give you and your family my condolences and thank you for coming forward to share the story of your daughter's life and death. I am currently a resident, not a psychiatrist, but I deal with suicidal, psychotic, addicted, and other mentally ill patients on a daily basis. Unfortunately, most of these people do not have someone to advocate for them the way you are there to advocate for Kaitlyn and other health professionals.*

*Medicine is not an easy career for a depressed person, particularly a sensitive and intelligent depressed person (and the three often go hand in hand). Being immersed in the suffering of others with limited outlets for debriefing and self-care does not make an introspective depressed person feel better about their own condition; it only intensifies and magnifies their awareness of the world's total burden of suffering, including their own. Every wisecrack by a colleague, every instance of others turning away when the subject of depression comes up, adds on ever more weight. Ultimately, the feeling of alienation and the loss of ability to compartmentalize in order to survive can tear a medical trainee apart. I liken it to the systemic sepsis that develops when the walls of an abscess break down, and its toxic contents spread throughout the body. Ironically, the body's attempts to protect itself against the onslaught of cytokines and pyrogens lead to its self-destruction.*

*I am older than Kaitlyn was, but I see a lot of myself in her; the perfectionism, the self-pressure, even down to being high school valedictorian. My family and I did not recognize that I was depressed as a child; when I was growing up, there was not as much awareness of depression in children and adolescents. Still, my parents were aware enough that they did take me to a psychologist once, who told them there was "nothing wrong" with me. The reason my parents took me to a psychologist is because I wasn't social. It's not that I had no friends at all, but I much preferred being by myself, reading, etc. to spending time with other kids. I was not yet a teenager when they took me to the psychologist. Even at that age, I was not interested in the things most kids were interested in, and I got along much better with adults than I did with other kids. (This was true when I was a teenager also). When the psychologist said there was nothing wrong with me, my dad snorted and said that I had managed to fool the psychologist.*

*The idea that a school age child could "fool" a psychologist is kind of preposterous to me, but this was the genesis of my understanding that there was something "wrong" with me because I wasn't like other kids. Of course, that belief made me even more anxious and withdrawn, and my parents and I fought about my lack of sociability regularly until I grew up and moved away. I do get along with peers better now, but I am still not a very social person as an adult. What you are saying about your daughter not showing any signs of depression resonates with me in the sense that I have learned to act more like other people. I sometimes say that I am an introvert who has learned to act like an extrovert. Maybe Kaitlyn did too. But acting like part of the group is not the same as being part of it.*

114

*As you and others have eloquently pointed out, the issue of mental illness among health professionals is an especially difficult problem. I agree that this is in part because of the culture of perfectionism in medicine. But it is also because of what some call the "unwritten curriculum," in which trainees learn by experience that our needs and feelings are not important and should not be expressed. All of the wellness centers and seminars in the world will do no good when the much stronger implicit message we get during our training tells us the exact opposite. To paraphrase Ralph Waldo Emerson: what our academic physicians and other role models DO speaks so loudly that the trainees can't hear what they SAY.*

*I finally went on medication during college, and I have been taking meds on and off since that time. I had some major depressive episodes in medical school, and I wanted to quit, but my family and dean always talked me out of it. Their intentions were good, but the results have most decidedly not been. As I approach the end of my residency, I look at myself in the mirror sometimes and wonder, how did I get to be this unkind, uncompassionate person? This is not me! This is not who I want to be! If I could go back in time, I would not have gone in medical school. I would have done something else that interested me. There was no overriding reason for me to make the kind of psychic sacrifices necessary to become a licensed, practicing physician. Unfortunately, figuring out how to extricate oneself from the medical field is not so easy, and the further along one goes in their training, the more difficult it becomes.*

*However, having matured beyond adolescence has been helpful in the sense that I have more experience in coping with depression. The seemingly insurmountable problems that made me contemplate suicide (and attempt it once) as an adolescent don't invoke active suicidal ideation now that I'm older. I have enough life experience to know that depression waxes and wanes, and I understand that things can eventually get better. Unfortunately, it is not easy to explain that to a young girl like your daughter. I couldn't conceive of how things could or would ever get better when I was her age either.*

*At any rate, your daughter was obviously intelligent and capable. I have to think that you didn't see her depression and suicidality in large part because she didn't want you to see them. The why...I don't have an answer for that. And I think that is what eats away at you more than anything; why she didn't come to you, trust you. I wish there were an answer to that question. I also wish the best to you and your family in your search for answers.*

The author chose to remain anonymous in this book but is a practicing MD.

The next entry is from a practicing psychiatrist. She had commented on my blog a couple of times and when I decided to write my book, I asked her if she would like to write a short segment about depression and about how it is often hidden. She gave me much more than I asked for because she also included a personal story about her own period of severe depression, which I had not known existed until she sent me this story.

**Silence About Suicide is Killing Physicians**

*The statistics for physicians and suicide are daunting. Physicians have the highest suicide rate of any professional group. Studies show that female physicians have an eight fold rate of suicide compared to their male colleagues. The suicide rate for female physicians in their 40s is increasing at an alarming rate.*

*There are many contributing factors such as the increasing expectations by their patients coupled with a system that is placing unprecedented burdens on*

116

*physicians. In my own practice setting, I am expected to do more and more with less time. For example, out of economic necessity, my employer recently switched to a cheaper, more time-consuming electronic medical record system.*

*One thing I have learned through both personal and professional experience is that silence about depression and suicidal ideation is also a major contributing factor. That is why I have decided to share my own experience.*

*I don't know why I was so driven when I left high school to go to college. I can't blame my parents. Neither one wanted me to go to college, and instead wanted me to continue working at my hospital job so I could help support the family. Rather than putting pressure on me, they were always fine with where I was. There was no one in my family who was "high achieving". My father had not worked in years, and was blissfully unconcerned about this, saying it gave him more time to work on his "writing" and his "inventions". I wasn't in competition with any of my four siblings, as they had made it clear for years they did not care about school or grades. No one ever looked at my report card.*

*I was determined to become a surgeon despite the many obstacles that were in my path: I had not taken the required college prep classes in high school so college was going to require an immense amount of studying. I had to work part time to pay for college. I didn't have any mentors; my family did not provide any emotional or financial support, and, in fact, shunned me due to my decision.*

*My determination made it possible for me to overcome these obstacles for the first three semesters of college. I excelled in my classes, earning a 3.8 GPA as a chemistry pre-med major by the end of first semester of sophomore year. I held down my job; I paid all my bills on time. I was referred to as cheerful, upbeat and optimistic by classmates, dorm mates, and employers. No one would*

117

*have predicted that within a year of the end of that third semester, I would have crumbled to the point of becoming suicidal, and that my academic career would be in tatters.*

*The trigger was the death of my only true friend, who was murdered the Christmas break following our third semester of college. Inwardly, I was devastated, but outwardly I remained upbeat and driven. People were impressed that I was so strong in the face of such a calamity. It was proof, I was told, that I had what it took to someday become a surgeon. However, I did not have the tools to weather this tragedy. First of all, I had no way of letting anyone know I was in trouble. I was trapped in the idea that because I wanted to become a doctor, I had to appear strong at all times. I did not recognize the signs of depression that I was experiencing: disturbed sleep, decreased appetite, loss of focus and concentration, increasing hopelessness about the future. I had severe guilt over my role in my friend's death: I had left her to Christmas shop alone, and she had been abducted from the mall parking lot. Understandably, her family was angry that I had "abandoned" her, which compounded these feelings.*

*My energy seeped away during the Christmas break, but I worked full time at my hospital job and then returned to school for the spring semester. I went through the motions of going to work and classes.*

*Because I had been so driven, and had needed to work 20 hours a week consistently, I had not formed any other true friendships. I had no one to talk to about my guilt and my feelings of profound loss. Although everyone on campus was aware of my friend's death and the manner in which she died, there were quite a few people in my college life, classmates, people at my job in the dorm cafeteria, who had no idea I had lost such a close friend in such a tragic manner. At her campus memorial service, I was surrounded by strangers. She had been a sociology major, and unlike*

118

*me, she had obviously grown close to quite a few of her classmates. They had collected more anecdotes about her in three semesters than what I had accumulated from knowing her all my life.*

*By the end of the spring semester, I had failing grades in all my classes. I had two choices: withdraw from school, or get Incompletes. Withdrawing from school would have resulted in having "Ws" on my transcript, which I was told, medical schools did not like to see. Incompletes would show up as regular grades once I completed the course work, and no one would ever have to know about them. They carried their own risk: it would require that I complete those classes by the end of the following fall semester while I also took my fall classes. I felt it was my only choice. I gave myself the unrealistic goal of completing the work over the summer. However, because I was continuing to experience symptoms of depression, I had made little headway by the time fall semester had started, and I sank deeper into both depression and academic disaster as I got further behind.*

*I did finally go to the counseling center for help and my therapist urged me to adopt a daily exercise routine. She gave me articles showing that engaging in daily aerobic exercise would elevate my mood. I took up cycling and joined a cycling club, and within weeks I was training for a 100 mile ride. My grades, however, did not budge. I got behind in my fall semester classes as well as in my Incomplete classes.*

*I did not plan my suicide attempt. In fact, I hadn't even thought of it until the day it happened. I remember that just before leaving for a training ride with the club, I went through the previous day's mail: there were several warning letters about my grades. I sat on my bed, in my cycling attire, paralyzed by the anxiety the letters had produced. I arrived at the cycling club meeting place too late: they had already left for the day's 50 mile ride. I*

119

*thought I would try and catch up with them, and as I rode my bike, the anxiety about my grades continued to mount. I began to think there was no way I could possibly face that failure. I remembered a hill that we had been warned never to attempt to descend on a bicycle. People have died on that hill, we were told. It is too steep, it ends at a major intersection, and it is almost impossible to stop. At the very least, you will get a ticket, as there are signs posted prohibiting bicycles on that hill.*

*I decided that hill was my "salvation". I became quickly convinced that this was my only choice, that this was the reason I had seen my mail a day late, just before the bike ride, because my friend was trying to tell me that the solution to my problems was to simply join her. These thoughts gave me an immediate sense of relief from the worry that had gnawed me over the previous months.*

*I should have died. The traffic on that hill was very light. I should have been going very fast by the time I reached the intersection at the bottom and hit the six lanes of traffic. But, apparently, a car entered the road very close to the top of the hill, then did an illegal U turn, hitting me before I had picked up speed. I suffered several broken bones and a concussion. I broke my jaw. A large amount of gravel became imbedded in my thigh. I suffered a loss of consciousness. While I was in the hospital, I was given a ticket.*

*I lost all sense of time as I recuperated from my injuries. By the time I left the hospital, I had been "kicked out" of college with failing grades in two semesters of classes. My GPA was 1.9, just half of what it had been the previous year.*

*It was during my physical therapy, when I mentioned that I didn't care if I ever got well, that I was finally referred to a psychiatrist. I was given a tricyclic antidepressant, and started therapy. I felt the heavy cape that had descended on me begin to lighten, and then lift.*

*Within weeks of starting treatment I became extremely grateful I had not died, and became fearful of dying. I was able to not just return to my previous level of optimism, but I learned important things about myself, and grew both emotionally and spiritually. I was able to finally grieve my loss, which focused and energized me.*

*It took just months for my depression to go into what is known as remission. It took YEARS, however, to repair the damage caused to my life by my untreated depression. Not only was my academic career derailed, but my attempt had left me with astronomical medical bills. I was a young college "flunk out" with no insurance and no marketable skills.*

*Although it took several years, I was able to repair the damage and get into medical school. In 2002, years "behind schedule", I became part of the class of 2006 at an osteopathic medical school that took into account my entire journey, not just my GPA. By the time I entered medical school, I had become the mother of two children, and changed my goal from becoming a surgeon to becoming a psychiatrist.*

*I did not know it at the time, but during the period of my application, a member of the class of 2005 committed suicide. I learned of this during orientation the week before classes started. As a result of that tragedy, our class received several types of suicide prevention educational activities and interventions. We were urged to reach out to and watch out for each other. We memorized the signs of depression (depressed mood, loss of interest, guilt, sleep disturbance, psychomotor retardation or agitation, appetite changes, concentration loss, energy loss, loss of sex drive). We were taught to prioritize our personal and spiritual well-being above all else. We received periodic workshops and lectures about suicide.*

*Our class quickly adopted the practice of a group hug before every exam. We had a record number of applications to psychiatry residency programs.*

*When I entered residency, I learned that suicide prevention and mental health awareness are not a standard part of most medical school curriculums. Most of my colleagues from other medical schools had received just a cursory lecture or two on suicide. Being in psychiatry, my colleagues quickly overcame those deficits. But, I have to wonder about the many medical students who do not receive mental health support and education about suicide and then enter specialties which do not help them overcome these deficits.*

*Medical students tend to be very driven. They tend to feel a great deal of pressure to be strong for others, and have difficulty admitting defeat. These personality traits enable them to cope with the rigors of medical education, to be strong for their patients and colleagues, and overcome the increasing obstacles present in health care. Unfortunately, these traits also put them at greater risk for depression and suicide. The only way this risk will be overcome is for suicide prevention to become a routine part of the medical curriculum. All medical students should be taught the symptoms of depression because a depressive episode is the biggest risk factor for suicide. Until this becomes routine, we will continue to risk losing medical students and physicians. Because, as I learned both in my personal life, and in my medical education, silence about suicide kills.*

*To save one life is as if you saved a whole world.*

*The Talmud*

What Dr. Wexler has written is alarming and hopeful at the same time. It's alarming that so many medical students and physicians are depressed or suicidal. It's also disturbing that so many medical schools do not give enough attention and focus to the risk of depression and suicide in medical school and to let students know regularly how important it is for them to seek help if they are struggling with these feelings. It is hopeful though, in that Dr Wexler's story tells of someone who was in the very depths of depression, survived a suicide attempt, received help and went on to become a doctor. This proves that if someone is depressed, a career in medicine is not the death sentence it is perceived to be. Another very positive aspect is that many medical schools are beginning to focus on improved education for students about depression. However, there are many medical schools that still have inadequate measures in place to deal with this problem. It seems to me some only react after a suicide occurs. All medical schools need to incorporate what Dr. Wexler's school did after the suicide in their school.

Next is an email that was sent to me by a medical student a few weeks after Kaitlyn died. She was just graduating medical school and was going on to her residency, but felt moved to email me about her own experiences. I have only included a small part of her letter to protect her identity and she has approved this portion of this letter to be put in my book.

*Dear Mrs. Elkins,*

*I cannot imagine the pain you are experiencing today, or any of the days following your daughter's death. I would like to offer my sincerest condolences. I am just graduating medical school. I have wanted to write you for weeks, but was hesitant for some reason. After seeing a friend's repost of your editorial on Facebook recently, I started this letter. I hope I send it. I am sorry I did not know your daughter, because I would like to offer a story you hadn't heard or a memory, although I am sure you have heard many recently because it's clear she was loved by many.*

*I have read so many things on her Facebook and on yours that I feel like a voyeur and I'm embarrassed to admit that to you. However, through reading your posts, I thought that you might appreciate this. I still want to apologize for the following paragraphs. They are about me and my struggle and my connection to your precious daughter's death. It feels selfish and insensitive to write that to you, especially because I didn't know her.*

*Like many people who have written to you or commented on your posts, I have suffered depression of differing degrees my entire life. Unlike Kaitlyn, I was more forthcoming. My first major depressive episode started in sixth grade and was severe. I did start seeing a psychologist and then psychiatrist. I started taking Prozac that same year and my life improved dramatically. My parents were confused and scared, especially my mom who was very uncomfortable with the idea of her young daughter on psychiatric medication, but came to accept it, especially when she saw how much I improved.*

*My depression was less pronounced in high school, but my junior year in college, my life started to spiral out of control. I struggled through this, asked for help, and saw a therapist for about a year.*

*Medical school was awful. It's so isolating. The people are perfectionists, and maybe not as similar to me as I thought they would be. I didn't have as many friends as I was used to having. There was a joint birthday party my first year, and sixty-four people out of 120 were invited; not me. This hurt my feelings so badly. I knew I didn't fit in. I went through the motions of the next few years doing what I needed to do, but not really feeling anything. At times I have even felt unsuccessful because my performance has been pretty average, never too far above or below. That's pretty damn good, just not to people like us; or it's not enough. To my parents I'm perfect; 100%. I'm also the only one. They think I'm brilliant, gorgeous, funny, and everything else you could ever want in a daughter. I know they beam with pride when they tell people about me. They don't understand my depression completely, but they support me in every way they know how.*

*I was injured in an auto accident. I stopped being able to sleep, and began showing textbook signs of PTSD (post traumatic stress disorder). As someone who has struggled with mental illness for 15 years (taking medication for it the entire time), I felt different and desperate. Luckily, my friend at school reminded me of our designated psychologist, who I began seeing almost weekly for months. I also awkwardly told my parents. They supported me, like always, but of course wish I had been more forthcoming earlier. It's so hard to explain. I don't want to guess how Kaitlyn felt, but personally I have felt hesitant because I don't want to bring them down or make them feel like bad parents because I have been cursed with sadness and insecurity (even though we are incredibly close).*

*The next few months were what I called "operation getting by". I tried to accept that medical school wasn't the best time of my life and that this was an anomalously sad time in my life and tried to focus on the light at the end of the tunnel (which got much brighter after I matched in what I wanted where I wanted). So I've been taking a knee and running out the clock, trusting that the next stage in my life will be better."*

I have often wondered since reading this if Kaitlyn may have felt many of the same things that this medical student (now a resident) felt during the time she was in medical school. I feel in my heart that she did, though she never admitted it. I did know that Kaitlyn was not happy in the city she lived in because she did not know many people there. She had told me this many times but whenever she did, she did so with the realization that she would only have to live there a few more years and that she would be able to deal with it until then. Meanwhile, she still kept in touch with her friends from other areas that she loved and often went out with them. So I did not worry. I now know that Kaitlyn kept 99.9 percent of her misery to herself unfortunately.

The following are words from a friend with whom I have become acquainted through my blog. She also provides an insight into the mind and feelings of a depressed, yet highly achieving young woman. I have chosen to use three separate writings of hers because in so many ways she does remind me of Kaitlyn.

*As someone whom you have said reminds you of your daughter, and as I have gotten to know you, I have been impacted by some of the things you do and the reactions you have had following your daughter's tragic death, because I can see my own mother doing the very same had my own attempt had a slightly different outcome just ten months ago.*

*I too am a "chronic overachiever and perfectionist" as my therapist has pointed out. She tells me I do this to overcompensate for what I feel I lack. NOT AT ALL because my parents put pressure on me. They have loved me unconditionally from the moment I was born (and even earlier, as my mother liked to tell me frequently) and have never put any kind of pressure on me to excel. They are just as proud of me for making a perfect score on my SAT and for being accepted into MENSA as they were for my sloppy giraffe painting I did in the 8th grade, which they have proudly displayed over their mantle in the living room. And I'll pointedly admit that I am NO artist.*

*In my recent research into my conditions (Major Depressive Disorder, OCD, and Post Traumatic Stress Disorder), I have also found that those with well above average to genius IQs who are self-motivating and extremely competitive (part of my OCD is intrusive thoughts of failure) work to mask their depressive episodes by accomplishing. This may mean making straight As; this could be represented by being class President and popular (Abraham Lincoln was extremely depressed for most of his life); it has been seen to manifest in completing detailed projects and innovative new discoveries and this has also meant conquering physical feats such as the marathon (as both your daughter and I have done). All this in the name of proving we are okay. We deserve to be here. Or that, "I just hate myself so much because I am such a horrible person and guttural failure that I need to do all of this to show that I am not the most detestable human on the earth." Because sometimes we feel that we are. But no one would know it.*

*I made my parents very proud and they had no reason at all to worry about me. Until they returned from a two week cruise to Alaska to learn that the child they never thought they would have to worry about was just released from the ICU with 50 stitches, having received a lifesaving blood transfusion and was now in a "Behavioral Rehab Hospital" for an undermined amount of time. Of course, they wondered how they had failed me. My mother particularly felt that she should have been able to see how much pain I was in. I would have never admitted to it. I would have just gone on to earn another promotion, or to begin training for an Ironman, or to write a new industry abstract to fund a research project....anything to prove to her that I was more than fine. I was thriving! But on the inside I was dying. No one knew.*

*Had my attempt been a completed suicide, and my parents returned and been as mystified as you were about why I was so depressed, I would expect nothing less from*

127

*my mother than to tear my house/computer/phone apart for any bit of information she could find to see what had haunted me so deeply. I would have anticipated her talking to all of my friends about my demeanor. I would want her to find peace and answers in any way she needed to. And if ANYONE made her feel badly about any of it for one second, I hope I could come back and haunt their ass for being such terrible human beings. I can't think of anything worse!! What a horrible, shameful thing to do to a grieving mother.*

*I did not know your daughter. From what I have read and seen she was beautiful, and brilliant, and obviously loved you very much and I have NO doubt she would want you to write this book, both to help you process and recover what has happened and also to honor her memory. Give her something tangible that she has accomplished. She HAS left behind something good here. She did accomplish something. Let that goodness and light be seen by others. Let it help others. And IT WILL. Maybe there are others out there like us who are contemplating letting go. I researched suicide and I am sure she did as well. What if we had found a book like this? What if we knew there were others like us? I wouldn't have felt so alone and she wouldn't have either. I would have known there are alternatives. There is a way to get better. Your book can help other people.*

*Rhonda. You are Kaitlyn's voice now. I can't wait to read what she has to say. I want to know more about who she was.*

*Christine O'Hagan*

She also told of her running and depression, which I can imagine is how Kaitlyn must have felt:

*I love to run. I haven't always. I despised running when I was younger. It was something we were made to do in gym class and then in dance team for punishment. But I had children and I got pretty pudgy doing so and very little time to remedy that, so I ran. More accurately, I joggled (a hybrid of waddling and jogging). I was determined to lose the 40 or so pounds I gained with my first child and honestly, the time spent outdoors got me away from the house and some free time to think, so I began to look forward to this time. Each day I ran a little more than I joggled and eventually I worked my way up to running three miles straight with no walk/joggle breaks. I felt my first "runner's high" and felt great. So I set a goal and accomplished it. I completed the 26.2 mile San Francisco marathon in 4.5 hours in 2001. Just because I thought the most difficult thing someone in my position could do was to travel across the country alone and finish one of man's toughest physical challenges. So I did it and then I stopped running for ten years.*

*It is not easy to train for and run a 26.2 mile event or even a 13.1 miler (half marathon). I have run these races in the heat of Southern Texas where I live; the winds of California seaside; and even straight up a mountain to the tune of an 8,000 foot increase in height, and what they say is true. It is more mental than physical. You have to be able to overcome your negative thoughts to be able to continue through the pain of a race like that. The training can be even more brutal; getting up early everyday when your friends are sleeping in. On cold mornings, running on sweltering hot days, in the rain...during all kinds of conditions, you still have to get out there or you will not be ready. But, if I am depressed, it is nearly impossible.*

*How is it that I can defeat all negative thoughts for a race but I cannot defeat them through depression fog and suicidal ideation to want to live? I can get through a Lupus flare because I have support and I am allowed to talk about that illness, but I cannot talk about the one that is even more scary. If I tell people, friends, coworkers I cannot leave my house because I have had a seizure and will have to begin treatment for another flare right away, I get immediate understanding and phone calls and even visits from friends, but if I were to tell them I don't want to get into my car to drive to work because I can't manage to shower and put on makeup and if I did, I am afraid I will want to drive into a tree, I will only get scared glances, lessened trusts and avoided interaction. That is IF I were to tell them. Because I don't tell anyone when I feel this way. I will throw my hair into a ponytail, wear comfortable clothes and pray that I can make it to the office without my compulsion and intrusive thoughts about dying overtaking my conscious actions. I have literally made myself make up stories all the way to work about the other people in their cars because I would NEVER hurt another person no matter how badly I felt. I know if I lost control of my car, even just trying to hurt myself, I could hurt someone else; an innocent person, or even a child. I hate myself even more for the possibility of this.*

*I read that paragraph above and know how serious an illness depression is. How can a healthy person not understand that? I don't want to feel this way. I would never choose this. And if I could just think happy thoughts to motivate myself to snap out of it I would. I would give anything if I could.*

*I will say this without hesitation: Nothing I have experienced is as painful as a major depressive episode. Not childbirth without pain meds (twice). Not repeated dialysis. Not a gallbladder gone bad with gangrene and filled with stones (which is pretty bad). Not a migraine. Not cancer treatment. I would do five marathons in a row, up a mountain, while giving birth, carrying a mountain lion, as I'm having a Lupus flare while on dialysis, than have one more depressive episode if I were given the choice. Picture*

130

*that in your head and it sounds ridiculous, but I am
absolutely serious. I would trade hours of torture in a
foreign country's prison to be able to experience a few
minutes of happiness like I did when I was a child. Running
does bring me close. I do find peace there before
exhaustion.*

*So far, I have managed to keep putting one foot in front
of the other. This is my mantra for both the marathon and
life. I almost didn't make it a time or two, but here I sit,
typing this for all of you nice people. Or maybe just myself,
but either way I am here. I do feel like a phony, but I am a
phony who is managing the best I can. I am going to work
and when I can't it is most likely due to a super scary
depression day (aka. Lupus flare) and I am training for my
7th marathon in Houston in January and my 8th in The
Woodlands in March. I keep hoping what is in me IS
stronger than what is before me.*

Another piece of writing from Christine is very
revealing:

*My parents had no idea I was depressed, let alone
suicidal. I was "high functioning" and had always been an
overachiever.*

*I always worked very hard to prove to everyone (and
myself) that I deserved to be here. I have always also felt
that living was painful. I never have liked myself, in spite of
any accomplishment or achievement. I dismissed praise
and compliments (I still do), yet felt this overwhelming need
to do well or I was even harder on myself. I can relate to
your daughter. Even after my attempt, in the hospital the
psychiatrist asked me, "Why are you here? You don't seem
at all in need of my help." Instead, he wanted to talk about
the marathons I had done and my college (the same he had
attended) experiences. I was even able to fool him. I was at*

131

*absolute rock bottom and put the happy face and cheerleader attitude right back on again.*

*I was able to open up to my therapist and some close friends, and now here. This is who I really am and being able to drop the "healthy, together" act has made a big difference. Now I feel like if I were to be at that point again where the pain was so great I couldn't imagine living one more day, I could reach out and get help. I never would have admitted that before.*

*I am so sorry you lost your lovely girl. I wish she had the same opportunity I had. I wish you had the chance my mother did, to understand that your daughter was in pain and then to realize this pain was NOT your fault; to get to hear her tell you that you could not have prevented the suicide attempt no matter what you might have tried. I have explained to my guilt ridden mom time and time again after she says that she should have noticed my pain that I would have just denied it. I would have just pushed her away and avoided her and undertaken one more task to prove that I was okay. Another marathon…another degree…another raise at work…to prove to everyone that I deserved to be here and I was ok. Even though I wasn't. That was what I did.*

*I wish you well and hope you are able to use your pain in the future in a way that can help you, and maybe others. Thank you for sharing your story so selflessly and for accepting people like me. I have no doubt your little girl looks down from heaven on you and knows you will be ok. She isn't hurting anymore.*

*Christine O'Hagan*

And I'd like to include a writing of an internal medical resident who didn't even know Kaitlyn but knows of her story through my blog. She wrote this on her blog and I thought it so very moving that I wanted to include it here:

132

## To Kaitlyn, a girl I will never know

*I've been wanting to write this to you for a while. I go to work, and though I've never met you, I think about you. I talk to a patient, and while I'm standing there, there you are again, tugging at my heart. Maybe it's because I know of your mom, and I know of her heartbreak. Maybe it's because I know you will never be able to do what you were meant to do.*

*This is what I know about you. You were a medical student. You went to school in North Carolina. You cared for people. And you wanted to care for them in the greatest capacity possible. You wanted to help people during their times of sickness, strengthen them in their weakness. But your life was robbed from beneath you. So this will never happen. And the world has lost another great physician.*

*I hear you were a loving person, one who illuminated the day of all whom you came across. Of course you did. You were your mother's shining star. But what no one knew, and what you didn't reveal until your departure, was that you were also suffering. Deeply. But you were good at hiding it with your smile. And because it was a genuine smile, we were beguiled. Especially those closest to you.*

*When I think of you, my heart aches. Maybe it's because I feel that I understand you better than I have a right to. Maybe it is because I once smiled a similar smile. I weep because of what you did, and because I think I understand why.*

*When I think of you, my soul is anguished. You were going to be a remarkable physician. You would have touched others with your empathy, changed lives with your care. They would have remembered you, not simply because you were the one who eased their suffering and comforted their souls, but because your spirit would have brightened their lives. No one had the right to take that away from you.*

133

*I'm sorry I never got to know you. But even now, you will not be forgotten.*

*Phoebe Chi*

As I continued to realize that many brilliant people, as demonstrated above, can become so deeply depressed, the overriding thought in my mind was that Kaitlyn's intelligence could have perhaps been a contributing factor to her depression. I am not saying all intelligent people have mental illnesses because that is not true. But what I am saying is that bright, gifted children often require close observation.

I will call attention again to the opening poem to this chapter that Kaitlyn wrote as a child. Obviously, she felt different, but I have discovered way too late that there were reasons she felt different. I came across an article online and asked the author for permission to include it in my book because it explains why gifted children often feel isolated and alone.

**Existential Depression in Gifted Individuals**

*It has been my experience that gifted and talented persons are more likely to experience a type of depression referred to as existential depression. Although an episode of existential depression may be precipitated in anyone by a major loss or the threat of a loss which highlights the transient nature of life, persons of higher intellectual ability are more prone to experience existential depression spontaneously. Sometimes this existential depression is tied into the positive disintegration experience referred to by Dabrowski (1996).*

*Existential depression is a depression that arises when an individual confronts certain basic issues of existence. Yalom (1980) describes four such issues (or "ultimate concerns") - death, freedom, isolation and*

*meaninglessness. Death is an inevitable occurrence.
Freedom, in an existential sense, refers to the absence of
external structure. That is, humans do not enter a world
which is inherently structured. We must give the world a
structure which we ourselves create. Isolation recognizes
that no matter how close we become to another person, a
gap always remains, and we are nonetheless alone.
Meaninglessness stems from the first three. If we must die,
if we construct our own world, and if each of us is
ultimately alone, then what meaning does life have?*

*Why should such existential concerns occur
disproportionately among gifted persons? Partially, it is
because substantial thought and reflection must occur to
even consider such notions, rather than simply focusing on
superficial day-to-day aspects of life. Other more specific
characteristics of gifted children are important
predisposers as well.*

*Because gifted children are able to consider the
possibilities of how things might be, they tend to be
idealists. However, they are simultaneously able to see that
the world is falling short of how it might be. Because they
are intense, gifted children feel keenly the disappointment
and frustration which occurs when ideals are not reached.
Similarly, these youngsters quickly spot the inconsistencies,
arbitrariness and absurdities in society and in the
behaviors of those around them. Traditions are questioned
or challenged. For example, why do we put such tight sex-
role or age-role restrictions on people? Why do people
engage in hypocritical behaviors in which they say one
thing and then do another? Why do people say things they
really do not mean at all? Why are so many people so
unthinking and uncaring in their dealings with others?
How much difference in the world can one person's life
make?*

135

*When gifted children try to share these concerns with others, they are usually met with reactions ranging from puzzlement to hostility. They discover that others, particularly of their age, clearly do not share these concerns, but instead are focused on more concrete issues and on fitting in with others' expectations. Often by even first grade, these youngsters, particularly the more highly gifted ones, feel isolated from their peers and perhaps from their families as they find that others are not prepared to discuss such weighty concerns.*

*When their intensity is combined with multi-potentiality, these youngsters become particularly frustrated with the existential limitations of space and time. There simply aren't enough hours in the day to develop all of the talents that many of these children have. Making choices among the possibilities is indeed arbitrary; there is no "ultimately right" choice. Even choosing a vocation can be difficult if one is trying to make a career decision between essentially equal passion, talents and potential in violin, neurology, theoretical mathematics and international relations.*

*The reaction of gifted youngsters (again with intensity) to these frustrations is often one of anger. But they quickly discover that their anger is futile, for it is really directed at "fate" or at other matters which they are not able to control. Anger that is powerless evolves quickly into depression.*

*In such depression, gifted children typically try to find some sense of meaning, some anchor point which they can grasp to pull themselves out of the mire of "unfairness". Often, though, the more they try to pull themselves out, the more they become acutely aware that their life is finite and brief, that they are alone and are only one very small organism in a quite large world, and that there is a frightening freedom regarding how one chooses to live one's life. It is at this point that they question life's meaning and ask, "Is this all there is to life? Is there not ultimate meaning? Does life only have meaning if I give it meaning? I am a small, insignificant organism who is alone in an absurd, arbitrary and capricious world where my life can have little impact, and then I die. Is this all there is?"*

*Such concerns are not too surprising in thoughtful adults who are going through mid-life crises. However, it is a matter of great concern when these existential questions are foremost in the mind of a twelve or fifteen year old. Such existential depressions deserve careful attention, since they can be precursors to suicide.*

*How can we help our bright youngsters cope with these questions? We cannot do much about the finiteness of our existence. However, we can help youngsters learn to feel that they are understood and not so alone and that there are ways to manage their freedom and their sense of isolation.*

*The isolation is helped to a degree by simply communicating to the youngster that someone else understands the issues that he/she is grappling with. Even though your experience is not exactly the same as mine, I feel far less alone if I know that you have had experiences that are reasonably similar. This is why relationships are so extremely important in the long-term adjustment of gifted children (Webb, Meckstroth and Tolan, 1982).*

*A particular way of breaking through the sense of isolation is through touch. In the same way that infants need to be held and touched, so do persons who are experiencing existential aloneness. Touch seems to be a fundamental and instinctual aspect of existence, as evidenced by mother-infant bonding or "failure to thrive" syndrome. Often, I have "prescribed" daily hugs for a youngster suffering existential depression and have advised parents of reluctant teenagers to say, "I know that you may not want a hug, but I need a hug." A hug, a touch on the arm, playful jostling, or even a "high five" can be very important to such a youngster, because it establishes at least some physical connection.*

*The issues and choices involved in managing one's freedom are more intellectual, as opposed to the reassuring aspects of touch as a sensory solution to an emotional crisis. Gifted children who feel overwhelmed by the myriad choices of an unstructured world can find a great deal of comfort in studying and exploring alternate ways in which other people have structured their lives. Through reading about people who have chosen specific paths to greatness and fulfillment, these youngsters can begin to use bibliotherapy as a method of understanding that choices are merely forks in the road of life, each of which can lead them to their own sense of fulfillment and accomplishment (Halsted, 1994). We all need to build our own personal philosophy of beliefs and values which will form meaningful frameworks for our lives.*

*It is such existential issues that lead many of our gifted individuals to bury themselves so intensively in "causes" (whether these causes are academics, political or social causes, or cults). Unfortunately, these existential issues can also prompt periods of depression, often mixed with desperate, thrashing attempts to "belong". Helping these individuals to recognize the basic existential issues may help, but only if done in a kind and accepting way. In addition, these youngsters will need to understand that existential issues are not ones that can be dealt with only once, but rather ones that will need frequent revisiting and reconsideration.*

*In essence, then, we can help many persons with existential depressions if we can get them to realize that they are not so alone and if we can encourage them to adopt the message of hope written by the African-American poet, Langston Hughes:*

*Hold fast to dreams,*
*For if dreams die,*
*Life is a broken-winged bird*
*That cannot fly.*
*Hold fast to dreams.*
*For if dreams go,*
*Life is a barren field*
*Covered with snow.*

*Langston Hughes*

*James T. Webb, Ph.D., President*
*Great Potential Press, Inc.*
*Supporting Emotional Needs of the Gifted (SENG)*
*http://www.sengifted.org/archives/articles/existential-*
*depression-in-gifted-individual*

According to the SENG website, "In 1981, SENG was formed to bring attention to the unique emotional needs of gifted children. It provided adults with guidance, information, resources, and a forum to communicate about raising and educating these children."

The author of this article told me that SENG was started years ago due the suicide of a brilliant young man whose parents had no knowledge of his depression. After I read this article, though it was very eye opening, I began to feel even stronger pangs of guilt that I did not conceive that Kaitlyn could possibly be depressed, that I did not see the meaning of her poem "Costume".

When I first began to become really aware of the extent of Kaitlyn's intelligence, I was excited. I was thrilled. I began to immerse myself in researching all I could about gifted children. I read many things about the subject. I wanted to make sure her life was challenging enough for her, which is why I had agreed to let her go to a residential high school for the math and science gifted, though she chose not to stay. She was challenged as much as possible in her classes as she took the hardest courses she could. I felt her need for intellectual stimulation was being met.

I also have heard that there are instances where highly intelligent children often begin to have problems with mental illness such as depression and bipolar disorder, but I never felt I had to worry about this with Kaitlyn, because again, I saw no signs, or at least no signs that I recognized. I wish I had enlightened myself about such things as this article discussed, but I simply never came across anything like that. Had I read such articles, maybe I would have been much more in tune to what could be going on in her mind and to question her more. I feel deeply saddened that I didn't. It's too late for articles like this to help my daughter, but it's not too late for other parents of gifted children to learn what I did not know.

### Blog Entry: Just How Deadly is Depression? You Might Ask

*In our society today, so many people tend to think that if some people have so much going for them, they have no right to be unhappy. Quite frankly, they are rather uncaring and unaccepting of the fact that someone can be blessed with what they term as "having it all" and yet still be unhappy. It's a "you have no right to be depressed" mentality in this world. Believe me, I have seen it personally. And the person who is depressed also thinks so. How can they be so sad and have so much going for them in their lives? They feel guilty, alone, scared and hope that they can handle it themselves. And no wonder. But I'm here to tell the WORLD that this mentality must STOP! Most of the time depression is a chemical imbalance; you can be a multimillionaire with everything you could ever ask for and STILL be depressed. Yes, some depression is situational, and some people live a life of so much self destruction, and their depression is obvious. That is also terrible. But in many cases, depression is a chemical imbalance that can be helped with medication.*

*One of the things Kaitlyn wrote to us in her suicide note is this: "I know I could have become a successful doctor, wife, and mother. But the only thing I ever really wanted was not to feel the way I have felt all my life." And that says it all. So my daughter that I thought was an angel on this earth, who was so accomplished and gifted and had a wonderful life ahead of her, was killed by depression. Depression overtook everything she could have continued to have accomplished.*

*So just how deadly is depression you might ask? THAT is how deadly it is and my daughter's story cries to be heard. It is a tragedy in every sense of the word and has left her family in some surreal world of which we can't make heads or tails. She left all who loved her with unanswered questions and no idea how to be happy again. Her passing has diminished us all because her presence illuminated our world.*

*On my determined days like today, I want to just shout to the world how horrible this disease is. It must be known that it is killing so many young people, so many that have so much to give and would have continued to change the world for the better. But they are gone.*

*As I mentioned earlier, ever since Kaitlyn was a little girl, right up till she was grown, I would often joke with her that before she was born and still in heaven and they were receiving all the gifts that they would take with them to earth, that she got into every single line, more than what she was supposed to and received most of them. Depression made her leave every one of her gifts behind. She laid them all down and went away. This should never happen to anyone.*

Kaitlyn relaxing in her apartment

Kaitlyn dressed for the high school prom, sweet smelling
Wisteria in the background in our yard

# Chapter 10

## Memories From Kaitlyn's Friends

### *Separation*

*Your absence has gone through me*
*Like thread through a needle.*
*Everything I do is stitched with its color.*

*W. S. Merwin*

After Kaitlyn's death I was so fortunate to have the words of her many friends, past and present, sent to me by email, cards or Facebook messages. All of them totally were shocked that this happened to Kaitlyn. Kaitlyn was a quiet and reserved person. She always chose her words well, and she chose her friends very carefully; each and every one of them with goodness and integrity. Kaitlyn had a great talent for acquiring meaningful relationships and most of the time, keeping them. She was not the type of person that loved going to big parties and I do think that she had a hard time fitting in with many people. However, the friends she did have who took time to know her, which were many spanning the years, found out just what a special person she was. The ones who did not take the time to know the quiet ones, missed out on knowing my daughter.

Following are some of the words from just a few of the many friends she had. I wanted to include these so you would not just have my opinion of my daughter, because what mother does not think their child wonderful? I wanted you to know the thoughts of those who knew Kaitlyn at one time or another and how she touched their lives. These are only a few selected pieces of the many messages I received.

*Rhonda, I can't begin to tell you how sad I am for you, Allyn and Stephanie. There are so many words that can't be said, so many memories that can't be shared. Please know you are all in my thoughts. There is nothing I can say to assuage the loss you all must feel, but I wanted to share a memory I have of Kaitlyn. Perhaps some comfort can be found in knowing how many lives your daughter touched.*

*I bought a print for her, a Dali poster that reminded me of her. I thought she may like it. I made a frame of West African mahogany from the region in Tanzania she would be staying soon and, on the last day Kaitlyn was here in May of 2010, she and I picked up some matting and glass and assembled it on my back deck. It was a beautiful warm May day and I could sense Kaitlyn was restless for her upcoming trip. As you and Allyn well know, Kaitlyn was all gas pedal. But, in putting that together, finishing the frame, on that day, there was a calmness about her I had rarely seen. It made me realize how complex and wonderful she was. How rare she was. I think of her often and fondly. I remember little moments like this one and feel eternally grateful that I got to share some time with her. I can't say anyone in my life has been better to me.*

*Rhonda, you and Allyn are good people; in a different world I would consider you to be good friends, good neighbors. I am so sorry you two have had to endure this. Please, if there is anything I can do, do not hesitate to ask. I loved your daughter.*

*Kristopher Williams, former boyfriend*

The following is from a man she became friends with when she lived in Cary, NC, before she went to medical school:

*Dear Mrs. and Mr. Elkins,*

*Scanning Facebook this morning, I just found out that Kaitlyn died. I can't believe it; I have rarely known anyone who shared her life and joy so well.*

*Kaitlyn and I met while she was living in Cary. She was a fantastic friend; open and honest, compassionate and caring. She was an incredible listener, sitting quietly and hearing everything I said or couldn't say. I can ramble on for hours - Kaitlyn never minded. She was just so empathetic.*

*One beautiful spring day three years ago, Kaitlyn spent the afternoon goofing around with me and my dog Molly. She took some incredible pictures of the two of us. I too have struggled with depression, but somehow in those pictures, all I can see of myself is a perfectly happy person. Kaitlyn somehow knew how to capture that.*

*My thoughts and prayers are with you and your husband. Your daughter gave so much to me. I am ever so thankful to have known her.*

*Again, Mrs. Elkins, your daughter brought me and so many others such joy. What an incredible woman she was. I am very lucky to have known her.*

*Sincerely yours,*
*Oren Abeles*

Just four days before Kaitlyn took her life, I saw a picture that was put on her Facebook page. As it turns out, it is the last known picture that was ever to be taken of her.

What the picture showed was Kaitlyn and a few other people in a gym. Kaitlyn and another girl were playing some type of game that I had no idea what it was. The picture was posted by the other person with whom Kaitlyn was playing the game. It was a happy post. It showed the other girl on the floor of the gym and Kaitlyn kneeling behind her.

After Kaitlyn died, I emailed the girl in the picture to let her know that Kaitlyn had died. I had no idea that it was one of Kaitlyn's fellow medical school classmates and I did not know that she knew. Following is the reply I received:

*Hi Mrs. Elkins. I just saw the picture posted on your page and the caption, so I wanted to fill you in on what we were doing that day. I admit that writing this to you is as much about getting my own thoughts out as it is about telling you about my experience with Kaitlyn. Our class is about 120 people, but we are split up into groups of about 10 at the beginning of 3rd year, and those 10-person groups are together all year on clinical rotations. Kaitlyn was in my group.*

*During orientation for 3rd year, the whole class had to go to Camp Hanes for team building exercises, and we did the exercises with our rotation groups. I wasn't that excited about the whole thing, because I didn't understand the point. The school began doing this team building thing with the class that is a year ahead of us. I felt like our class got along really well and we didn't need the team building. I had spent a few days telling everyone I know how stupid it was that the school was going to make us spend all day getting sweaty doing stupid exercises so we could bond. I was wrong.*

*The game we're playing in that picture is a bit complicated, but was really fun. Basically the whole group (about 30 of us) split into pairs. Kaitlyn was my partner, because she had been standing near me when we were told to pair up and we were told to pair with someone we didn't know well. I had assumed Kaitlyn was really shy or odd, since I had never really spoken to her, but I was immediately struck by how wrong I was about that. We talked and joked easily for a few minutes before the game started. In each pair, one person gave directions and the other one followed. I'll call them leader and follower for*

146

*ease of explanation. The follower had to stay inside the lines of the basketball court, could only move by walking like a crab, and was blindfolded. The leader had to stay outside the court and would call out to the follower, telling the follower to move left or right, forward or backward, etc. There were a few foam balls in the mix, and the goal was for the leader to: 1. Give directions so the follower could avoid getting hit by a ball (that would mean the team was out) and 2. Guide the follower to a ball and direct the follower on how far and in what direction to throw the ball to attempt to hit another follower (thereby getting that other team out).*

*In the first game, Kaitlyn was the follower (blindfolded, crawling around) as I called out directions. We didn't last very long. In the second game, we switched positions. In the picture, you can see Kaitlyn's strategy for us, which was that I would sort of hang out by the edge for a while to let the other teams battle it out, leaving fewer people for us to have to get out, and leaving fewer people who could get us out. The game was a blast. Kaitlyn and I actually won! We were the last team standing. She was a great coach, keeping me out of range of other players and giving really good directions so I knew exactly where to find a ball and how far to throw it in which direction to get another team out.*

*That game was at the beginning of the day, but it was the best part for me. Before that day, I would have had trouble picking Kaitlyn out of a crowd and didn't know anything about her, yet I knew I would be spending the next year in close contact with her. I think I had only met her one time but I had never really spoken to her.*

*After the day at Camp Hanes was over, people asked me how it went. I told everyone who would listen that I was wrong to be so negative about the trip. I had actually met Kaitlyn and had a really fun time with her. I was so excited that I had discovered another sweet, funny, nice person who would be rotating with me. I told my family and friends and anyone I spoke to about how great this day was because I got to meet this girl, Kaitlyn, whom I hardly knew and now was really excited to be working with.*

*That was early in the week, and I told this story for days afterwards. When I found out Kaitlyn had taken her life, I was overcome with grief. I was also stunned and confused. Here was this person, someone I had never really spoken to and would hardly recognize until a week before, whose name had now come out of my mouth every day for the past week. I spoke to many people about my feelings after hearing about Kaitlyn's death, but I can't seem to shake this weird feeling. It seems so strange that she would come into my life in such an important way, and then be taken away.*

*I really had a moment of clarity after meeting Kaitlyn. I decided I'd be less quick to assume someone was odd just because I didn't know them well. I realized there are people in my class, even though I feel we are generally a close group, whom I don't know well and from whom I might gain a lot if I became acquainted with them. And I thought I had made a new friend and was really excited to get to know Kaitlyn better. I regret that my interaction with Kaitlyn was too little too late. It wasn't enough to make her feel included and understood. And I didn't have time to create a deep enough friendship with her so that we could share our feelings of depression and hopelessness, and help each other, even if all we could do was support each other.*

*Although I didn't get to help Kaitlyn, she helped me. I had so much fun playing that game, and Kaitlyn did too. And I will always remember Kaitlyn for being the one who taught me how much I have to gain by seeking out the quiet ones, and by reaching out to people. I do not know what Kaitlyn expressed to you in her letter, but I do know how deep and intense her pain must have been for her to do what she did. But I also know that even though it wasn't*

148

*enough to turn everything around, Kaitlyn broke through her depression that day, even if only for a little while, and had fun and felt genuinely happy. Losing a loved one who is young makes a kind of ripped open hole inside you, which is unfathomably deep and dark. I hope these words don't make you sad; I just want to express that I have some sense of what you must be feeling, and that I am really deeply sorry. I promise to work towards making the school a friendlier place for students who are struggling (and I can tell you so far that it is actually the majority of us, and not just a small segregated minority). It will never be worth Kaitlyn's life, but since we cannot get her back, I want to make sure that we can at least gain as much from her life and her pain as possible.*

*Kaitlyn's classmate*

Kaitlyn started going to the gym maybe about a year before she died. She always told me how very much she enjoyed it, along with her running. I think she must have alternated running and gym days and she would go very early in the morning before school started. Some days after she died, I received an email from a friend of hers that she met there.

*Rhonda,*

*Thank you for allowing me to contact you this way. I have been following your wall on Facebook and feeling your pain. Your thoughts, words, and questions are the same ones I have floating around in my head and as the tears roll down my cheeks, I share your grief.*

*I know the bond a parent has with his/her child and I grieve with you as only a parent can. I also grieve at the loss of Kaitlyn as my wonderful friend. The news was so shocking to me that I did not believe it and thought it to be a cruel prank on Facebook when another gym friend called me and said he thought she took her life. So much so that I called her phone immediately only to get no answer. I have been in shock ever since.*

*I last texted with Kaitlyn the Monday before she left us. She would often send me an early morning text and ask me "How is your day so far?" She knew I was an early riser and that if I didn't see her at the gym at 5am, I would be up as she started her studies for the day. I shared with her that I was not feeling well and I actually ended up in the hospital with severe abdominal pain that turned out to be a nasty virus. Of course, Kaitlyn being Kaitlyn, she asked if she could do anything for me, which I thanked her for, and that was our last conversation.*

*I remained under the weather, away from the gym and in bed on pain meds for the rest of the week. Our friends at the gym told me she came in on that Tuesday to work out and one of them even asked her if she could check his body fat with her calipers later that week. He told me she smiled and said she would be happy to. So, like you I have been beating myself up wondering what happened between Tuesday and Thursday and I hate that I didn't get a chance to see her because of my illness. In my head, and on occasion even out loud, I have found myself asking Kaitlyn why she didn't call or text me that she needed to talk? I asked myself if I missed any signs. Could I have done more? I can't imagine the pain she must have been in and when I try, my heart breaks and the tears flow as they are flowing now just talking about it. The only comfort I have is to pray and to remember the person that I was immediately drawn to.*

*I met Kaitlyn at the gym in the fall. I am always there very early in the morning and normally it's the same few people day in and day out, so it wasn't hard to spot that a "newbie" was there. I was attracted to her instantly. Not only because of her beauty, but she had a silent confidence and gentleness about her. I remember thinking that she*

150

*was in her early thirties because of the way she carried
herself. I introduced myself and told her if she needed any
help, to let me know. She gave me one of those Kaitlyn
smiles and I was hooked to her personality instantly.*

*We felt comfortable with each other straight away and
struck up a lasting friendship. A few weeks later we decided
to run together. I had not run in some time due to an injury
and she was just starting to increase her mileage after fully
recovering from her marathon some months before. We
decided to run a three miler at a family park. I only bring
up this run because this is where we truly got to know each
other. There is something about running and talking that
makes runners open up with one another.*

*We talked about everything from family, to religion, to
relationships. Though our views differed on many subjects,
we bonded on our openness with one another. We would
talk for hours! Not only did we share conversation, but I
was fortunate to be Kaitlyn's taster for the many healthy
dishes she would prepare. What a great cook she was! Not
only were her meals delicious, but healthy as well. If she
wasn't cooking us a meal, we would go to our favorite Thai
restaurant. This was great for me because she wouldn't eat
her rice, so I got a double portion. I don't think I will be
able to go back there again. Way too many memories!*

*Getting back to running; I showed Kaitlyn a greenway
that she was not aware of that was only a few miles from
her apartment that she fell in love with. It snaked through
the woods and around a lake and if you did the whole thing,
you could get in a 15+ mile run in without having to dodge
traffic. I remember one time she wanted to do her fastest
5k on the greenway. She knew my regular pace would help
her accomplish her goal so we set out to conquer this. Long
story short, she hadn't prepared and fell short. She was so
upset with herself that she began to cry. I held her and
understood her frustration because we were a lot alike in
the aspect of having that "all or none" personality. It took*

*me the rest of that day to get her over it. However, she wasn't going to be defeated and proudly announced that she did it just a few weeks later. I admired her fortitude and saw a lot of myself in her.*

*As she moved forward in a new relationship, and her studies increased to get ready for her boards, we spent less time together, but always kept in touch at the gym and over the phone. We still made time to meet for dinner and I took her out to a fancy restaurant for her birthday which we both enjoyed tremendously.*

*During our time together, she talked about you, her father and Stephanie often and with great love. I could tell how close you guys were. She made it perfectly clear that her family and her cat came first above all things. I know that if she could have helped it, she would not have hurt you guys for any reason! Depression is so silent and hidden and overwhelms a person beyond any logic. Kaitlyn was the smartest person I ever met and if anyone could have conquered this silent enemy, she could have! The only solace I cling to is that she is no longer suffering and the smile that she displayed to all who knew her is now permanently fixed upon her face.*

*I could go on about the person that became my friend, a workout partner and my inspiration to succeed in all we do, but it's still too painful and I miss her too much to continue at this time.*

*I hope in some way by sharing the experience I had with your daughter that it will help comfort you. I know it doesn't make it easier, but I hope this email conveys how deeply she touched my heart and the hearts of all who knew her. My prayers continue to be with you and your family.*

*Christopher Small*

Shannon Massman was Kaitlyn's boyfriend for about 2 years and they remained friends after they broke up and moved on to other relationships. I have included his writings throughout my book because they are so beautiful and moving.

*Kaitlyn.*

*Yesterday I said goodbye, but I still hear you in my thoughts, and you still lead me. Your deep convictions, so honestly shared, still serve as guideposts. Your determined habits still motivate me. Your beautiful, inquisitive joy reminds me how I simply need to seize the happiness offered to me. Your moment of terrible sadness teaches me how much I depend on others. I promise you that I will make it, and I will be the person you saw in me.*

*Even now, you are introducing me to incredible people. They are people I wouldn't have thought to meet on my own, perhaps for their differences, their similarities, or their situation. That was one of the many amazing things about you, your eagerness to embrace the whole world. And yet, they are all beautiful, quality people. Today you taught me how much richer my life can be with those people in it. I promise to be more like you in that way.*

*I'm still here, Kaitlyn.*

*Shannon Massman 4-16-13*

*Kaitlyn.*

*Of course I miss you fiercely. Other feelings are ever-evolving. The sense of personal loss, the sadness for your family and friends, and the echo of your own terrible sadness you finally shared with us. Each is built on the shadows of the last, and each is fleeting as I struggle in turbulence seeking something solid to build tomorrow upon.*

*The panic and despair has mostly retreated to the silence. It now waits in those times I used to be most at peace and insightful; in a quiet moment over coffee, or under the rush of water as I bathe.*

*The overwhelming regret I felt/feel for not having foreseen or prevented this grew daily at first, escalating with each of your good friends and loved ones telling me how you respected me, valued me. Although there are still places inside me that I fear to look, and I still imagine specific ways I could have perhaps given you the strength you needed, with the help of those same beautiful and generous people that you kept so wisely, that sense of personal responsibility is finally easing. In its place, I'm left with still more questions. Confusion. How could this possibly have come to pass? The world was yours! You blazed a trail everywhere you chose to tread. I and many others followed your fearless lead on many journeys, and we all struggled to keep pace.*

*You said that this would hurt me more than anything. But did you consider that I would gladly suffer this to keep you? You hoped I would forgive you, but I can't bear to think you might have believed I wouldn't. I'm not angry, never angry... just...lost. I find that I can throw myself into work finally, and it masks the loss; but this safety also terrifies me, because even the terrible grief is something of you that I cherish. It still connects me to you, it keeps you close, and I fear to relinquish it.*

*My increased sensitivity to your amazing qualities emboldens me to strive to be more like you in many ways. I've already promised you that I would learn to seek out more amazing people to enrich and be enriched by; a talent of yours. But there are so many things I respect you for. I'm afraid to promise to do these things, because many of them, although I wish to attain, are such departures from my skills. I'll do what I can, but some of these things were uniquely you.*

*Somehow, you were always able to sit and write, eloquently and with no hesitation, the distilled, elegant, and uncompromising truth, with kindness in your heart. To compete with you required hours of reconsideration and revision. But you, you merely opened your soul to your pen and you were done.*

*You never hesitated or procrastinated, simply doing what seemed right immediately, unstoppable...and so I tended to envy your life experiences. This too I want to learn from you. I suppose we talked about this...but I wish you had known just how right you had gotten it.*

*While I'm hurt and diminished, you've also given me a new responsibility - to realize how much more I can be. I have to continue. Keeping your counsel helps me even now, but it saddens me too. I wonder, am I getting it right, Kaitlyn?*

*I'm still here, Kaitlyn.*

*Shannon Massman 4-24-13*


*On the surface, my feelings are somewhat numbed, but my dreams of you continue to evolve.*

*It seems my subconscious finally understood the trauma caused, waking each day to discover anew that I have not actually saved you. Yet its confused efforts to heal me persist. As a new perverse 'peace', it offers a fantasy where you are terminally ill. I come to you to tell you how wonderful you are. I retell stories of our time spent together.*

*You are strangely silent.*

*Shannon Massman 6-9-13*


*I received terrible news this morning. My POMS (\*where Kaitlyn worked as a surgical assistant) partner in crime is no longer with us. I am completely heartbroken. She was one of the most beautiful, brightest and inspiring* individuals that I had ever met .We started our fight to get into graduate school together. I still remember the look on her face when she found out that she would be attending Wake Forest Med. She inspired me to never give up.

I am going to miss our random hikes at Umstead, attempting Lord of the Rings marathons, and our random dinner nights. I will never forget the night we celebrated your 21st birthday, the mischief we'd get into at Dr. Won's parties, and how ecstatic we were about the midnight premiere to the final Harry Potter installment. She was the turkey and I was the whole wheat. I'm going to miss you beautiful girl.

*Shalu Bhalu*

### Dragonfly

*Your beautiful, albescent skin*
*Never again to see the sun's rays*
*My tears cut my own skin*
*Like mini scalpels*
*When I reminisce of you*
*My entire body shakes*
*As I weep*
*My mourning is from*
*The depths of my soul*
*It can find no solace*
*Except for mere fragments*
*Of our times together*
*Times when I could protect you*
*But from this*
*I could not save you*
*And it kills me as well*
*The words of your letter*
*Bruise the skin of my own psyche*
*Purple, like lilacs*
*Covering my skin*

*My heart feels atrophied, almost*
*Yet I can still feel it*
*Only as it breaks*
*Into those fragments*
*That will forever remain shattered*
*I know I'll do well in life*
*Because your letter told me so*
*It's all I have left*
*I can't let you down*
*My precious dragonfly*
*One day soon, we'll soar together.*

Stephanie Elkins Alford, Kaitlyn's sister

*I only just saw this tonight, which mortifies me. I want to echo all the words that other people have left. And I'll add this: Even among all the wonderful qualities Kaitlyn had, she was so, so, so kind. It's wonderful that she was brilliant, athletic, ambitious, etc. But ultimately, what is more important than the way we treat others? And Kaitlyn was \*ferociously\* kind. The way she cared about other people and devoted her time and emotional energy to making others feel loved... wow... she's been a model for me in my own life. Rhonda, Stephanie, et al, I'm so sorry.*

Roman Testroet 4-26-13

This is another note from one of Kaitlyn's friends:

*There are few people in the world whose lives could be so widely regarded as special and inspiring as Kaitlyn Elkins' was. Virtually everyone she came in contact with admired her in one way or another. She had one of the strongest minds of anyone I ever met; even when she was so quiet and reserved as a little girl back in school, everyone knew that she was determined, independent and insurmountably smart. It seems like everywhere she went,*

157

*she had a book with her. She was a gifted writer and a talented artist, among so many other things. She simply excelled at everything she put her mind to.*

*The woman she grew up to be was equally inspiring. She was bold, articulate and kept that same sense of determination that she was so well known for. It seems like every time I saw her on Facebook, she was telling about her 10 or 12 mile early morning run that she loved to take so much. She was the kind of person who would never give up until she had accomplished her goal, and she's one of those people who you never forget about, even now that she's gone. She will be missed.*

*Aaron Cartrette, friend*

Here is something written by Kaitlyn's good friend and running partner Neal.

*I was never closer to anyone than I was to Kaitlyn. She inspired me to be a better person. She was all the things I dreamed I was, but wasn't quite. She helped me realize how good I could be.*

*When I first met her, she was finishing college and applying to medical school. I asked her what she would do if she wasn't accepted. She said she would apply again and that being a doctor was the only thing she ever wanted to be. I was wary when she told me she didn't have a backup plan. I knew tons of people who had planned to go to med school and didn't even get close. I never discouraged her. But even if I had, it wouldn't have made a difference. She was driven and in charge of her destiny in a way that I had never seen before.*

*She did so many things so well. She was impossible to categorize because everything she did was superlative. I was really happy when she started running and sharing her experiences with me after I hadn't been in contact with her for nearly a year. I was shocked when, soon after, she decided she was training to run a marathon. She set an ambitious training schedule and an ambitious finishing time. But, I knew better than to argue with her. By the time she told me she was running a marathon, she already knew more about running a marathon than I did and had made her training plan. She met her goal time and went from not running at all to running a marathon in about eight months. She was planning an ultra-marathon after medical school.*

*She wasn't just successful. Everything she did, she did beautifully. She seemed to achieve with ease. She moved elegantly and artfully.*

*I spent most of my time with Kaitlyn just trying to keep up. She grew so much in the time I knew her, I was excited to see what she would learn next. I grew a tremendous amount too. She introduced me to things I wanted to learn. She knew me very well and knew what I would find interesting.*

*Kaitlyn made my life so much better when she was in it. She made it worse by leaving it. I've spent the time since she died falling apart. I've read and reread the text messages she sent me and the suicide note she left me. We spoke nearly every day for her last year. I've gone through our conversations - especially the ones from her last weeks and months. I had no idea her world was crumbling. She had just finished taking her Medical Licensing Exam. She was doing team building exercises with the other medical students at a retreat. She was starting the last 2 years of medical school, and she seemed so happy to be so close to her goal. She had spent months and months studying for the exam and finishing her second year of medical school. She would have been an excellent doctor.*

*We talked and laughed like normal. She was planning to meet me that weekend to run in a race. She canceled the race with me the week before, but still planned to visit.*

*I wish I had known what she was thinking. I wish I had seen her cancellation as a sign. I wish I had known her as well as she knew me. I wish she were still here. I am left with a scar that will never heal.*

*Some day, I hope that I can find the strength to live a life that I would be proud to share with her.*

Neal Timpe 1-16-14

Next are the written feelings of Kaitlyn's suicide by her sister Stephanie:

*"I have something terrible to tell you," my mother said to me in between sobs on what is now the bleakest day of my existence. My thoughts immediately flashed to the future, thinking that she would tell me that something happened to either my Nanny or my Daddy, because I always worry about that phone call. The next sentence proved my thoughts untrue. "Your sister Kaitlyn has killed herself."*

*After the involuntary scream and tears spilled from my eyes, I thought that surely my heart would cease beating altogether from the magnitude of what was just said to me. My sister was dead; I knew that to be true cognitively, but mentally I hoped that it was just a sordid prank. "I'm going to kill Kaitlyn for playing such a cruel joke," I tried to reason with myself. But I knew that she had already taken her own life. My baby sister was gone, and there was nothing that I could do about it. My mom was still on the phone with me, so I asked all of the normal questions: why, when, how? etc. These only provoked even more questions. I could give in to my emotions and go crazy, or act rationally. I knew that, in private, I could lash out at the world for this happening, but I had to be strong for my family.*

*Through tears, I said goodbye to my mom and told her*
*that I would be heading home, which is an hour away.*
*They (my mom, dad, uncle and Nanny) were already*
*making the three hour trek to Kaitlyn's apartment. I had to*
*take leave of my emotions long enough to call my work and*
*let them know what had happened. I wrote a quick poem in*
*between about my sister, because I knew if I didn't do it*
*then, my thoughts would be lost later. Afterwards, it hit*
*me: I was just about to go shopping for her. You see, I was*
*a coupon junkie and I always managed to get an*
*abundance of free food that way. When Kaitlyn was home*
*for Easter, I told her that I could get a bunch of oatmeal for*
*her for free. Before my mom had called, I was getting*
*ready to leave my house on my oatmeal quest. Talk about*
*the horrible irony. I would later personally give her a box*
*of oatmeal while she lay in her casket, never to be able to*
*enjoy it.*

*After I somehow managed to call work, I told my*
*husband, who was also extremely upset, that I would be*
*driving home by myself. Knowing better than to argue with*
*me, we said our goodbyes and out the door I went. I can*
*still remember the drive home so vividly. I made it to my*
*Nanny's house in good time. She had gone with my*
*parents, but my aunt, uncle and a woman from church were*
*there. As soon as I entered the living room, my aunt was*
*waiting for me and gave me a tearful hug. All eyes in the*
*room were red with sadness. We talked about Kaitlyn and*
*pondered why she did what she did. My two cousins*
*arrived after a while and we talked for a bit. I had always*
*been very close to my cousins, especially when we were*
*very young, so I was grateful for their company.*

*I walked through the yard and by the pond that we all*
*loved when we were youngsters. It provided me with a*
*small degree of inner peace, but I knew then that things*
*would never be the same. After staying at my Nanny's*
*house for a few hours, I went to my parents' house once I*

161

*knew they had returned home. My parents live across the road and to the side, so thankfully I did not have far to go. There were several family members sitting with my parents; aunts, cousins, grandparents. All were there to comfort us, but no amount of words can heal a freshly damaged heart; at least, when you are in a sea of sadness, this appears to be true.*

*I would like to say that the pain subsides, but it doesn't. It does, however, become somewhat easier to manage (at least, it does for me). And this is what I live with every day: my sister will never be an aunt, mom, or wife. Not only was her precious life taken away, but ours were robbed as well. This is a story that, although morose, needs to be told. More importantly, it needs to be heard.*

As I have mentioned previously, Kaitlyn's last boyfriend was a long distance boyfriend she had met on an online dating site like so many people do these days. Kaitlyn knew that I didn't feel that long distance relationships were good for people as they are so hard on the people involved because they cannot see each other often. I did not know about Shai until just before she came home for Easter and she was nervous telling me about him because she knew I may not approve due to the distance. She was a grown woman and did not need my approval, but she did worry about what I thought, although it still did not prevent her from doing what she felt in her heart was something she wanted to do, and she had fallen in love with him.

Kaitlyn had the amazing ability from the time she was a little girl, to "present her case" - if she was trying to get me to see things her way - in such a way that would usually make me feel good about any decision she had made or wanted to implement. She would always explain to me rationally, intelligently and calmly her thoughts and ideas and, far more often than not, she would have me seeing things her way.

After she told me everything about Shai via email, I again told her of my concerns, but told her that she was a grown woman and always made good decisions, so I wished her the best in her relationship with him, hoping with all my heart that it would not cause her to be lonely. Shai was older than Kaitlyn by about 17 years or so, but Kaitlyn was usually drawn to older men because they were so much more mature than people her own age and I think she found much more in common with them. He was divorced and had two children.

Though I have said all through my book that no one knew of Kaitlyn's depression, that is not altogether true, because near the end of her life, she chose to put it on her dating profile and confided in Shai about it. I don't know what prompted her to finally tell someone, but he did not see that she was suicidal during her visit because she was so good at hiding it from all of us. She also hid the severity of it from him too. Kaitlyn had told Shai that we were aware of her depression, but the reality is we were not. She was not in the habit of lying to us but I believe she told him that so he would not be alarmed by her depression and tell us.

I feel with all my heart that she did not go home with the intention of ending her life after seeing him, because she participated in everything she usually did; going to school, going to the gym, logging on and posting her dietary intake for the morning on an online site that she belonged to, just as she always did. I feel that the depression that in hindsight was apparent, fluctuated in its intensity and during that week she spiraled into a deep depression and acted upon it. I know from her note it was not the only time she had thought about killing herself, but I don't think she had planned on doing it when she did until the last day when she stayed out of school. These are just things I think. However, I still don't know what was fact and never will in this life.

I asked Shai if he would like to write something about her for my book and he eagerly agreed to do so, and for this I am grateful. I am also grateful that he was in her life, though far away. She loved him and he loved her and he gave her as much happiness as her mind would allow at that time. It's just that just like the rest of us; his love or ours was not enough to keep her, because depression does not care who loves you or who you love.

Here is Shai's letter about Kaitlyn:

*Today the grief hit me again, and I was crying as I walked into the airport. The same terminal, the same stop. The place where I watched her walk away that last time, sad for the end of her visit yet flooded with a fierce and wild joy for having such a wonderful girlfriend. I am Kaitlyn's last boyfriend. On Sunday, April 7th, I drove her to the airport, and on Friday that week, after 48 terrifying hours of silence, I heard she was dead by her own hand. I have been grieving for the loss of her longer than our actual acquaintance, and that speaks volumes as to the kind of woman she was in life.*

*Kaitlyn and I started communicating with each other in September of the previous year, through an online dating site. Although I was living very far away from Winston-Salem, I would occasionally look for compatible matches without any geographic limits on the query – more than anything else to give myself hope that women who are right for me do exist, even if none of them are nearby.*

*In the computer, Kaitlyn's profile came up as a perfect match against the many hundreds of questions both she and I filled in. Even upon my careful reading, she was perfect. Obviously bright, articulate, successful and stunningly beautiful. She was too young for me to consider it appropriate to date her, and too far away. Her profile said that she "was born in sadness" and expressed a poignant loneliness – speaking of her sense of isolation in Winston-Salem, and her need to find like-minded souls to connect with. I wrote her a short note saying "I don't expect we'll ever meet, but I want you to know you're wonderful; keep doing what you're doing; don't give up on being you". And that was it. I heard nothing back.*

*In January the following year, I saw that she visited my profile. Needless to say, I was surprised – why would this amazing woman show up at my electronic doorstep? So I sent her a message saying "I was surprised to see you visiting my profile. Thank you for dropping by". Kaitlyn replied with a long letter confessing that she had been "profile enjoying" me since September, but had been doing that in the "stealth" mode available to paying members of the site. She felt I was perfect for her, and was correspondingly finding it really intimidating to contact me. From that start, we started a flurry of text conversations and video calls. A couple of weeks later she visited for the first time – for just over a day. It was heavenly.*

*Kaitlyn and I communicated almost daily. She was a morning person, and often went running at dawn, whereas I am a night owl. The joy of my day was to wake up every morning to a message from her. We would video-conference almost every night – both of us working on our respective academic pursuits: she studying for her medical board exams, and I reading and writing papers related to my scientific work. When she was ready for bed, I would "tuck her in" by talking about our day, our plans for tomorrow, and our growing love for each other.*

*During the weeks leading up to her medical board exams, Kaitlyn felt even more isolated and stressed, having little opportunity to interact face-to-face with anyone, so I visited her for a week. In April, right after her exam, she came to visit me for a similarly long stay. Then she was gone.*

*We spoke often of our future together, which she looked forward to very much. She felt uncomfortable with the religiosity of the North Carolina, and yearned to live in a more liberal environment. The excellent research hospitals in my area appealed to her, and the hope of finding a residency in one of them once her rotations were over was a common topic for our conversations. She really wanted to have kids, and I too was hoping to start a new family, after my marriage dissolved. In most things, we saw eye to eye, but in those things we didn't, Kaitlyn would often bring me around to her point of view with grace and eloquence. She was truly my match; more so than I had ever dared to hope to find.*

*Kaitlyn also became close to my dearest friend, Margaret. The two of them enjoyed a warm and affectionate connection that grew independently of my connection with either. During Kaitlyn's last visit, the three of us spent many happy times together.*

*Throughout my relationship with Kaitlyn I was aware of her sadness; that very sadness prompted my first message to her. I spoke with her about it, and never once felt that it was dangerous or out of control – her hope; her infectious joy; her fierceness in pursuing the future she was building for us – all spoke of a woman who is passionate about her life and future. Who is aware of her sadness when it appears, and makes no attempt to hide it from me.*

*In her suicide letter to me, Kaitlyn wished for me to find happiness, and apologized for taking away all that we had hoped for together. That is a hollow farce – Kaitlyn sentenced all of us who loved her for a lifetime of grief for her loss, by never having given us the chance to treat her condition. She had contracted a lethal disease; one that not only kills those who succumb to it, but also leaves all those who love them indelibly scarred and wracked by pain and grief for many years.*

166

*On April 7th I watched Kaitlyn walk away for the last time, waving me goodbye and smiling; a vision of beauty and grace. "Classy", I thought to myself, "you lucked out, this time". Almost a year later, I can't walk into that terminal without crying for the loss of my fierce and wonderful pixie lover; the pain is still raw and burning when it hits. Having her in my life was worth every moment of this excruciating pain. She was worth spending a lifetime with.*

*Shai Revzen*

I have saved Shai's writings about Kaitlyn for the final part of this chapter because I wanted to express some feelings I have about some of the things he has written.

I have spent hours upon hours reflecting on some things that he has shared in this letter and during our correspondence since Kaitlyn's death. The reason being is that so many of the things he told me that she said are such a departure from the Kaitlyn I have known all my life; the parts of Kaitlyn I thought I knew at the end.

He writes that Kaitlyn was uncomfortable with the religiosity of the area she lived in, particularly the south in general. She also indicated she felt this way to me in the last year of her life, telling me she wanted to go into residency in a more liberal place such as San Francisco or Seattle (before she met Shai). This seems to imply that Kaitlyn felt this way all her life. (I'm not saying that he made it sound that way; I'm saying that in the end, Kaitlyn actually felt this way because I believe him and from what she told me herself). I fought the urge not to include that sentence that he wrote, but I did include it because I wanted to leave what he had written and how he knew her. Besides, I have not left out any of the other things her friends have written about her, but I would like to write a bit about Kaitlyn's religious experiences as she was growing up.

167

From the time our children were born, we took them to Sunday school and church with us. We attended a very old (established in 1850) Presbyterian church, which by that time had a pretty small congregation. However, there were a reasonable number of children their age. Our children always seemed to enjoy church and happily attended on Sundays and in the summer during Bible School. Our congregation was so small there was no Wednesday night service or many extra services, except during revival. If one knows how Presbyterian churches are, they know that during service it's very quiet and low key.

Once Kaitlyn reached adolescence, I knew that she began to question certain things in the bible and other beliefs. She had a very open mind and never, ever believed in anything just because it was taught to her, or because it had been taught to millions of people for thousands of years. She always questioned, always searched. She did not do it in a disrespectful way, but a way that was sincere.

Our preacher had been with us for years and he and Kaitlyn developed a close relationship. On many occasions he and his wife would have sessions where they would discuss the bible and her educational pursuits with her. Kaitlyn loved our preacher and was always eager for these talks.

At some point during her early teenage years, she began studying, on her own, all the major religions of the world. I knew this because I would see the books on different religions in her room. I asked her about this and she said that she was just trying to learn about the different religions. She always asked me how we were to know which religion was right, that each religion thought theirs was the only correct one. She was searching. Years later I asked her about her search and why she felt the need to do it and she said, "I was just trying to find something to believe in Momma."

When Kaitlyn was around 16 years of age, she began dating a boy steadily and she then started to go to his church. This church was much more demonstrative in its services than our quiet Presbyterian church was. She enjoyed that church and became a Sunday school teacher for the youth. She attended many extra things that the church did and also went to a Christian concert in another state. At this time, Kaitlyn was greatly immersed in the church's activities and continued to date the same boy and attend his church for 2 years until they broke up and then went away to college. Kaitlyn even partly chose the college she went to due to its base in religion. It was a regular private college but it also held some mandatory religious courses. This is what Kaitlyn wanted at the time.

Once Kaitlyn was in college, I think she went to a few churches trying to find one to belong to, and when she came home she would attend the church she and her ex-boyfriend attended. However, after a time, she just stopped. Somewhere along the line Kaitlyn became disillusioned with religion. She went from full force religious beliefs to not going to church at all.

It took me three years to finally redecorate her room once she went away to college. I begged her all those years to please go through everything she left behind and decide what she wanted to do with it. Years later, she finally just said, "Momma, you just decide what to do with it and it will be ok." So I did. It took me a long time to decide what to keep, what to give away and what to throw away. Even then, she had still left the many scriptures she had written on paper and hung on her closet wall; the many different bibles left in her book shelf, the books of C.S. Lewis and all her books I saved.

As she became involved with her medical school studies, and maybe before, her scientific beliefs just collided with anything having to do with religion and I think she became disillusioned. I don't know why, but I feel she was searching for something that she never found. This was Kaitlyn's religious upbringing. She was never forced to go to church; she did question many things, but she believed and she seemingly embraced and enjoyed everything she did concerning the church. Shai's revelation that Kaitlyn felt uncomfortable with the religiosity of the area where she lived confounds me. I knew about Kaitlyn's feelings of cynicism concerning religion before she died, but I did not know that she harbored the memories of a childhood and an adulthood where she felt "uncomfortable" with the religion around her. Though this is not what Shai said she felt like when she was growing up, it made me think that perhaps she felt that way and it made me a little confused. I don't know when Kaitlyn started feeling this way. I don't know whether her illness made her believe that religion had been forced upon her in childhood, but she had certainly not been bombarded with it. I think that maybe that towards the end of her life, she started remembering things differently to how they actually occurred. Or maybe she felt pressured into practicing her religious beliefs because it was expected of everyone around here. I have no idea. In her journal that ended in 2008, she expressed a great belief in God.

As her parents, though we went to church regularly, we never really discussed much about religion and church outside of it. I often felt guilty about this. But I was just not the type of person who was very outspoken in my beliefs with other people, but I believed in all that I was taught and I tried to be a good role model for my children. However, I believed there was more to our creation and past as a human species than what the bible revealed and I had an open mind about it, believing that the teachings of the bible and science and evolution could have worked together in some way. So strict religious beliefs were never forced upon our children.

Shai had also told me before that she felt isolated as a child due to her intellect and this is something else I did not see. She had such a close group of nice, intelligent friends. She never appeared lonely. She went to sleepovers and parties, and she usually always had a boyfriend. If she felt isolated, she never, ever showed it. She was a quiet person, but so am I and I simply did not see it as a problem. As I mentioned earlier, Shai was the only person that I have found in whom she confided about her depression. She told him she was "born into sadness." It hurts to know this because I never knew she felt this way. I did not know sadness could be completely veiled by a facade of happiness.

One of the saddest things of all is Shai telling me that she had confided in him that she was, "…a fake, lazy, and would wind up disappointing everyone" and that she was broken. A fake? How? Because she faked being happy when she was not? Possibly. I don't know what else she could have been faking. She could not have faked intelligence, or ability, or being a wonderful, caring person. Lazy? The only time I ever saw her lazy was with me when we would vegetate on the couch for hours when she came home, watching our favorite movies and talking. Otherwise she was totally devoted to studying, running and being with friends. Disappoint everyone? She could never have disappointed anyone, including us, even if she had packed her bags and left medical school in pursuit of something else. Never, ever. I think she cared more than she would admit what other people thought of her. I never knew this. Broken? My baby was broken? How was she broken? What made her broken? This breaks my heart so very much that my baby felt broken and I didn't know it.

All of the things that Shai told me were huge indications that my daughter was very ill. She was still highly functioning. She dressed well and took care of herself and her body until she died, but she was very ill because she had never told anyone anything like she told him at the end of her life. If she had told me her thoughts like this I would have taken her to get help. The things she expressed to Shai were things that I never knew she thought. But he didn't know she wasn't getting help. He thought I knew all this.

He told me that she had told him that he was the only one who really saw who she was. It was because she chose to show him who she was. I think in the end she needed to at least tell someone how she felt.

So, in a book that I have written that indicated she showed no signs of depression, I have now said that she did. But she only did it at the end of her life to only ONE person and that person thought we knew. The things she told him did indicate someone who was clearly depressed, who had a very low opinion of herself; something no one else knew. But I do not blame him for not knowing that something was seriously wrong, because she told him we knew and he thought she was getting help and support from those she loved.

Kaitlyn, January 28, 2013 (Photo ©Neil Timpe)

# Chapter 11

## Signs and Dreams

*For in grief nothing "stays put." One keeps on emerging
from a phase, but it always recurs. Round and round.
Everything repeats. Am I going in circles, or dare I hope I
am on a spiral?
But if a spiral, am I going up or down it?
How often - will it be for always? - how often will the vast
emptiness astonish me like a complete novelty and make me
say, "I never realized my loss till this moment"? The same
leg is cut off time after time.*

*C.S. Lewis, A Grief Observed*

In the early days after Kaitlyn's death, I longed to have
some sign from her. I needed some acknowledgement of
her continuing existence in the universe somewhere,
somehow.

I knew that many times loved ones who have passed
over would often visit those they left behind in vivid,
meaningful dreams. I also knew that sometimes they were
given some sort of sign to let it be known that they still
existed. Oh, how I longed for these signs!

As I stated before, I was brought up in a Christian home,
but I was always so open minded. I believed in the bible
but I also believed that there was so much more that we as
humans do not know and could never comprehend until we
die ourselves. Who really knows what heaven is like?
Who knows where it is? Does it exist right beside us on
some different plane that we cannot see? Or does it exist
far away into the cosmos, or even past the edge of the
universe? What form do we assume when we die? Do we
lay asleep in our graves until the Lord calls us, or do we
immediately go to wherever it is we go?

Different religions believe different things. Who is to say who is right? Do we reincarnate into a different body? If so, do we do that immediately or do we have to wait a certain time? Do we exist in any form close to how we were before we died, or do we become a part of all the energy within the universe? Energy never dies, but is just transferred into a different form. Sometimes an open mind is a mind that cannot rest for trying to figure out the answers. My mind was and still is like this. It makes me not know where Kaitlyn is. Is she somewhere near me, is she all around me, or has she already been born into a different body? Is she in heaven knowing how much I suffer, or is she there oblivious to my suffering? Does she still remember me in whatever form she is in? These wonderings torment me and never let my mind rest.

My relationship to Kaitlyn was and still is so very important that it hurts me profoundly to even think that she is somewhere and does not remember me, or how close we were, or just how much we meant to each other. If this is true, what is the point of our life here on this earth if we can't continue the strong bonds formed here on earth to wherever it is we go? So knowing she still exists somewhere is so very important to my ability to survive her loss. She must exist. She must still be somewhere. Most of all, she must be happy.

Now I know there are religions that say that if one takes their own life, one will go straight to hell. Fortunately, no one has said or even implied this to me at all since Kaitlyn died. I have never believed this. I know that someone who takes their own life is depressed and depression is an illness. I know God would not send someone to hell for being sick in body OR in their mind. I do not give much thought to this for in my mind and heart, my Kaitlyn is not in any kind of hell. No one that wonderful would go to hell.

This is my belief and my energy is not wasted in wondering this, but I did want to at least mention how I feel.

As I continued to wish and hope for signs from Kaitlyn, I dreamed nothing at all. My sleep was deep blackness induced by anti-anxiety medication prescribed by my doctor. Nothing could penetrate that blackness. It was the only way I escaped my nightmare in life; having sleep that allowed me to go into nothingness.

One day, however, my niece, (who was near Kaitlyn's age), sent me a message saying she had dreamed about Kaitlyn several times. She and Kaitlyn did not have much in common, but they respected each other very much and they shared the gift of being artists. She said the first dream came to her a week after Kaitlyn died, but she didn't know if she should tell me or not. Then she had another dream about her the week after that. Still she didn't tell me. Then soon after that she had another one and at that time she felt she must tell me. This is the message I received:

*Rhonda, I have had three dreams about Kaitlyn. I haven't said anything because I didn't know what to think of it or whether it was just my mind playing tricks on me. I honestly don't know if any of this means anything but I really think it does. Also, I dream every night and I've dreamed things before and the next day, whatever I dreamed will happen.*

*So the first dream that I had, it was you, Allyn, Kaitlyn and I in a small room. Kaitlyn looked like she did before lost weight and cut her hair. Nobody could see her except me, but she was happy and smiling and she told me to tell you that she was there and that she was happy and loved you both very much. She said that she was exactly where she was supposed to be and it was neither of your faults that she did what she did. Then she told me to tell you to*

175

*hug her, even though you still couldn't see her, but you hugged her and I could see it. You were happy, and so were Allyn and Kaitlyn. This dream was the one that was very significant to me.*

*The second dream is very foggy to me, but I just know she was there looking at me.*

*The third dream I have only just awoken from. Kaitlyn was sitting down and she looked the way that she did when she died; she was cold and I hugged her to warm her up. The only thing she said was, "Why haven't you told my mom?" I know she was talking about the first dream I had and I know that is probably why she keeps appearing in my dreams. Believe me, this sounds as strange to me as it does to you, but I think she really wanted me to tell you this. Seems very real to me. I love you and I hope this brings you comfort.*

I cannot describe just how this dream touched me. I really felt that it was a sign from Kaitlyn and she was trying to reach me through someone else. I believe in signs like this. I believe that those that have died can come to us or others through dreams. I know there are many fake mediums, psychics, etc. out there, but I do believe that there are real ones in this world. I also believe that anyone can be the recipient of dreams from our loved ones and receive signs. Those dreams gave me so much peace, yet I was still miserable. I have found the two can go hand and hand, impossible as that may sound.

Finally, one night at the end of June, I had my own dream of Kaitlyn. It was so vivid and I felt as if we were really together and that the dream had great significance.

Kaitlyn and I were walking together. She looked like she did the last time I saw her with her short hair. She was smiling her usual sweet smile and displaying the charming demeanor she always had. She seemed happy and excited. She had both of her hands around my upper arm as we

176

walked together. While we were walking, there were visions above us. The only way I can describe these visions is that they were scenes of the way people were once treated years ago when they had mental illness. One person was confined to a small, enclosed space and not allowed out. There were other scenes, but those are too foggy to remember. It was probably just the result of my fitful sleep and distraught state that caused this strange dream. But if I wanted to think it real, I would interpret it as Kaitlyn telling me why she didn't tell anyone about her depression; because of the stigma attached to it and the problems it may cause by admitting to it and seeking help. Even though it's not as bad as it once was, it is still an uncomfortable topic. That's the way I interpreted the dream anyway. But it was good to see her smile, if only in my dream; Kaitlyn was very happy.

And then I started seeing some signs.

Kaitlyn knew I loved the movie "Dragonfly" and she had bought me a teapot with dragonflies on it. Two months after she died, when my husband and I went on the 2-week trip to South Dakota, mentioned earlier, I saw dragonflies everywhere and even bought two necklaces with dragonflies on them. The Native American from whom I bought one of the necklaces said that the dragonfly was a sign of protection to them. When we got home, there was a dragonfly on my front door. Was this a message or just my mind's desperate attempt to make some connection with Kaitlyn; to somehow know that she is somewhere safe and happy? I don't know, but I took it as a sign. I can do that. It made me feel better. Also, as the summer went on, I saw an unusually large number of dragonflies everywhere. Sometimes, when I was having one of my worst days and I was outside playing with our dog, I would see one or two dragonflies flying around me for a long time.

There was one summer night when my husband brought me a coin that he said he just found in our spare change tin. It was a thick brown coin, which I knew from the look and feel that it was not from the United States or Canada. I collect coins and I could tell. However, at that time (my interest in everything has declined since Kaitlyn died), I was not even interested in looking more closely at the coin, so I just laid it down. A couple of days later, I decided to take a closer look at it. The coin was from Tanzania, the country Kaitlyn had visited when she was in undergrad at Campbell University. I do not remember her giving me coins from there when she arrived home. I don't remember seeing them in her personal belongings that I have either. So how did that coin get there? There has never been an instance where I have seen any foreign coin other than Canadian or British in change. Could this have been a sign? I happily took it as one.

My husband and I were in the yard one day in September 2013, as we always are in the afternoon, playing with our dog Savannah. My husband asked me if I had seen the bud that was on one of our azalea bushes. I looked at him as though he were crazy. It is SEPTEMBER; azaleas only bloom once a year and that is in the spring around April. I thought he must have seen a pink piece of paper or something and thought it was a flower. Now sometimes azaleas may bloom too early when we've had a few warm days in the winter, but I've never seen one bloom in September. He told me to go over and look for myself, because it might still be there. So I walked over to it and, lo and behold, there it was; one tiny pink bloom on one of my huge azalea bushes. Pretty as can be. No other bloom on the bush and no other blooms on any of the many azalea bushes I have in my yard. In the 26 years we'd lived in our house, I had never seen any of the azalea bushes bloom in September. Kaitlyn died when my azaleas were in full bloom. I wonder if it was a sign from her.

One morning in October I awoke from a vivid dream about Kaitlyn. We were sitting in a parked car somewhere; she was on the driver's side and I was on the passenger's side. She looked just like she did when she was 18 before she went away to college. She looked at me with that worried look on her face (a face she always had if she was very concerned about something; you could see it in her eyes and expression, her little forehead all furrowed up). She looked at me and said, "You're worried about me, aren't you Momma?" I said "Of course I'm worried about you. You're here but you're not really here."

I had a pack in my hands like Goodie Powders except that it contained some kind of medicine that was a strong painkiller like Darvocet (this kind of medicine does not exist that I know of). Kaitlyn looked at me and asked, "Why do you take that stuff?" I said, "I have to because I am in so much pain. And besides, this is probably how you died." (I know that drugs were not involved in her death, and I do not take narcotic pain medication of any sort unless prescribed by an MD or dentist).

I looked up to see where we were and it was like a school. Then I turned to face her again, but she was gone. And I woke up.

I'm not sure exactly what this dream meant, but it could be one of two things to me. Perhaps she was trying to tell me that I should no longer worry about her, that she was alright and at peace. But perhaps she was trying to tell me that she was in fact, worried about me. I don't know, but it was so very real, as though she had really been beside me. I can see her worried face now.

Just before 7 on the morning of 11-11-13, the seven month mark of when Kaitlyn took her life, I awoke from a vivid dream. I got up and fed my dog since she was out there barking and came to type my dream down while it was still clear in my mind.

179

I dreamed I was working at a hospital as a floor nurse. I have these dreams often even though I've not been a floor nurse for over six years. As usual, I have never seen this hospital before; it's always a different one. But in this dream I was my current age of 53. I had been assigned seven patients for that morning. I went into each patient's room and carried out my assessment of them, writing down important information on my little pad as I always did. I remember them. I remember one of them had a urinary catheter bag I almost forgot to check. The last patient I went to check on was a large man with oxygen tubing lying beside him. His chart read, "If he turns blue, put oxygen back on." Well that's just ridiculous in real life, because if someone turns blue you make sure the oxygen is on and call a code. But he was not blue; he was a healthy color. He was a nice man with black hair and was my seventh and last patient to check on before I started passing out medications etc.

Getting ready to do those things, I passed a small lobby that appeared to be some type of daycare. The hospital must have a daycare facility for its employees' children. How convenient I thought that was. But as I passed, I looked on the floor next to a bookshelf of toys and books and there sat Kaitlyn, totally immersed in playing. She was about 2 or 3-years-old. All of a sudden, I forgot about space and time and the present and I just ran over to her and said "Kaitlyn, what are you doing here?" I thought, "Gosh, she's wound up in the wrong daycare somehow. I bet her daddy brought her in as a surprise." I was SO glad to see her!

Her blonde hair was up in pigtails and she was wearing a little matching shorts' outfit with large stripes on the shirt and little polka dots on the pants. The stripes and polka dots were purple and the rest of the set was yellow. This does not sound pretty, but it was. This was one of her outfits.

I ran to her, so very happy to see her, and I sat on the floor where she was at and held her little warm body close to mine, smelling her hair like I always did. Smelling her hair was always like going to heaven for me. It was like getting a glimpse of her soul somehow. She just felt so good in my arms.

Then, all of a sudden, I remembered how old I was and that Kaitlyn had really grown up and died. I knew right then that this was just a gift that I was receiving, that I got to talk to and hold my girl one last time as a young child. She smiled so sweetly, looking up at me with those little glasses on. I held onto her tightly and she held onto me tightly as she always had done throughout her life. I told her, "Honey, I know I can't keep you here; this time has long gone and passed." She just smiled at me, and I hugged her again and told her, "Goodbye Kaitlyn. Goodbye my little girl. I love you and I miss you. I always will."

And my dream was over. I woke up with the smell of her hair and her warmth still with me.

On the day before Thanksgiving I had the following dream that I wrote about in my blog:

*I woke up as usual this morning around 5:30 at the request of my cats to feed them. This time, it wasn't so very hard to get up because I did not feel the overwhelming sleepiness that I usually feel when I have to get up to feed them. After I fed them, I was not going to go back to bed because I was not sleepy, even though I had stayed up very late last night. But I decided to go back to bed since I didn't think 4 hours of sleep was enough.*

*I soon drifted off to sleep to my surprise and as I was lightly sleeping, I heard my cat Dagny running around all over the house; he's so big and heavy he sounds like a horse. It seemed like he was doing this forever, but as I heard him in the background, those sounds became the sounds of Kaitlyn running around the house playing, jumping in my bed like she used to do to talk excitedly to me. She was so happy and looked around 8-years-old.*

*As dreams sometimes do weird things, we were suddenly outside on a warm sunny day at my mother-in-law's house. The sprinkler was on and Kaitlyn was having fun running in and out of the water having a wonderful time. She was wearing a green shirt and yellow shorts. I remember those clothes well.*

*All of a sudden the playing stopped and she ran to me as I was kneeling down watching her, her hair in a messy ponytail due to all her playing and her hair, skin and clothes damp from the sprinkler. She ran into my arms and we hugged so tightly; not the little hugs one gets sometimes, but a full on neck-to-neck, our arms around each other. She was crying so hard and I started crying too. She said, "Oh momma, I'm so sorry, but I tried so very hard, so very hard, but I couldn't stay. I hope so much that I gave you happiness and that I didn't disappoint you." She was crying so hard. Still holding each other, my hand touching the back of her hair, I told her, "Kaitlyn you gave me the most happiness in the world and I could never be disappointed in you, never."*

*We were still hugging each other full on when I woke up. I can still feel her hair and her damp little body. And I cried and cried as I woke up remembering the feeling of her in my arms and the hurt in her voice that she had to leave. As I lay there, I whispered out loud as I cried, "Thank you Kaitlyn for coming to see me again. Please never stop even though it makes me cry."*

*I need her so much all the time, but in my darkest hours sometimes she comes.*

# Blog post July 3, 2013: It Was in the Spring

*It was in spring, my favorite time of year, when the azaleas of my yard were in full bloom and the green grass of my yard started taking over from beneath the brown of winter. The cool chill was giving way to warm breezes and the pollen was starting to fall. Yes, spring, my favorite time of year when new life is emerging, when everything starts anew and there is freshness in the air. On one of these fine spring days my daughter, as life burst forth, the deep hidden darkness you held secret inside of you for so long caused your heart not to see the promise of new life everywhere. It caused you to go into winter, when everything seems dead. In the gray, black and white that is depression, it wiped away, in your mind, all the color of spring, all the color of your beautiful life, your beautiful mind, your beautiful future, your beautiful self, all hopes of a future you deserve and took you away from us all. You saw yourself as winter.*

*You were always the spring bursting forth in a world that was dark. You blazed your light across a sky that was black. You, who I never knew had winter in your soul, always shined with spring.*

*So you took your life in spring taking with you the world I had once known, the realities I thought I knew and my life as I knew it. But you never took my love away. It went with you, but is also in my heart to stay.*

*I will never see you as anything but spring.*

Kaitlyn in 2010

# Chapter 12

## Similar Experiences

*Be kind, for everyone you meet is fighting a hard battle.*

*Socrates*

Since Kaitlyn took her life, as I have mentioned before, I have had an outpouring of sympathy from many people across the world due to my openness about her death on Facebook and my blog. Online, I have met so many parents, wives, husband's, siblings and so on whose lives have been touched by suicide. Trying so desperately to find somewhere where I could relate to other people that have been through this, I have come across and joined many online forums on Facebook and other sites that are dedicated to people who have lost loved ones to suicide.

Again, though it helps so much to have the support of these wonderful people, almost all of the loved ones left behind said that their children always showed signs of depression before taking their lives. I have read about many brilliant, talented, creative and driven young people taking their lives, but the majority of them displayed symptoms. That's not to say that I cannot relate to them. It doesn't mean that I don't feel for them greatly. If it had not been for these relationships I have formed with these devastated people, I don't know if I could have survived. Having access to a place, even online, where bereaved families are able to talk about their feelings, is a life saver for many people, including myself. There are forums where you don't even have to reveal your true identity, so you are free to talk about your true feelings of sadness and despair. Those forums are invaluable.

Though these sites have helped me immensely, nowhere could I find anyone who had lost someone to suicide who seemed totally happy and had no observable problems prior to the tragedy.

As time went on, it just reaffirmed my belief that Kaitlyn's situation was unique. Was my daughter the only one in the world that showed no signs at all before killing herself? I was beginning to think so.

One day, I came home to find a message on my answering machine. It was from a man calling all the way from Oklahoma. He had found my blog, read it and called to say that he could relate to me so well because about six months before Kaitlyn took her life, his 15-year-old son did the same thing. He went on to say that his son was also very intelligent, succeeded at everything he did and showed so much potential. He said my daughter very much reminded him of his son.

I called him back and we had a nice conversation until he had to return to work. Since that time we have become very good online friends and he has helped me along so much. I feel a kinship to him due to the fact that his son, like my daughter, showed no signs of depression whatsoever and by all accounts was happy and successful. He writes so beautifully about his son, and I wanted to include his words here. He wrote the following about his son two and a half months after he took his life:

## My Personal Tsunami

*The year 2012 arrived innocuously and inauspiciously enough. Throughout three-fourths of the year just past, I was lulled into a false sense of security that 2012 would be just another mundane year in the steady progression of time. The days rolled by one-by-one with the same unrelenting predictability as waves rolling in one-after-the-other upon the seashore. There is a relaxing comfort to be*

186

*derived when you are basking in the sun with the rhythmic waves lapping at your feet in the surf.*

*But then, on October 17, 2012, seemingly out of nowhere, there arose a dark towering wave and within seconds, before I could even catch my breath, it blocked out the sun with its massive proportions and in a split-second of sheer terror it descended upon my placid yet precarious existence. And then it struck with obliterating force. For the longest time there was total and complete darkness. The life air was sucked out of my lungs as I was plunged into the chaos of disorientation, confusion, and disbelief. One minute I was living just another ordinary day and the next I was thrown about like a rag doll in the hands of a sociopathic sadist. I didn't know up from down. I no longer recognized my surroundings. I couldn't get my bearings. In the turbulent dark water I tumbled head over heels as I was buffeted by forces totally beyond my control.*

*I descended into my deep, dark, watery grave. A lifetime of memories crossed my mind. I couldn't breathe. I was suffocating in the dark abyss. I could hear the faint sound of familiar voices in the background of people who were trying to help me. In the blur of the moment, I could hear their words but I could attach no meaning to what they were saying to me. I saw multitudes of familiar faces, yet I couldn't begin to tell you who was there with me, save a few.*

*I'm sure that I was very, very close to completely giving up. I had no strength left or comprehension of what was happening to me. My life was over. I had given up.*

*But then I called upon Him. I thought He had abandoned me. I screamed at Him. I cursed Him. I was very, very angry at Him. I wanted to turn my back on Him as I had done so many times before. And then He reached down through the dark murky depths of my despair. He wrapped His mighty and powerful arms around me and He rescued me. He brought me out of the depths of my sorrow and He breathed new life into my lungs. He gently placed me back upon the placid shores from which I had been eviscerated.*

*I looked around and everything was different. I knew that I was in the same place, but my surroundings had completely changed. I knew that I was different, too. My entire body ached with unimaginable pain. My mind no longer seemed to work the same way as before. I was devastated and wrapped in suffocating grief. Suddenly, I felt very alone as a though a part of me, perhaps the best part of me, had been ripped out of my body. The black towering wave that had descended upon me without warning receded back out to sea as quickly as it had engulfed me. Now the real pain would begin.*

*I will concede that I was completely numb when that dark force reached down into the depths of my soul and tore out a third of my heart. I sensed immediately that I had been grievously wounded, perhaps mortally so. I didn't know if I could survive or even if I wanted to carry on living. But I sensed that I had to, for there were others who depended upon me. I also wanted to survive out of sheer defiance against the rogue wave that damn near killed me. I just didn't know how incredibly difficult it would be just to survive as I tried to heal my bleeding heart.*

*As I surveyed the landscape around me, nothing looked familiar. Everything was essentially the same around me, yet I knew that I would never be the same person again. The sun still shined during the day. The moon still gathered the stars at night. Life went on without skipping a beat around me. How could it be so? How dare the earth continue to rotate with the days turning into night and dawn returning again and again every morning when my life was stopped dead in its tracks and frozen in time! But as the brightly flowering red and yellow chrysanthemums in my garden faded to brown decay and the last hardy leaves fiercely clinging to the skeletal trees in my yard lost their tenuous grip on the branches and gently succumbed to their fate below on my dormant lawn, I instinctively knew that the winter of my despair had just begun.*

*Am I losing my mind? I can still hear my son speaking to me, but he only speaks to me with a single word. I strain to remember and hear the sound of his voice. It terrifies me that I might forget the sound of that adolescent 15-year-old boy's voice. But I hear it constantly in my mind over and over again in monosyllabic fashion. The word reverberates through my mind with the same kind of consistency as the waves lapping the ocean shore. I hear my son calling me "Dad". Sometimes his utterances are happy and other times he sounds sad. Oftentimes, the sound of his voice is exasperated with me as it was when I might tease him about a girl or some other thing that he thought to be foolish. Maybe the reason I only hear my son saying but a single word is because I long to hear him call me "Dad" again. Maybe it's because I know that my son was forever lost in that deep dark wave that took him away from me. Whatever the cause, if I only remember the sound of my son saying but a single word to me in the subtle nuances of his various tones of voice, I suppose that the word "Dad" is as good as any.*

*I can still remember all the familiar places before that fateful day, but now the landscape is permanently and irrevocably changed. To be honest, I don't like my surroundings much anymore. I'm uncomfortable in my own skin. My priorities in life have all changed. Many of the things I once considered important now have little meaning or value to me. I don't particularly like the person I have become and I'm not sure that others would have much patience or tolerance for me, either. I understand that. I am now damaged goods. I am but a shadow of my former self. I am among the walking dead. I live in the moment. I try to avoid thinking about the past because it is just too painful to contemplate. My plans for the future have been so*

189

*radically altered that I have surrendered my goals and aspirations for the future upon the altar of despair. I live one day at a time.*

*But I have not given up! Having been dealt one of the most devastatingly painful and crippling blows that any parent can possibly endure in life, I am bloodied but determined to rise again upon my wobbly legs to fight for living yet another day. I've had the life knocked out of me and though I often feel defeated, I am not vanquished. I will live to fight another day and another day and another day until ONE DAY I might possibly be rewarded with my hoped-for reunion with my son. I only wish that I had been able to impart to him the virtue and the courage that is often required to face the painful struggles in life in the face of seemingly overwhelming challenges. So now, Sam, I will pick up where you left off as my way of attempting to honor your memory. May you always gently speak the encouraging word of "Dad" in my ear.*

*Randall Robinson*

Reading these beautiful words from my friend made me realize that I had a kindred spirit across the states. I could relate so much to what he wrote, his beautiful, eloquent words of pain and loss. But I also knew I had much to learn from him; that desire to live and to defy the horrors of that terrible foe that took the life of our beloved children. Where did the desire to fight come from? How can one climb out of the pits of hell into which one has descended and fight this horrible thing that took our children? I knew I must find it, but at that time, the jury was still out on whether or not I could even live any longer.

These are the words that Randall wrote about his son on the one year anniversary of his son's death:

## Reflections on the One-Year Anniversary of My Son's Death by Suicide

*One year ago, my first public statement about my son's suicide began with the following words:*

*"Two days ago, my precious 15-year-old only son, Samuel P. Robinson, scrawled a hastily prepared handwritten note in his bedroom and then quietly retreated into the cool autumn night at the bottom of my ex-wife's large backyard. I have replayed in my mind hundreds and hundreds of times what might have been going through his tortured mind when he finally raised the barrel of the handgun that he pressed against the very center of his forehead before squeezing off a single round that instantly killed all of my dreams and aspirations for my youngest child."*

*In the year that has passed since then, it would be an understatement to say that things have changed in my life. It might be more accurate to say that my old life ended on October 17, 2012 - the day my son, Sam, ended his life. When my only son died, a part of me died with him...perhaps, the best part of me. The world, as I knew it, ceased to exist when my child breathed his last breath. On that day, my entire world slipped off its axis, leaving everything in chaos and confusion.*

*Sam's suicide was as sudden as it was unexpected. There was no time to prepare or brace ourselves for what has justifiably been called "every parent's worst nightmare". The pain of losing a child to suicide is more horrific than the most terrifying nightmares. Grieving the suicide death of a child is like living in a recurring nightmare from which there is no waking. Indeed, peaceful slumber evades the newly bereaved parent who learns that their child has taken their life. Sleepless and fitful nights become the norm when your dead child is the last person that you think about before drifting off to sleep and the first thought that enters your mind when you wake up in the morning. Throughout the day, not 10 or 15 minutes go by without intrusive thoughts of your child's suicide. The most painful thoughts are those that recall every grisly and bloody detail of the scene where I reacted in horror at the sight of my son's lifeless body.*

*I'm sure that it took me every bit of six months, if not longer, for the shock and the numbness to begin to wear off and the awful reality finally began to set in that I would never see my son again. (Not in this lifetime, anyway.) That's when the real work begins in grieving the loss of a loved one. Fortunately, by the time the thin veneer of denial and disbelief began to fade, I was already involved in a support group that was meeting me at my point of need. Meeting once a week at my church, the Survivors of Suicide support group gave me an opportunity to discover that my grief was neither extremely uncommon or unique. In fact, I have discovered that suicide crosses all ethnic, socio-economic, religious and cultural barriers. No one is entirely immune from either suicide itself, or the effects of suicide, which are far-reaching upon the families that it touches.*

*Surrounded by so-called "survivors of suicide", as we refer to those who are bereaved by the suicide death of a loved one, it does not take long to discover that we survivors share many of the same questions about the deaths of our loved ones. Of course, THE central question is usually simply "Why?" i.e. Why did you choose to leave me? Why didn't you get help? Why didn't you tell me you were in trouble? Why couldn't you have found another way? Why wasn't my love good enough to keep you here? Why?! Why?! Why?!*

*It also does not take long to discover that the only person who could satisfactorily answer any of these questions is no longer talking. Even those who do choose to leave suicide notes (who, curiously, are statistically in the minority) generally leave many questions unanswered and their motivation unclear. It soon becomes apparent that we will never have completely satisfactory answers to the questions we have about why our loved ones chose to leave their bodies. Partial answers and some strong clues are sometimes capable of being gleaned from the behavior and activities of those who have completed suicide; but, as with all suicides, there is simply a mystery about the unknowable that must be accepted and embraced by those who are trying to make sense of what amounts to a senseless act. There are some questions for which we will not find satisfactory answers...at least, not in this lifetime.*

*A close cousin of the "why" questions is the whole category of speculation dealing with the "what-ifs" i.e. What if I had only done this, that, or the other? What if I hadn't done this thing or that thing? What if I could do this over again, what would I change or do differently? There are hundreds of what-if questions that constantly undermine the thinking of survivors of suicide, forcing them to re-examine every angle of their prior interactions with their loved one with the hope of identifying something that might have, or could have, made the difference. Mostly, the "what-if" questions that we survivors bombard ourselves with are an exercise in futility, since nothing that we could say now or nothing that we have said or done in the past is now going to change the outcome. Still, it is human nature to assume that we have a great deal more power or control over the actions of people than is actually the case. Ultimately, my son and my son alone is responsible for the choice that he made for himself. Obviously, I would have chosen a different outcome for my son or at least a different approach to the handling of his undisclosed problems. But I was not permitted the luxury of any input, advice, or counsel concerning my teenager's unilateral decision to end his life. I regret that, but it does not change the outcome.*

*Once you are left with the conclusion that you will never have full or complete information as to why your loved one took their life and once you have come to accept that all of the what-ifs in the world are not going to change the final ugly reality of the suicide death...it is at that point that we finally come full circle and return to the ageless question that so many of us must confront in facing any type of painful circumstance in life. Why did this happen to me and what can I learn from it? The noted French philosopher Jean-Paul Sartre once said, "What is important is not what happens to us, but how we respond to what happens to us."*

*I have not yet fully determined how I will respond to my 15-year-old son's death from suicide exactly one year ago today. But I have already seen a few profound changes in my life and I don't mind sharing a few of those things with you before I close. My son's death has helped me to feel profoundly more empathy toward other people who are suffering from bereavement. People who suffer in silence with debilitating mental depression that they either cannot or will not discuss with others are now heavy on my heart. But the people with whom I feel a particular kinship are those who have similarly experienced the unimaginably painful loss of losing a loved one to suicide. There are no words to describe their pain; but, I have felt or experienced it myself. I have seen the shell-shocked look of devastation on the faces of family members who have wandered into my support group shortly after the funeral of a spouse, a child, or a sibling who has died of suicide. I know how hard it is for them. I have the heart of a servant toward them now. I want them to know that they CAN survive the death of a loved one!*

*Toward that end, I have poured myself into my local suicide survivors' support group where I have received training and assumed a leadership role in co-facilitating our group at the invitation of our group's leader. I'm also active in an online suicide survivors' support group on Facebook which, sadly, claims almost four thousand members whose lives have been directly impacted by suicide.*

*Suicide - the very name is probably the ugliest word in the English language. Yet it is a word that describes the fatal culmination of a painful condition from which our loved ones were unable to free themselves despite their best efforts. My son was drowning in depression right before my very eyes and I didn't see it. Nobody saw his head slip underwater repeatedly during the five previous suicide attempts he alluded to in his terse suicide note. Nothing is known about those five prior attempts at suicide. To this day, I do not know how those earlier attempts were accomplished or how close he came to succeeding with the plan that he eventually brought to completion. I have only my son's belated confession in his suicide note that he had been "suicidal since the sixth grade" and that he had previously attempted suicide five times. Again, I just don't know whether the earlier suicide "attempts" that my son recounted in his note consisted of holding a gun to his head and not being able to pull the trigger, swallowing a handful of pills without the intended effect, slipping a noose around his neck and not being able to follow through with it, or some other cause. It really doesn't matter now whether his earlier suicide attempts came close to succeeding or if they were merely half-hearted trial runs. Since nobody knew anything about the earlier suicide attempts and the first time we learned about them was in my son's suicide note, we were effectively denied the opportunity to intervene. The fact remains that Sam succeeded at just about everything that he set his mind to doing...and suicide was no exception.*

*Sam didn't fit the profile of the kind of person that you might think to be at risk for suicide. He was popular and well-liked. He had good friends who came from good families. Sam was especially gifted academically. He was a straight-A student. Outwardly, he seemed reasonably well-adjusted. He was well-groomed and maintained good personal hygiene. He was conscientious about what he ate and he tried to maintain himself in good physical condition. If you were to describe a desirable type of son to have, he would possess many of the qualities and traits of my beloved Sam. But Sam was no more perfect than any of the rest of us are. His greatest defect was that which he managed to hide with the greatest of skill. I believe it was the pervasive sadness that, by his own account, took root early in his life while he was going through adolescence and increasingly debilitated him as he progressed toward high school. One of Sam's best friends said, "He wore his mask well." He didn't breathe a word of his unhappiness to anyone.*

*Could anyone have made a difference with Sam? Could anyone slow that train of emotions before Sam allowed himself to derail? Would anti-depressants and cognitive therapy have made a difference in Sam's life or would he have struggled for a lifetime with debilitating mental depression? Again, these are the kinds of questions for which there are no satisfactory answers. This is the mystery of suicide.*

*In the midst of all of the confusion and mystery that surrounds my son's death by suicide, let me conclude with certain truths about which there can be no doubt. Samuel Philip Robinson was unique and precious in God's eyes. He was loved by a mother and father who would have unhesitatingly sacrificed their own lives to save his. He had two older sisters who loved and cared for him as well. He showed great promise and potential during his abbreviated life. He had a great number of friends who cherished him. He also, in all likelihood, suffered from undiagnosed and untreated mental depression, which ultimately claimed his life. The depth of his depression and unhappiness remained carefully concealed from view and was never honestly acknowledged or admitted. His passing will leave a permanent tear in the fabric of our family life that can never fully be repaired.*

*As I write this, it was exactly one year ago today at roughly this same time of the night when my son Samuel contemplated ending it all. Oh, how I wish that he might have abandoned his plans that grew in the Petri dish of hopelessness. How I wish I could have instilled at least some minimal sense of hopefulness in my lost Sam. How I wish I could have saved him...if only I could have seen him struggling. If only...if only...if only..."*

*Randall Robinson*

When I read this very moving, articulate telling of my new friend son's suicide, I realized, among many other things, just how far my friend has come in the one year that he lost his son. When I first read it, I told him that I can only hope to come to the terms of understanding that he has reached in the aftermath of this devastating loss. He suffers greatly I know, and he always will, but he is using his pain to help others and to assume a leadership role in helping others. I admire him so much. It takes such great strength to do that. I can only hope to one day attain his level of strength.

I have recently met another grieving mother online whose life has been turned inside out and upside down by her daughter's suicide. Her daughter was very talented and sweet. It took much courage for this mother to write this for my book and I appreciate her contribution about her wonderful daughter so much.

*My only daughter, Amy, took her life eight days before her 24th birthday. She left behind her cat, Grace, her two dogs, Lavinia and Cody, three unpublished novels,*

197

*numerous works of her own art, a purple bike we had picked out together for her birthday and a family who still can't believe she is gone. She also left a suicide note that was written on a yellow sticky pad saying, "I am sorry. I knew this was coming and I couldn't stop it. I can't fight it anymore. Please don't hate me. I am finally free." Amy was funny, smart and beautiful and I know now that she didn't value herself at all.*

*A few days before she died I sensed something was very, very wrong. She had been living in Denver and going to college but she came home for a few weeks towards the end of this past summer. I realize now that she left this world unwillingly because she was no longer able to stand the pain of continuing to stay. But I never expected the phone call - the shock of someone telling you that your daughter is dead. Dead means never seeing her face again, never hearing her laughing, never hugging her as hard as I can and living with the excruciating grief that never ends from missing her in my life.*

*I remember saying at her funeral that her life felt like an old fashioned movie in two reels. The first reel was her childhood. I took care of her as a baby and then helped her grow and become more independent. I worried about her and prayed and hoped she would be safe and lead a happy life. The second reel is the one I was waiting to watch. In this reel, she would find someone she could make a life with and have children and also hopefully have the career she worked so hard for that would bring her satisfaction. But I never got to watch it. The second reel is gone now. Stolen away from me forever. All my hopes and dreams for her will never be realized.*

*I feel now like I am Alice in Wonderland. I have stepped through the looking glass into a new world. I can't seem to find my bearings in this new world without Amy. I am lost, confused, in pain, and grieving. Her brother, who is 15 months younger than Amy, is lost too. Now we mark*

*everything together as BAD and AAD - before Amy died
and after Amy died. The hard reality that I have yet to
really accept is that it will be that way now for the rest of
our lives.*

Lisa Koumis

**Blog Entry:** *Sadder than Sad*

*I wake up every single morning to the realization that
my sweet 23-year-old youngest daughter took her own life.
I lie in bed and ponder that fact, in the place where we
spent many Saturday mornings talking since she was very
little. Before I get up I look at my dresser with the photo of
all of us at Disney World when she was little, a photo of her
and her sister when they were little, and a school picture of
Kaitlyn with a frame made from her Popsicle sticks. You
can still see the red dye where the Popsicle was. There's
her last bottle of perfume. On my side of the bed, where I
grab my glasses before I put my contact lenses in, there's
the old shelf with some of my books and a few of the
ceramic angels Kaitlyn gave me when she was little. This is
all before I make it out of bed.*

*As I walk around the bed, there is the beautiful photo of
her taken at daycare when she was around 4-years-old,
with her straight blonde hair and glasses in a pretty dress
in front of a picture of a big apple. I turn to walk out of my
bedroom door, but before I do I pass the photo of her when
she was in high school and the very last picture I see in that
room is the one of Kaitlyn and me that she had beautifully
framed in her apartment. It's the one we took in
Washington, DC. That is the one where I run my fingers
across her image daily. Then I look down and there is the
box made from some type of stone that she bought for me
once as she knew how I loved decorative boxes.*

199

*Then I enter the hall and there is the frame containing all the photos of our family in our early years; Stephanie is very young and Kaitlyn is a baby. On the other side of the hall is the small spare room where I put so many of Kaitlyn's things from her apartment after she died. I feel her presence so much there; her scent often fills the room.*

*Then I go to my bathroom. It is filled with things she helped me pick out from Bed, Bath, and Beyond when I finally redecorated some of the things in there after years. She helped me pick out some towels and the pretty shower curtain that has butterflies all over it, the beautiful trash can and the toothbrush holder and soap dispenser. The beautiful "Falling Water" soap still sits on my soap holder unused. It's the last thing she ever gave me, on the last day I ever saw her alive. I can't use it or it will disappear like she did. Next to the sink is the washcloth holder that she had in her bathroom with nothing on it. In my tub are still remnants of the nonslip decals that are on the bottom that she had applied so expertly and precisely. When she was a teenager and in her bright pink and bright color phase, I let her decorate this bathroom herself, which was mainly used by her (we have 2). After I redecorated, some of the pink flowers and butterflies could not be removed from the bottom of the tub, so they remain. Then there's Kaitlyn's shaving cream for her legs I still have and have not used up yet.*

*I walk out of the bathroom and to the kitchen where I am immediately met by the left end of my refrigerator where I have to this day, and since the very day I put them there, some of the things Kaitlyn drew and made as a child. I still have some of her report cards and even her high school transcript there. On the other side is a postcard she sent me from Africa when she went in 2010. It starts, "Dear Parents". She has never addressed us that way, always "Dear Momma and Daddy" the way she addressed her suicide note. I guess she wanted to sound a little more formal in her postcard.*

*I go to make my coffee and there is her mixer, her spice rack with all the spices and her nice toaster. I look out my kitchen window and there sits the red wicker sleigh on the ledge that she had put there when she was a little girl, now faded, never having been removed from that spot. I walk past the kitchen table and look at the chair where she always sat. I walk past one of my bookshelves to see another decorative box she bought me with two pictures of her in Africa on either side.*

*Before I make it to the couch with my coffee, I pass another bookshelf where her bronze baby shoes are and her little porcelain blonde child figurine with the number 7 at the bottom, which was given to her by one of her teachers on her 7th birthday because she loved Kaitlyn so much. They all did. She was their dream student and so very sweet. There also sits a beautifully framed picture of her when she was around 17.*

*I sit down in my den and look to the left of me on my fireplace mantle and there is a photo of her as a baby looking out to me and beside of it is her footprint that was framed by her grandmother Elkins.*

*I look to the right of me and in my living room is a room filled with all her living room furniture that inhabited her apartment complete with the large beautiful self-portrait she drew and I had framed. That picture was not in her apartment as she had left all her artwork at home when she left for college.*

*This is what I am faced with EVERY SINGLE DAY when I get out of bed and EVERY SINGLE DAY my heart breaks off into even smaller pieces until I'm sure there will be nothing left to it one day. The intensity of the pain I experience in all of this never decreases. Ever.*

*Then when I go outside or leave the house, I start this same process with things that remind me of her out there.*

201

*Then at night the whole process I described for the morning starts over again only backward. I trace the image of her picture where she and I look out of that photo with happiness in our eyes. I get into bed and again the last thought I have is that my daughter killed herself, that she is no longer here and that I am sadder than sad and I wonder how a mother can live like this for the rest of her life. I wonder.....and I am sad. So very, very sad.*

*And then in the morning I awake to the realization that my sweet 23 year old youngest daughter......*

A daycare picture of Kaitlyn

# Chapter 13

## Personal Stories of Depression

*There are wounds that never show on the body that are deeper and more hurtful than anything that bleeds.*

*Laurell K. Hamilton, Mistral's Kiss*

While my focus of this book is about the many people that suffer depression in silence, I also want to include the stories of people that suffer depression and thankfully reached out for help before they went past the point of no return and ended their lives. For many of these people, their symptoms were evident, which forced them to obtain help.

It is also extremely important to make people aware of the stigma attached to mental illness. Yes, we have come far from the days where mentally ill people were locked up and the key thrown away forever, but we still very much live in a society that places a heavy stigma on any form of mental illness. One of the reasons I think my daughter did not share her depression with anyone or reach out for help is due to this stigma. I have no way of knowing this for sure because she never shared this with me, but after losing her I have reflected a million times on the possible reasons why she did not seek help, and the stigma is one of the most likely reasons.

Here are some of the stories of successful people that did not want to reach out for help initially, but when they finally did they were met with adverse reactions, some even from healthcare professionals who should know better. How can we as a society implore people to reach out for help, when they are met with criticism. So many people are ignorant about what depression is; a disease that should be given the same attention as any other medical condition.

*In my most severe depressive episode, I lost 30 lbs in three weeks. I wasn't at the point in my life yet where I really knew how to reach out to people to help me, so I was all alone in my one room apartment. I literally lay on the living room floor for weeks, I think actually, two months. From time to time, I would crawl/stagger/walk-holding-the-wall to the bathroom and then either just go to sleep on the bathroom floor or on the floor between the living room and the bathroom because it was too much energy to get into my bed. And I think part of me also just thought I belonged on the floor, you know.*

*Sometimes I would realize that I needed to drink some water or eat something, although I had absolutely zero interest in either, so I would make my way the few steps over to the kitchen and find something old in the cabinet, like crackers, and drink some tap water in a cup. I didn't want to die; I just didn't know how to live anymore. I was doing all I knew how to do, which was hang on. I felt very sad and I hoped that maybe I would just accidentally die and go to sleep there on the floor and not wake up so it wouldn't be a suicide. I would lay as still as possible to try to quiet things that were happening in my head; memories, bad things. I felt like I was disappearing day by day. It was an emotional pain that I am unable to describe; vast, profound, nearly beyond my human ability to withstand, so I would just lay very still day after day.*

*I wish I could tell you I did something brilliant, but I just lay on the floor. One day, I felt kind of sick like I was going to throw up, so I went to the bathroom and was on my knees in front of the toilet. I felt like I was going to faint and the next thing I remember was waking up on the floor of the bathroom and my head hurting. I slowly stood up and saw in the mirror that the whole left side of my face was swollen to where my eye was completely shut. From where I had been laying, I figured I had fainted and hit my head on the side of the tub and knocked myself out. It was actually a moment of change, because after weeks and weeks of total pain and nothingness, I thought, "If you don't do something that makes you get out of this apartment, you are going to die in here. Either you are going to hit your head like this and just die, or you will die from just not eating and not wake up." And I didn't really want to die. I just didn't want to hurt so badly all the time and I didn't know what to do.*

*I called my brother who lived nearby who knew nothing. I just told him I was sick because I was ashamed to tell him I was depressed. He said I could come and stay with him and his wife that night and that they would take me to the emergency room. I felt a little relieved, but still embarrassed. I was glad to finally have human contact.*

*We went to ER. They did a whole workup. At the end of it, my brother said this to me, "The Dr. tells me there is nothing wrong with you and you need to stop acting like this; you can't stay with us anymore and you need to just get yourself together and do whatever you normally do to just get on with your life." I felt so incredibly ashamed and I knew I should not have reached out for help, because I didn't even know how to do that.*

*As I lay in bed on the night I spent at my brother's, a verse of Scripture I hadn't thought of in years came floating into my head, as I felt like I was drifting out into space, lost, alone. "Peace I give you, My peace I give you, let not your heart be troubled, neither let it be afraid." The words had the effect of what I imagined it would feel like for someone to hold me in their arms and rock me softly to sleep.*

*The next day I went back to my lonely apartment. I felt deep despair that I am unable to describe. I gathered all the change I had in my car and in my apt and drove to the local grocery store where I knew exactly where the medicine aisle was. I only had very limited energy, so my plan was to go there, go directly to that aisle, buy as much* medicine as my money allowed, and take it all, hoping it would end my pain.

I walked in, went to the aisle and there, to my surprise, both sides of the entire aisle all the way down were completely empty. I stood there wondering, is this real, is God shielding my eyes or are they redoing the store or what in the world? The next thing I remember was a remarkably strong and warm sense of God's sure presence, like a hug from someone who knows you, then I actually smiled. It was like God had smiled at me and said, "Dorian, really? C'mon now!"

Next in the sequence I remember becoming aware of how my clothes were just literally hanging on me and how I was incredibly hungry. So I took the little money I had and went over to the bakery section, bought two chocolate donuts, ate them before I made it back to my car, drove back to my apartment and went to sleep. Still the best donuts I've ever eaten in my entire life.

The next morning, I remembered what I had thought before, that if I didn't have something to do to leave my apartment, I would likely just die there and someone would eventually just find my body. So as awful as I looked, I gathered myself, one of the hardest things I have ever done - and I have done some very hard things - and I drove a block to Taco Bell to apply for a job. There, I had a divine appointment, which I describe in another piece of writing. It was a turning point, yet still a very long journey.

What I can say, now that I have had nine years of being totally free of depression (due to mental health help), is this: When someone you know who has had a track record of success suddenly becomes incapacitated, they need help! Remarkably, that ER Dr was, in my opinion now as a well person, an idiot! It should have been very clear to him that SOMETHING was VERY wrong! I did not even LOOK right. My clothes were hanging off of me. Half my face was swollen. If I had been a person who had been lazy all my *life, a slacker, had always laid around, never accomplished anything and just expected other people to take care of me, then I could see my brother saying those things to me. But you know what? I already had a college degree, magna cum laude, Phi Beta Kappa. I had won awards as a journalist. I had worked four jobs at a time. I had been working since I was 14. I had never asked anyone for anything. I had accomplished every single goal I had ever set out to do. Something is wrong when you tell someone like that, well, you need to just get yourself together and quit acting like this! Really?*

*Now that I'm well, it makes me mad because I know it is still happening to someone today who is alone like I was. People - depression is not a character flaw; it is not a personal weakness. When people do things that create illnesses by lifestyle choices, we don't even criticize them! Yet people who have depression, which is basically a broken brain, we attach a stigma, we act like they need to just straighten up and act better. You know what? I will never be ashamed of it again! Done with it! I will forever speak out about it. Because I don't want anyone else to ever feel like I did when I went to that ER for help. It's unacceptable. When someone has a broken bone, we don't say, "Oh, you need to be tougher." Yet when they have a broken brain from depression or trauma or both, we act like they don't deserve our love and kindness. We live in the 21st century, people, not 1900. It's time to catch up! There are amazing treatments to save people's lives, but people won't even seek them out if there continues to be a stigma attached to just saying, "Hey, I really hurt so bad and I need someone to help me."*

*Just some thoughts from someone who's definitely been there and who can tell you that we are not designed to live like that. We are not meant to live without hope. The Bible says, "Without hope, the heart is sick." There is hope and as human beings we should be about the business of helping others who are suffering FIND IT.*

*Dorian Quillen*

The following is a story from a new friend I have found via my blog. I asked her if she would include her story as an example of what it feels like to be depressed:

*I was my parents' firstborn - a chubby, adorable baby and, in their eyes, utterly perfect. I don't know when the idea of being perfect entered my little head but it was probably around the time I was four-years-old and both of my little brothers had been born. We were brought up inside a house of absolute love mixed with a kind of fundamentalist Christianity; i.e. we were loved, we were disciplined, and then we were loved again. I remember being terrified of doing something wrong - terrified of even thinking something wrong - and at night I would kneel beside my bed with my beautiful mother and ask forgiveness for all of my many sins. I vividly remember not particularly liking my little brothers and the dreadful guilt of this, but I was too young to be able to express this to my parents.*

*Back then (the 1960s), "depression" wasn't used as it is now. I knew something was very wrong with me from the age of four, but I didn't know what it was. I was the perfect Sunday School child, the perfect big sister and the perfect kindergarten student but, behind the scenes, I wet my bed and sometimes my underwear intentionally, hiding it underneath the chest of drawers; I threw my precious hanky into the dog yard as a dare, and, one day (and I remember it vividly), I was walking up our driveway and I think I was about 7-years-old and I whispered, "I hate you, God," hoping that I would be struck dead immediately, but*

208

*obviously I wasn't. Instead I became tortured and secretive
about what I had said to God.*

*At the age of five, at kindergarten, I used to write my
worries at the back of my notebook and sometimes I would
show my parents and they would try to solve each one. This
was a daily ritual and, as an adult, I look back and my
heart goes out to my child self whose 'Worry List' became
longer each day. As I recall, most of the worries were to do
with not being perfect, of not being kind enough, of not
understanding the teacher, of being afraid of the big girls,
of feeling angry or hurt, of not praying enough, of not being
a good Christian etc.*

*My parents were wonderfully reassuring, but must have
wondered! In today's world a child like me would probably
be sent to a psychologist but back then childhood
depression, chronic anxiety and OCD, were not terms
anyone used. I believe I had all of these syndromes, but I
think my parents just saw me as a strangely intense, sweet
and good little girl.*

*Later in my childhood, I became a high achieving
student but also a loner. During lunch time at school, I
would go to the back of the school yard and climb a very
tall tree, right to the top. I would hide there until the bell
rang. Eventually, this was discovered by one of my teachers
who apparently spoke to my parents and to the children in
my class and for about a week everyone was very kind to
me. I felt watched and uneasy and relieved all at the same
time, but I was never allowed to climb that tree again.*

*After that, my main anxiety became that something was
odd about me and my poor parents had to continually
reassure me that nothing was wrong with me, but their
reassurances didn't work and by the time I was entering
adolescence, I was in a constant state of deep, painful,
relentless guilt and anxiety. I was friendly but so shy that I
didn't make friends easily. I was teased a lot, but not
exactly bullied, except by exclusion.*

*At 17, I fell deeply in love for the first time, but the romance didn't work. However, my love for the man (who is incidentally now my husband) was unrequited for years and then, when my father died suddenly when I was 19, I fell apart inside, but couldn't show this because I wanted to be supportive to my mother. I became thin and withdrawn and I can still taste the horror of those dark years, despite my memories being somewhat blurry.*

*One day, I began to cry and it just wouldn't stop. I rang my mother who lived two hours away and she came straight away and took me to a psychologist who recommended I be institutionalized for a little while. It was a horrible place, like a prison, but I stayed in my little room and took the little yellow pills (I guess valium) and gradually emerged, but with no solutions to what I now know was, and is, Depression.*

*I continued to struggle with feelings of utter hopelessness. I trained as a nurse, held down jobs, got a degree, then a PhD, married the love of my life and had our baby son, began getting my stories and a book published, and all seemed well, until one day, when Ming's Grade 1 teacher reminded me for the second time to get him some left-handed scissors, something once again snapped. Driving into town for a routine doctor's appointment, I couldn't stop crying at what a failure I was for not having gotten those scissors earlier. In the doctor's office, I sobbed and sobbed about the stupid scissors but, once I had calmed down a bit, he looked at me kindly and said, "You have Depression." This had never been said to me and in a way it was a relief and yet it also filled me with a sense of shame. He prescribed me with 50 mgs of Zoloft per day and eventually this had to be increased to 100mgs and now it is 200mgs. The diagnosis and the medication, I believe, saved my life.*

*And yet, despite the wonderfulness of this, I still keep my Depression a secret and hardly anybody knows – close*

*family and friends have no idea. Perhaps, having hidden it
for my whole life (despite the signs), I feel embarrassed
still? I don't know. Also, I wonder if there is any point in
sharing this aspect of myself with others. I don't want
people to worry about me (that is a huge factor come to
think of it); I don't want people's advice; I don't want
sympathy; and I don't want (a remnant from my childhood)
people to think I am strange, or weak, or faulty.*

*If it hadn't been for Rhonda asking me to contribute a
bit of my story to her book, and if I hadn't been touched
deeply by her daughter, Kaitlyn's suicide, I would never
have thought to write anything like this about myself. But,
just by doing so, I have realized that "coming out" of the
Depression closet might just be helpful to others. I don't
know.*

*Julie Goyder*

Thank you to all these wonderful people that agreed to
put part of their lives in my book. It will go far, I hope, to
reassuring others who experience some of these feelings
that they are not alone and that by seeking help their lives
can be drastically improved.

## Blog entry 1-30-14: What Transcends Death

*Yes, I am in deep horrible grief about the death of
Kaitlyn. I isolate myself a lot but I do not imagine things. I
know I've mentioned incidences with Kaitlyn's cat Gatito
before, but last night really made me think there may be
something to this.*

*The things that have happened before that I've
mentioned are these: He will sit in the middle of the floor,
look straight up at the ceiling and meow. Well maybe he
just likes to meow at the ceiling and nothing more. Then
along with that, he sometimes gets on top of my dresser*

211

where Kaitlyn's pictures and her perfume are and meows at them. The thing is though, these pictures are of when she was a child, not an adult, but the perfume was the last perfume she used. This is the only furniture other than our couches and chairs that he will get on top of. He does not jump on tables or counters or anything like that. Then the other day he got on top of the back of Kaitlyn's couch and meowed to the self-portrait that Kaitlyn drew that I have hung behind the couch on the wall. Last night, I was sitting on the couch in my den, feeling horrible. Gatito got on the back of our small couch that we keep in front of our never used fire place. He sat on top of the back of the couch, turned around towards our mantel and started meowing in the direction of Kaitlyn's baby picture and framed footprint. He was looking directly at them, not looking at anything else I had on the mantel.

Maybe he just likes to meow at things, but they just happen to involve Kaitlyn's things, or things pertaining to her and nothing else. This cat does not get on top of anything, nor does he meow at other random objects, only hers. Coincidence....I don't know.

No, I'm not hallucinating.

Kaitlyn loved this cat VERY, VERY much. Every time I called Kaitlyn and asked where Gatito was, she would always say "Right here" in her lap. She used to talk to me about how very much she loved him and how much he kept her company. I know that he must have been the last being that she talked to before she took her life. There are connections some people just don't understand and they transcend death.

Gatito and Kaitlyn

Stephanie, Kaitlyn, Allyn and me

# Chapter 14

## Some Things I've Come to Understand

*That's the thing about depression: A human being can survive almost anything, as long as she sees the end in sight. But depression is so insidious, and it compounds daily, that it's impossible to ever see the end.*

*Elizabeth Wurtzel, Prozac Nation*

In all my questioning and all my research, my grief, my disbelief, my horror of losing my daughter to suicide, and all my attempts to find the answer to that persistent question "Why?" I have come to realize that I will never completely know. I have however, come to learn many things that accompany the things I already know. The things I do know are these; depression is a disease that can affect anyone at any stage of their life and it does not discriminate. It can attack all races, genders, people of different religious groups, people who have no religion, people from abusive homes and personal situations, people from loving, stable backgrounds, poor, rich, young, old or in between. In short, it can and does happen to anyone.

Depression is not something someone can control. It is not a life choice. It is not a sign of weakness. It is an illness in the same way as diabetes, high blood pressure, heart disease or cancer are illnesses. And like many other diseases, if not treated, you may die from it. Depression shouldn't be regarded as a choice that the person has made, nor should it be viewed as a weakness, because it is not. Who would choose such a horrible state of mind?

I know that depression and all forms of mental illness carry with it a stigma that has been imposed by our society since the beginning of human existence. I personally have witnessed this often. You hear it in groups of people who

215

talk about that "crazy" person. You hear and read all the jokes that are "not meant to offend anyone." You know about it from all the talk you hear about people who are known to suffer from it. Most unfortunately of all, you hear it from some healthcare professionals themselves. I personally heard this uttered by a fellow professional about an attempted suicide in the hospital: "They didn't want to die or they would be dead. They just want attention" and "They should know how to do it right the next time." I've heard these things from healthcare professionals who ought to know better, but yet choose to act like ignorant people who see depression, attempted suicide and suicide as someone's weakness or attempt to seek attention. I hesitate to write these things because I don't want anyone that is depressed or suicidal to be deterred from seeking help. However, I need to say this so people in the healthcare profession will see just what their callous remarks can do to further stigmatize mental illness, thus preventing some people obtaining help. I also want to mention that most healthcare professionals show compassion for this illness and the insensitive ones are in the minority.

The major thing that I have learned is that there are many people out there who hide their depression completely. Kaitlyn was one such person. I have been continually researching the reasons why such people simply do not seek help of any kind and keep their depression hidden.

From all the writings from people who were similar to my daughter who have also suffered from depression and suicidal ideation and have even attempted suicide, I have pieced together some of my theories as to why my daughter and so many other people like her do not report or show their depression at all.

Even though I am an RN by profession, in no way does that make me eligible to state that it is absolutely the truth in all cases. The fact is, I don't know for sure about any of them. But from all that I have sought out, all that I have learned from others and my own personal experience with my daughter, there are many assumptions that I have come to believe. For some people, all of my theories as to why they do not seek help may apply, for some people, only a few may apply and for others, perhaps none of them apply. But here are my theories.

I feel that perhaps Kaitlyn as a young child may have felt different from other people due to her intellect. Even though she had friends that were also very intelligent and shared many good times with them, she felt alone and isolated because the large majority of people that she was around did not share her same interests and her thought processes. That's not to say that she thought she was any better than anyone else. I did know my daughter enough to know that she was very modest and felt she was no better than anyone else, but that she just couldn't relate to many people. I think the older she got, the more pronounced these feelings became. When she was little, she said that everyone expected her to be the best at everything and she did not like that. To me, in hindsight, I feel that she felt under pressure to be perfect and that she was held apart from everyone else. Another clue is the poem she wrote that I included earlier in this book named, "Costume" where she said she had to hide who she truly was because she was different.

I think those early attempts to let people know that she felt different were the very last times she ever tried to reach out, to say that she felt alone and different. I tried my best to assure her, when she came to me about people expecting her to be perfect, that she only needed to do her best. And my interpretation of her "Costume" poem as nothing more than a teenager's normal feelings of being different, scream at me from the past as something I should have taken more seriously. I feel so guilty about this now. But I knew Kaitlyn was different, and not in a bad way. She was

217

special and she was brilliant. I knew brilliant children thought differently to the average person and I thought those feelings were normal for them. Perhaps all very smart children feel as she did; different.

As time went on, Kaitlyn continued to achieve and to be the perfect student and daughter. We never pushed her to achieve; she did this all on her own, but I wonder now whether she thought that was what we and everyone else expected of her. Maybe she felt she simply could not let people and herself down by doing any less than what she had always done and so this piled even more pressure on her to achieve and to be the best at everything. This pressure on my child is something I did not know existed. I thought her achievements all came from within her and were easily attained. I thought she thrived on excelling. By all appearances this was the case. What if she simply felt she had to do it? Wanting to please everyone and herself may have put so much pressure on her that it caused her to start feeling depressed. Perhaps this is how other children like Kaitlyn feel. As I have said, I simply don't know. But this could be true.

As the years passed, maybe Kaitlyn realized she had a problem with depression, but how can anyone that has succeeded at everything in her life up until this point ever admit to anyone that she had a problem? What if all her friends found out? What if they did not think as highly of her anymore? What if she had to admit that there was something wrong with her? All of those thoughts and feelings could have very well been the reason why she did not come to us. Again, this is only my theory.

As she continued through high school and began the college applications' process, how would that affect her chances of getting into medical school if she were to admit that she was suffering from depression? What medical school would want someone that has any form of mental illness? Perhaps this was her thinking. Again, I don't know for sure.

Once she began medical school, perhaps the enormous stress that one encounters worsened her depression, though she never even admitted to it. But what if it did? What if it got worse and she knew she was in trouble? But how could she get help? If she tried to get help perhaps her medical school would find out and she would be kicked out of school, or if she were permitted to stay, what if her fellow classmates found out? What would they think of her? What if she made it through medical school and got treatment, but then was excluded from obtaining a good residency due to her mental health diagnosis? What then? I don't know if she was thinking that, but those were very legitimate fears and could have very well been a factor in her reluctance to seek help.

What if Kaitlyn simply did not want to be seen as having any kind of weakness? She was driven to succeed and there were occasions when, if she felt she fell short on achieving, she would be distressed. Perhaps she saw depression as a weakness. We depression sufferers feel that we are viewed with caution. We feel as if we have the plague. This needs to stop or we will continue to lose so many people to suicide and it will only get worse with time.

What if Kaitlyn didn't want to worry us or bother us with her depression? (Though of course we would not have seen it that way, but she may have). What if she thought we would be disappointed in her if she told us she was depressed? (We would not have been). What if she saw all the problems I was having with depression and didn't want to add to my burden and therefore decided to keep it to herself? What if she saw the struggles I had to find the right medications for depression and to locate the right professional to help me? Perhaps she wanted no part of that kind of life for herself.

Perhaps my daughter's perfectionism prevented her from even admitting to herself that she had a problem and even if she did admit it, I do believe she did everything in her power to self-medicate herself through all of her achievements and activities. She took up running to get her body in perfect condition and to benefit from the endorphins it releases. She ate healthily; she climbed mountains and she sought out relationships in distant states because she could find no one to really relate to easily where she lived. She tried many new adventures. I think all of them were fun to her, but I think they were also determined attempts to make her depression go away, or at least be manageable. I really think that perhaps she thought she could help herself without medical help, until it just became too much to handle.

I think many people such as my daughter have these thoughts, feelings and reasons why they don't seek help; they simply think they have too much to lose.

Again, I don't know if these things were what went on in my daughter's head. The only thing I was privileged to learn from her suicide note is that she was terribly sad. She could not even explain why she didn't get help, so I was left to try to piece that together myself. I still don't really know, but can only guess from all I have learned since the tragedy.

What has never ceased to amaze me is the extent of how well she was able to function right up until the very moment she took her life. Many suicidal people are barely able to write a note, can't think logically and hastily carry out the act, giving no forethought to anything. However, Kaitlyn went to orientation for medical school starting on the Monday she returned to school. She also went to her second day of orientation on the Tuesday. She was with two different medical students on those days and none of them say they saw a depressed girl. She even went to the gym on the Tuesday morning. On the Wednesday morning,

220

she even entered what she had for breakfast on the online diet forum to which she belonged. But she did not go to school that day. She called her boyfriend and told him that they could not have their usual Skype lunch together as they always did because she had "errands to run". He thought that very odd because she would never have chosen to run errands instead of talking to him, but would have carried them out at a later time. The last time he ever heard from her was when she texted him at 4pm that day and said, "I love you". She knew that he could not respond to her text at that time because he was at work. He never heard from her again, despite many attempts to reach her by text and phone.

What could have happened to Kaitlyn from Tuesday to Wednesday to make her decide to stay out of school that day and plan her death? Was it some event that no one knows about? Or was it simply a final realization that no matter what she did in her life, no matter how smart she was and what she could achieve, no matter how much she loved her boyfriend and wanted to spend a life with him, no matter how much she loved her parents, her friends and her cat and no matter how many people loved her dearly, none of that had, or ever would, make her feel better. Another question that remains unanswered.

To me, a suicidal mind does not think rationally. Their mind is focused on one command: "Kill yourself to escape from this pain!" Their planning is sporadic and they are haphazardly trying to end their life. Though undoubtedly Kaitlyn was not of sound mind, she was still able to plan and execute her suicide with the acute organizational skills that she had always possessed. Even in her suicidal mind, she was achieving and she would not fail at this either.

Weeks after her death, I was looking through her pocketbook again for the hundredth time. I always saw her grocery lists that she left in there. I looked at one or two, but no more, since they were probably all the same;

221

asparagus, fruit, vegetables, grilled chicken, etc. But one day I decided to look at every single one of them and on one list were the following items: Helium tank, tubing (this even had the size listed), clamp, rubber band, roasting bag, dessert and wine. My daughter had compiled a grocery list for her exit from this world. She had a list of the materials she would need for her suicide, as I'm sure she researched the method many times and well. She also probably included the wine as she did love to drink good wine on occasions. This could have been just one last drink of fine wine, or it could have been a means to get her nerve up to do what she was planning, or both. The dessert, of which kind I have no idea, was probably just her last enjoyment of something sweet, since she rarely enjoyed such treats due to her health conscience diet. That list haunts me and is still in her pocketbook where all of its other contents remain, just the way she left them.

As I said earlier in my book, Kaitlyn planned her death like one of her many projects. How can someone so ill in her mind be still so much together that she could plan everything so perfectly and precisely? That is something I will also never know.

I often wonder what an amazing feat of strength it was for Kaitlyn to do all she did from day to day, to put on a happy face for years, when all she felt inside was bleakness. I don't know how anyone could go so long feeling so bad. I admired all her strengths in life, but I regret that one strength she had, because if she had just let her guard down just a little, maybe she would have made her way to us, to anyone, to ask for help.

## Blog Entry 10-20-13: The Gummy Vitamins

*As I reached for the gummy multi vitamins and the gummy calcium vitamins this morning, I realize they will soon all be gone. I remember the day we cleaned out your apartment after your funeral and as I was cleaning out the pantry, there they were. The two biggest bottles of gummy vitamins I had ever seen. A few had been taken, but for the most part there were many left in both bottles. All of the things in your pantry and in your refrigerator that had been opened, we trashed, but I kept the vitamins. I take multi vitamins and calcium, but not the gummies. I took calcium chews because regular calcium tablets are big enough to choke a horse, and I have almost choked to death once taking them. So I thought I would not waste your vitamins; I would take them myself.*

*We asked some of your fellow med school classmates to come and take all of the healthy foods in your refrigerator that had not been opened to Goodwill. All those healthy foods....you were so very health conscious.*

*I looked at the two bottles of gummy vitamins this morning, which look like they had come from a special vitamin store. I bet they did. You only bought the best of everything. It took me three whole months to be able to even take the first vitamin out of your bottles. I didn't even take any of my own; I didn't even care. Actually, they looked like they would taste nasty. But one day, I decided to take them and they were actually very good. I started taking them every day. Now they are almost gone and I know what I will do with the empty bottles. I will put them away with the rest of your things and keep them forever.*

*I looked at the bottles. I remembered the health food. I thought of the irony of someone that took such great care of her mind and body, who then laid down one night, put a bag over her head, filled it with helium and put an end to all that she had worked so hard to build.*

223

*What did you think in those last few minutes before you lost consciousness Kaitlyn? Did you think of the endless hard effort that you put forth all of your life? Did you think of the bedtimes stories I told you at night, of Harry Potter, of the times I held you with all of my might? Did you think of your boyfriend and good friends that you held so dearly in your heart? Did you think of all the work you put into medical school, only to end it here in the middle? Did you think of the future that will no longer be and the doctor that the world will lose? Did you think of the husband and the children and the home you will never have? Did you think of me Kaitlyn? Or did you simply feel relief that your pain would now come to an end?*

*Visions of the things I saw when I first walked into your apartment after your death; half a glass of wine, the wine bottle, Sylvia Plath's poems and the book "The Bell Jar" sitting on your living room table in front of your couch. I can see you in my mind, sipping the wine and eating the dessert you bought especially for this occasion, as you wrote your suicide notes to your family and those to whom you were closest at the end; notes that were neatly written and carefully thought out. I imagine you had written these words in your mind many times over the years, and researched your method of death methodically and carefully like you did everything else. Your father cannot bear to think of these things; my mind won't let these visions stop.*

*I imagine you bought the wine to muster up the courage to do what you thought you had to do; bought the dessert because you wanted to enjoy your last moments. You bought "The Bell Jar" a week before, I imagine to read about someone that went through what you were going through. I can see you getting up after finishing your tasks, saying goodbye to your cat Gatito, going into your bedroom and closing the door to die in the "comfort of your own home".*

224

*Those gummy vitamins. The irony of what they represent and what ultimately transpired with the young woman, who so carefully chose them to keep her body strong, leaps out at me every time I touch the bottles; every time I taste their sweetness. All this flashes by in my mind when I look at the bottles. Those bottles.*

Kaitlyn at the White Coat Ceremony at Wake Forest School of Medicine, 2011, a rite of passage for first year medical students

Graduation from Campbell University, December 2010

# Chapter 15

## What Suicide Leaves Behind

*They say time heals all wounds, but that presumes the source of the grief is finite.*

*Cassandra Clare (Clockwork Prince)*

There is the huge misconception that people who take their own lives are cowards. They think they simply don't care about the people and loved ones they leave behind. Some critics believe that the suicide victim must have done something awful to render them incapable of facing life anymore. It is true, that some people use suicide as a means of escaping the shame they feel for a heinous act they committed, or to evade punishment for such a crime, or as a religious/political statement, but the majority of suicides are the result of severe mental pain that the sufferers just could not tolerate anymore. Though they know they will hurt the people who love them (but I don't think that they really realize the extent at that time), their mental pain is so intense that all they want is out of it. It's not that they really want to die; it's that they cannot stand feeling like that anymore. Anyone who has not experienced depression will find it very hard to understand how someone can feel like this. The worst kind of ignorance comes from those who think you can just "pull yourself together".

I found a quote by a man that explained very well how someone that is suicidal feels:

*The so-called "psychotically depressed" person who tries to kill herself doesn't do so out of, quote, "hopelessness" or any abstract conviction that life's assets and debits do not square. And surely not because death*

*seems suddenly appealing. The person in whom its invisible*
*agony reaches a certain unendurable level will kill herself*
*the same way a trapped person will eventually jump from*
*the window of a burning high-rise. Make no mistake about*
*people who leap from burning windows. Their terror of*
*falling from a great height is still just as great as it would*
*be for you or me standing speculatively at the same window*
*just checking out the view; i.e. the fear of falling remains a*
*constant. The variable here is the other terror, the fire's*
*flames: when the flames get close enough, falling to death*
*becomes the slightly less terrible of two terrors. It's not*
*desiring the fall; it's terror of the flames. And yet nobody*
*down on the sidewalk, looking up and yelling "Don't!" and*
*"Hang on!" can understand the jump. Not really. You'd*
*have to have personally been trapped and felt flames to*
*really understand a terror way beyond falling.*

*David Foster Wallace*

David Foster Wallace (February 21, 1962 – September
12, 2008) was an award-winning American novelist, short
story writer, essayist, professor of English at Illinois State
University, and professor of creative writing at Pomona
College. Wallace died by hanging himself on September
12, 2008.

The strongest drive in a human being is to remain alive,
to defend oneself, to avoid death. When someone is so
depressed and at the point of suicide, that drive has gone.
No one can understand it truly if they've not been through
it and that is why so many misconceptions about depression
and suicide abound.

Though my daughter did know that her suicide would
hurt those who loved her (I know this from her suicide
note), she fought the desire to die for many years before she
actually took her life. However, I believe with all my heart
that though her note sounded very lucid and articulate,

there is no way she could possibly have anticipated the impact that her suicide would have on her family and friends.

People who are suicidal to the point of carrying out that act do not fully realize the devastation that their exit from this world will cause to their surviving families and friends. Depression is so horrible that all you want to do is end your pain.

I've never been angry with Kaitlyn, because I've always understood what depression can do to a person and their will to live. But I'm here to tell you, though she did not mean it, a path of excruciating grief and torment so long, so wide, and so pervasive has been forever thrust into the entire fabric of our lives. Some days I can barely function. The rest of the family is heartbroken, as are Kaitlyn's friends. None of us will ever be the same; not I, not Allyn, who tries to be so strong to help me when he hurts so much himself, not my parents or my sisters, nieces nephews, brother-in-law, mother-in-law, nor any of her friends.

Sometimes, I feel so dark and lonely and quite frankly don't even want to talk to anyone at all. I go from appearing to be aloof (about which I feel so guilty), to talking nonstop, to crying my heart out, to feelings of feeling numb. My mom has lost two people. She has lost Kaitlyn and she has lost the daughter she once had. I'm not better. I don't even have the will to be better. And I do think about my surviving family; they are hurting terribly as well and it NEVER ceases for any of us.

Since Kaitlyn has died, as I've mentioned before, I've encountered so many people who have lost loved ones to suicide and the pain is ceaseless. I am told that over time, it softens, or you just learn to live with it. I hope that this is true, although it's hard to imagine right now as I am still in the early days of grief.

229

I see an endless sea of parents who wonder what more they could have done, even though they did everything they possibly could for those who did show signs. I see so many posts on suicide survivor websites that say things such as: "It's been 5 years now since…." or "It's been 10 years since…" and this goes on and on and there remains a hole in their hearts that can never be mended. Even if their lives are still full of people they love and who love them in return, this hole remains and it is filled only with pain.

I'm sorry if this does not promote the feeling that a person that has lost someone to suicide can go on to lead a normal life. I'm sorry if I cannot give more hope to the those out there who have lost someone. But I want to be honest with you and let you know the utter devastation that remains. Yes, most people carry on and learn to live alongside the grief as best they can and some even go on to be an advocate for suicide prevention, but the pain of their loss will stay with them until the day they die themselves. There is no getting over it, ever, although most survivors will find ways to be happy again.

The point I'm trying to make in this chapter is that there are so many people out there casting judgment on people who complete suicide. They are angry at them for being so "selfish". But they are not selfish; they are suffering from unspeakable mental anguish and this is their last resort. I am certain that if they did not fear being judged for admitting to their mental illness, so many lives would be saved. They would go straight to the doctor in the same way that they would for any other illness or injury. They would not sit at home and try to self-medicate, or try to walk on a broken leg. But many people who are depressed or suicidal do just that. They try to manage it themselves, cover it up and battle on until the pain becomes so unbearable that they can see no other option than to end their lives.

I guarantee you that whenever mental illness is seen for what it really is, a disease and nothing to be ashamed of, we will see a significant decrease in suicide.

## Blog Entry: Here I Sit

*Here I sit in the ninth month that Kaitlyn has been gone and I am no further away from the grief that I experienced at the moment I learned of her death. No matter what I know or continue to learn about depression, or even my own battle with it, I still cannot believe that my daughter killed herself. I have no illusions that she did not do this, but I still can't believe it.*

*It's still very hard for me to grasp that the person that illuminated happiness and light more than anyone I know could possibly hide so much unhappiness that she ended her life. The wonderful person that she was and the talents that she took with her makes it so hard to comprehend.*

*I know beyond a shadow of a doubt that fathers love their children as much as a mother does, but I can only speak of my own devastation at losing my daughter. My daughter (as they both are) was a part of me. I would say that I lost part of myself when she left, an amputation of a vital part of me, but actually, it is so much more than that. I lost a person in my life that was so much more important to me than myself.*

*Sometimes I wonder if I have not died and have actually gone to hell. I'm living in hell. My life is a huge vacuum. I am a shell of my former self. The void in my heart is filled with pain. However, no matter how sad I am for myself, it pales in comparison to the magnitude of the unexpected suicide and discovery of my daughter's deep sadness.*

*Oh I've said all these things here so many times and I keep grasping at more ways to describe the complete annihilation of one's spirit and drive after they lose a child; a child that turned their world into complete sunshine. How could she illuminate so much sunshine when her inner being was suffering from bleakness?*

*Kaitlyn lost her life, but I have lost mine as well. I cannot see myself ten years from now still suffering this horrendous loss. People do, but I just don't know how they do it.*

*I often sit and think that if I were to take all the bad experiences I've had in my entire life, and multiply them by a billion, it still would not come close to being as horrific as what I am going through now.*

*Kaitlyn's suicide makes me realize that my child was not happy, even though happiness is all I ever wanted for her. She deserved it. She was amazing. Oh I would have given anything to have known of her pain and consequently been in a position to help her. I would gladly have given up everything I had for her, to help her.*

*The idea of her death is so complex. I realize from her note that she was depressed, but I believe that she could never quite find something; something very important. I don't know what it was. It haunts me.*

*Today was bleak, gray and raining. When it is sunny outside I still see it as bleak, gray and raining. She took my sunshine away. She took her beautiful self away and I just cannot deal with it. I cannot come to terms with it. My heart is so broken; I am broken.*

*Oh Kaitlyn, how I miss you so. How so important you were to me, how much I love you...and I love you still. I love you so; I love you "very so".*

# Chapter 16

## The Stigma of Mental Illness

*"Did you really want to die?"*
*"No one commits suicide because they want to die."*
*"Then why do they do it?"*
*"Because they want to stop the pain."*

*Tiffanie DeBartolo (How to Kill a Rock Star)*

What infuriates me the most is the general lack of understanding and compassion towards people suffering from mental illness. I feel this is the reason why some people fail to seek professional help, and even those who do sneak around in secret, hoping that no one will see them in that psychiatrist's office, or else travel great distances to these appointments so no one they know will see them. I know this to be true, because I was one such person.

Back in 1999, when I first had my severe episode of depression, I slinked around like a cat in the dark trying to get to my appointments. The only people who knew were a few members of my family, my best friend at the time who encouraged me to seek treatment, and my boss and supervisor. The reality is, everyone at my workplace probably knew. In addition to feeling hopeless, it felt as though I had some vile disease.

Why do you think I felt this way? It's because I didn't want people to think there was anything wrong with me. And I didn't want anyone to think that because I was depressed, I was incapable of doing my nursing job.

Certainly, the stigma associated with mental illness is not as bad as it was many decades ago, but it still exists. It is perpetuated by the mass murders that are committed by seriously mentally ill people. Take the Colorado theater massacre, for example, or the mother suffering from postpartum psychosis who posed a threat to the White House and was killed by the police. How can we as a society disassociate everyday mental disorders suffered by many from those terrible tragedies committed by a minority? The answer is, one can't. Some sufferers believe that if they report their illness, they may be regarded as unstable enough to be a danger to the public, when in the majority of cases they are only a danger to themselves. I do believe, however, that some of those who resorted to such dreadful acts were not treated for their mental illness, inadequately treated, or else stopped their medication.

Somehow, we as a society need to put an end to the shame and lack of education about mental illness. Schools need to incorporate life skills into their curriculum, initially as a preventative measure, but then to subsequently reassure children that suffering from depression is normal and that they should seek help. Even more than that, we need to convince everyone that mental illness is not a weakness, so that they will be in a better position to recognize the signs and offer help.

Mental illness is a disease! I can't say this enough times. Sometimes, it can be circumstantial (bereavement, abuse, bullying etc.), but in many cases it is believed by many to be caused by a chemical imbalance in the brain. The medicines that are prescribed for patients are designed to regulate these chemicals. There are some scientists, however, who are skeptical about the chemical imbalance theory and yet there is no doubt that the correct medication can be hugely beneficial to sufferers. It doesn't matter how it works; just that it does is sufficient.

I feel that everyone knows what depression is, but some may not know what bipolar disorder is. Very simply put, bipolar is a mental illness that was once called manic depression. This term is not professionally used anymore. When someone is bipolar they have extreme moods that

234

alternate. They have what may be considered highs and lows. When they are on a "high", they may engage in irrational behavior, talk excessively, suffer from insomnia and decreased appetite, occasionally overspend, feel invincible, feel elated, experience a creative burst and sometimes become extremely irritable. Some, or all of these symptoms can occur and there are even more possible symptoms. This can go on for days. Then they can plunge into a "low" of deep depression.

What I have just described is bipolar type 1. There is also bipolar type 2 where the manic phases are not as severe and sometimes nothing more noticeable than a good mood. However, the depression that it alternates with is extremely severe. Even worse is when the bipolar manic and depressive states intermingle and they feel some of both at the same time. That is called a mixed state and is also incredibly dangerous.

That is a simple explanation of bipolar disorder for those who don't already know. Depression and bipolar are classified as mood disorders (but not the only mood disorders) and mood disorders have the highest incidence of suicide. I acquired my knowledge of these disorders from my years of studying in nursing school, my extended reading after nursing school and my research into my own depression. They are certainly not in depth explanations, but simple enough for a lay person to understand.

We are callous as a society. How many times have you heard the phrase "She's crazy" or "She just came out of the nut house"? For every phrase a mentally ill person hears like this, the more alone and isolated they feel and the less likely they will ever feel to talk about their illness or even seek help. I have said "She's crazy" myself in my life and not even mean it as an insult, just an expression that I did not even think about. We all need to stop and think before we say such things, even if we think them harmless at the time, because they most certainly are not.

We need to put more programs in place to teach people about mental illness. The government needs to invest more money into helping the mentally ill receive treatment. There is so much that needs to be done. Vast amounts of money are raised for cancer research and so much progress has been made in its treatment, which is a wonderful thing. We've poured endless funds into other causes, such as AIDS' research, Alzheimer's research and so on, which is also commendable, but how much time and effort do we spend on suicide prevention? Not as much.

There are more deaths each year in the United States from suicide than from auto accidents and yet it is still vastly underreported, so the true extent of this "epidemic" is not truly known. This should be a huge wake up call to the nation.

The simple fact is that most people fail to realize the extent of the problem unless their own lives have been touched by the suicide of a loved one. They don't want to think about it. They don't want to believe that it could never happen in their family, or to one of their friends, but it could and does.

According to the Center for Disease Control and prevention:

*Suicide (i.e. taking one's own life) is a serious public health problem that affects even young people. For youth between the ages of 10 and 24, suicide is the third leading cause of death. It results in approximately 4600 lives lost each year. The top three methods used in suicides of young people include firearm (45%), suffocation (40%), and poisoning (8%).*

*Most people are uncomfortable with the topic of suicide. Too often, victims are blamed, and their families and friends are left stigmatized. As a result, people do not communicate openly about suicide.*

*Thus an important public health problem is left shrouded in secrecy, which limits the amount of information available to those working to prevent suicide.*

The World Health Organization offers these worldwide statistics:

*Every year, almost one million people die from suicide; a "global" mortality rate of 16 per 100,000, or one death every 40 seconds.*

*In the last 45 years suicide rates have increased by 60% worldwide. Suicide is among the three leading causes of death among those aged 15-44 years in some countries, and the second leading cause of death in the 10-24 years age group; these figures do not include suicide attempts which are up to 20 times more frequent than completed suicide.*

*Suicide worldwide is estimated to represent 1.8% of the total global burden of disease in 1998, and 2.4% in countries with market and former socialist economies in 2020.*

*Although traditionally suicide rates have been highest among the male elderly, rates among young people have been increasing to such an extent that they are now the group at highest risk in a third of countries, in both developed and developing countries.*

*Mental disorders (particularly depression and alcohol use disorders) are a major risk factor for suicide in Europe and North America; however, in Asian countries impulsiveness plays an important role. Suicide is complex with psychological, social, biological, cultural and environmental factors involved."*

The World Health Organization also goes on to say:

### Effective interventions

*Strategies involving restriction of access to common methods of suicide, such as firearms or toxic substances like pesticides, have proved to be effective in reducing suicide rates; however, there is a need to adopt multi-sectoral approaches involving many levels of intervention and activities.*

*There is compelling evidence indicating that adequate prevention and treatment of depression and alcohol and substance abuse can reduce suicide rates, as well as follow-up contact with those who have attempted suicide.*

### Challenges and obstacles

*Worldwide, the prevention of suicide has not been adequately addressed due to basically a lack of awareness of suicide as a major problem and the taboo in many societies to discuss openly about it. In fact, only a few countries have included prevention of suicide among their priorities.*

*Reliability of suicide certification and reporting is an issue in great need of improvement.*

*It is clear that suicide prevention requires intervention also from outside the health sector and calls for an innovative, comprehensive multi-sectoral approach, including both health and non-health sectors, e.g. education, labor, police, justice, religion, law, politics, the media.*

**Blog entry 1-24-14: Mauled**

*I continue to wake up every morning to the reality of the impossible. Knowing that my youngest, beautiful daughter killed herself is the mental equivalent to being continuously mauled by a bear.....all day and night, every day and night.*

*I once heard of the true story about a group of fur trappers in the early 1800s that were traveling out west. One of the men in the group was mauled by a grizzly bear. His group decided to leave him there to die, for surely he would die. They left. This man, after awakening after some time, his body a mass of bleeding flesh, exposed ribs, broken leg, crawled and clawed his way many, many miles, many, many days, to civilization. He somehow lived.*

*I'm still at the gaining consciousness stage wondering whether I can crawl that far.*

Kaitlyn aged 8

Kaitlyn and me in 2007 when she was a high school
Marshal

# Chapter 17

## A Mother's Plea

*Young Life Cut Short*

*Do not judge a song by its duration*
*Nor by the number of its notes*
*Judge it by the richness of its contents*
*Sometimes those unfinished are among the most poignant...*
*Do not judge a song by its duration*
*Nor by the number of its notes*
*Judge it by the way it touches and lifts the soul*
*Sometimes those unfinished are among the most beautiful...*
*And when something has enriched your life*
*And when its melody lingers on in your heart.*
*Is it unfinished?*
*Or is it endless?*

*Author unknown*

The one thing I knew within only a short time after Kaitlyn's death is that I wanted to give a warning to all parents out there. Only a few days after the tragedy, I wrote an article and sent it to about four or five newspapers that were located within an hour of where I live. I wanted to warn parents and I want to do this here and now towards the end of my book. Everything I have written about up until this point has lead me to what I want to write now.

To all parents of children that you see as gifted, intelligent, creative, brilliant, driven and seemingly happy, please don't just assume that what you see is all there is. Things aren't always as they seem. Please heed this advice from a devastated, grieving parent who has been forced to realize that her apparently successful, happy daughter, was not happy at all. Not only that, she admitted in her suicide note that she had been sad ever since she could remember and only had "occasions" of happiness in her life.

Her home life was not dysfunctional; she had two parents that loved her more than life, a loving sister, and a huge extended family that loved her. We were not wealthy and she was not spoiled, but we gave her what she needed and we supported her in everything she wanted to do. We did not ever push her to do anything. If anything traumatic or horrible ever occurred in her life, we did not know about it. Kaitlyn was the victim of severe depression, but never admitted it, nor sought medical help. I'm here to tell you that this happens, and it happens far more frequently than most people believe. I didn't realize it, until we lost our beautiful daughter to this insidious disease. Unfortunately, I know it now.

For me, as I've often stated in my book, Kaitlyn was one of the few people that I knew, if not the only one, that had her life perfectly planned out. She succeeded at everything she ever did and did so for most of her life. She had a zest and love for life I've seldom seen. She was blessed with great intelligence. She was sweet, loving and just an overall wonderful and apparently well adjusted child/teenager/and then young woman. All these things were true. Nothing about her was a lie. You cannot fake intelligence, not for more than a few minutes anyway. You cannot fake being loving, not all your life anyway. She was all these things. The only thing that was a lie was her happiness.

As Kaitlyn's parents, her father and I were so extremely proud of her. We bragged about her to everyone all the time. We were proud. I thought one should be proud and give your child praise when it's due, and I still feel that is true. But what I didn't know is that a brilliant child needs just as much care with their emotions as anyone else, irrespective of their circumstances. For brilliant children often feel isolated and alone. Sometimes they may feel under pressure from others, but often they place enormous pressure upon themselves. Such children may fear failure and consequently may perceive an admission of depression as a failure. Through all of my research, I have learned that they often hide it more expertly than anyone else. These "golden children" seem so perfect that no one would believe that depression could affect their lives. That is why we do not press them and sit them down and ask often whether they are feeling fine emotionally. We assume they are ok because they exude an aura of wellbeing.

I beg all of you parents out there with gifted children, not to assume they are happy just because it appears to be so. Please sit them down often and just talk to them about how they feel inside. Clearly, every child is different, so there is no single approach that will work for everyone. In some cases, it may be appropriate to be forthright and ask, "Are you depressed?" In other cases, however, a more subtle approach may be required. Saying something along the lines of, "If something was bothering you, I hope you would feel able tell me", may work better. What is most important though is to reassure a child that there is nothing wrong with suffering from depression; it is not a weakness or a sign of failure, or something shameful.

If they don't want anyone else to know, assure them that no one has to know except you, their doctor and/or counselor. Start these talks and questions early in their life in an age-appropriate way that they can understand. Depression can start at an early age, in adolescence or young adulthood. Since no one knows when it can strike, openness about the topic must be started early on. I'm not trying to say that you need to sit them down every single day and question them, but occasionally reinforce the knowledge that they can come to you about anything at all. And if they do admit to feeling depressed, don't be afraid to ask the question "Do you ever feel like harming or killing yourself?" Contrary to some people's beliefs, asking this question does not instill the notion into them and make them more likely to commit the act. However, if they are thinking about it, at least you know and can take the necessary steps to help prevent it happening. Most importantly, if they do admit to depression or suicidal ideation, take it very seriously and don't assume that it's merely a phase or a normal part of life that they will get over. One of the biggest myths about suicide is that people who talk about it rarely complete the act. Tragically, many do go on to succeed in ending their lives.

Gifted, intelligent and creative children are usually so much more introspective than most people are. They do a great deal of soul searching, thinking about the meaning of life and are so easily prone to being depressed for a variety of reasons. Sometimes they are profoundly affected by the atrocities in this world that so many other people do not even think about. Sometimes they just feel so alone and isolated because they feel different to others. They are often introverts who have more difficulty socializing and forming friendships than extroverts, which complicates the problem.

I've lost the bright shining star of my life. Kaitlyn was not perfect. I didn't expect her to be; no one is. But maybe she thought I expected her to be. Maybe that's why she didn't tell me. But I do know that if she had told me about it, I would have done everything in my power to help her in any way I could. If she wanted to quit medical school, we would have helped her pay her student loan back if it meant we had to live in a tent. But she would have never asked that of us. That is how she was. She thought of others more than herself.

If I had it to do all over again, I would have been more in tune with her feelings and read between the lines of those prophetic poems she wrote. I would have sat her down often to find out just how she was feeling inside. I would still have boasted about her, but I would have let her know more often that though we were proud of all she achieved, she did not have to succeed at everything and that we would still love her just as much if she didn't. I did tell her these things during her life, but I would have done it more often and more thoroughly. I wouldn't simply have asked "Are you happy?" and accepted an affirmative response. I would have sat her down and talked about her happiness in depth, praying with all my heart that she would be honest with me. Nevertheless, even in doing all that, she may still not have confided in me about her unhappiness. I admit that I still might not have been able to change the outcome, but I'll never have that chance again; I'll never know.

In my quest to find answers and in my communications with other people who were similar to Kaitlyn, I encountered a couple of young women who really gave me something to think about and sent me into the depths of guilt that I had not expected. They told me that in describing my daughter, all I seemed to be doing was talking of her achievements and not the person she was inside. One suggested that I was still trying to see my daughter as perfect instead of the imperfect person she was; as we all are. They went on to say that that is exactly the kind of pressure that was put on them; people expecting them to be perfect and the reluctance of people seeing them as anything but a list of achievements. This hurt me to the core of my being. Guilt sprang out of every pore and I wondered, "Is that what I did to my child? It's my fault, it's all my fault. I bragged about her all the time; to her and to anyone who would listen. No wonder she couldn't bear it, no wonder."

In voicing my feelings to one of these young women, she then went on to admit that of course parents talk proudly about their children; what parent doesn't? But I wondered if that's how Kaitlyn felt. To me, the things Kaitlyn did WERE a part of her. Her art, which she was so very talented at, was an achievement, but it was part of her.

245

Her brilliance was a part of her; her gift of writing was a part of her. I not only loved her for what she could do, I loved her mind and her heart and soul. Her accomplishments were part of who she was. This is who she presented to me and all the world, so what else was I supposed to see? I saw the person she wanted me to see. I had no way of seeing anything else; the parts she kept hidden. What people do is part of them, but it does not mean that is all they are to you.

If it seems as though I do harp on about her achievements in this book, it's because I was proud of her. Her talents were a huge part of who she was, and it's important that I mention them because it highlights the fact that there are other talented young people out there who are hiding depression and may well be thinking about suicide.

My book is not about guilt. Yes, I do feel guilty that I may not have seen some of the signs I should have and guilt is one of the legacies of suicide, even when a parent was aware of their child's depression. They will still ask the same questions, "What if I had done this? What if I had done that? What is it I didn't see? Was I a good enough parent? Would I have been able to change the outcome?" My book is primarily about heartache, grief, disbelief, horror, searching, railing against the stigma that prevents people from seeking help, and a warning to parents, counselors, leaders and those brilliant young people who feel unable to ask for help. It's my plea to parents to keep a close eye on their children. Talk to them. Don't think that what happened to my daughter could not happen to yours, because it can. I hope that all of you reading this will begin to question your children, whatever their age, because I do not wish another precious child to die by their own hands, nor do I want another family to endure the same torment that we are experiencing.

To all those brilliant young people out there; please don't be ashamed to admit that you are depressed and need help. Always remember that seeking help is much better than being where my daughter is now; three miles down the road and in her grave, so far away from the wonderful life that she envisaged for herself.

## Blog entry 1-19-14: Kaitlyn Would Have Been 24 Today

*Kaitlyn, today, 1-19-14 is your birthday. 24 years ago today was the day that you came into our lives. I had no way of knowing what a great experience was awaiting me in the years ahead.*

*I am not going to wish you a happy 24th birthday in heaven, because you are not 24. You will never be 24. You were 23 when you left this earthly life and I'm almost sure that where you are time is not measured in the same way it is here on earth. Actually, I'm almost sure of it. We measure years from how long it takes the earth to circle the sun, and earth is not where you are anymore. Instead, you are somewhere that I have not the capability to imagine. I hope it is the paradise that you so very much deserve, because when you graced this earth you made my life a paradise just by being your mother, of experiencing your wonderful presence, for giving me all the love that I could ever ask for, and for being such a wonderful daughter your entire life.*

*Today is one of the hardest days I have experienced since your death. I can't celebrate another year of your life, because you are no longer here and it makes me so unbearably sad to know this. Your sister, her husband Steve, and one of your friends Neal are going out to eat sushi in your honor at the place we went to that time. But I cannot go. I am not ready to go out in public to celebrate your birthday, but it's very important to your sister to do this and I'm so happy Neal is going too. I can't do that yet; maybe next year. For this year I will stay home with your daddy. Stephanie and Steve are going to come over and*

247

*celebrate your birthday. Stephanie felt that I would need her on that day, and I will. She's going to make a cake and we will eat it for you. We will light a candle in your memory and then go visit your grave. This is how I want to do it this year; at home and in private because that is all I can bear right now.*

*To know that you are no longer here to turn 24 breaks my heart so very much. You deserve to be 24 and continue on until you are 100, and in between that time to live the fullest, happiest life possible. But that is never to be and I can't do a thing to change it. If I could, I would not hesitate for a second to give my life to make it happen.*

*I love you Kaitlyn. You made an impact on all the lives that you brushed by. You made me happier than I could ever have imagined and gave me so much unconditional love. You were so very, very special. I know you still are…somewhere out there.*

*Until we meet again my wonderful daughter, I will miss you and forever mourn your loss. But I thank God for every single second I had with you, you wonderful girl.*

*So, no "Happy 24th birthday in heaven", just "Happy birthday my sweet daughter". A day that I could not have imagined would be the beginning of someone so wonderful.*

*I love you with all my heart and soul. Until I see you again……*

*Love,*
*Momma*

# Chapter 18

## Things That Are Being Done

*If you know someone who's depressed, please resolve never to ask them why. Depression isn't a straightforward response to a bad situation; depression just is, like the weather.*
*Try to understand the blackness, lethargy, hopelessness, and loneliness they're going through. Be there for them when they come through the other side. It's hard to be a friend to someone who's depressed, but it is one of the kindest, noblest, and best things you will ever do.*

*Stephen Fry*

Significant progress towards helping medical school students who are struggling with depression actually happened at Kaitlyn's visitation. Someone from the Kaitlyn's medical school attended and enquired about flowers for Kaitlyn's funeral. At that time my husband told them that Kaitlyn had always loved flowers, but that what he thought she would like more would be for people to donate money to the school to help other students who were battling depression. At that very moment an idea was born.

After her funeral, two of the deans kept in contact with me by phone and email. During one phone call, one of the deans asked for my permission to undertake a number of things. The first was to dedicate the next school publication to Kaitlyn. (This is a something they publish every 3 months or so). It would contain letters from Kaitlyn's classmates about their thoughts and experiences of her. They also wanted to include two of her poems that she had written while she was still at Campbell. Naturally, I agreed to these requests.

In addition, the dean told me that the school was going to create a fund for their wellness center in Kaitlyn's name, which would be ongoing and to which the students, their parents, the faculty and members of the community wanted to contribute. The fund would be dedicated entirely to helping the students of that school who suffer with problems of depression and other forms of mental illness. It would also focus on mental health awareness. He wanted to borrow one of her pictures that she had drawn (her self-portrait), make a full size copy of it, frame it and hang it at the wellness center. Of course, I gave permission for that too.

Efforts are being made in the school to encourage students to seek help for mental problems without fear and stigma. They also have hired another psychologist for the school, which is being funded from their own budget.

I feel from the above that progress is being made - at least at Wake Forest School of Medicine. I don't know how most medical schools handle this situation, but at least I know that the one Kaitlyn attended, is making strides to address this problem.

I also feel that each and every fellow classmate of Kaitlyn's has been forever touched and changed by Kaitlyn's death. It is something they will never forget and hopefully it will enable them to show greater compassion in their personal and professional lives. This is a drastic way to learn about compassion, but at least her death has not been in vain and she is still helping people. She would like that.

I recently read an article in the Medical School of South Carolina's publication "The Catalyst" that they are also making changes to help students at their school who are suffering from depression. Following are some excerpts:

## Prevention of depression, suicide among students a priority at MUSC

*On average, 400 physicians commit suicide in the United States each year according to the Psychiatric Clinics of North America. The male physician is two times more likely to commit suicide than the average male, and the female physician is three times more likely to commit suicide than the average female.*

*Many of the psychological issues that physicians face start when they are in medical school, which is something that MUSC is addressing through the Counseling and Psychological Services Program.*

*Kelly Anne Holes-Lewis, M.D., one of two attending physicians who see student patients at CAPS, said that in 2012 there were 2,894 MUSC student visits to address these issues.*

*The main reasons for the visits were anxiety (31 percent) and depression or problems with mood (20 percent). Academic and learning problems (16 percent) was the third largest reason followed by relationship problems (9 percent), adjustment concerns (8 percent), alcohol or substance abuse or dependence (7 percent), eating disorders (3 percent) and other mental health problems (6 percent).*

*Holes-Lewis estimates that 33 percent of all of those visits were from College of Medicine students.*

*"It's a problem I'm very passionate about," Holes-Lewis said. "When adequately treated, we can help these students fulfill their full potential."*

*Any student who is enrolled in a health-based or research-based academic program on campus is eligible for free services at CAPS. Everything that they need is financially provided through a fee linked to their tuition bill.*

"Students can come in for evaluation and receive appropriate treatment and services for as long as it takes to resolve the issue and restore wellness. I believe this is one of the most helpful and efficacious programs I have ever seen on a university campus," Holes-Lewis said. "Oftentimes, these students are leaving home for the first time and are away from their support group. Additionally, they are often starting or in the midst of academically intensive programs. Depressive and anxious symptoms can develop that overwhelm a student's ability to cope in these circumstances."

There are numerous barriers in place that are currently holding back health care students and professionals from getting the care they need. Holes-Lewis said one of the main reasons is the stigma of mental illness. Many of those in the medical field fear that if they are labeled with something like depression or anxiety, they will appear to be less effective or unable to cope.

The fear of lack of confidentiality is also a problem among students and physicians. With the use of the electronic medical record, access to diagnoses and medications is something that many physicians worry about before seeking help from another health care professional. CAPS has its own internal electronic medical record, not accessible through other MUSC systems, so student confidentiality is ensured.

Many of the students at MUSC and other medical universities are high functioning and may not realize there is a possibility of a mental issue like a learning disorder because they've always been able to keep up. The CAPS Program also offers extensive diagnostic testing for learning disorders, which can cause anxiety. If a learning disability is diagnosed, the CAPS staff will then take it a step further and recommend the necessary accommodations for that student to have within the classroom or during the board exam testing.

*"We want our students to be able to work to their full potential and help them succeed in any way that we can,"* Holes-Lewis said.

The same stressors that students go through continue, and in some ways are magnified, when they become physicians, according to Holes-Lewis.

*"It is widely recognized that physicians and other people regularly engaged in end-point decision making are at increased risk for developing heart disease, hypertension and depression,"* she said. *"The goal of our program is to intervene in a meaningful way so as to reduce these comorbidities and overall provide effective treatment strategies for greater health and well-being."*

Holes-Lewis is currently proposing an executive wellness program to include providing care for MUSC physicians who are struggling with depression, stress, anxiety and other psychological concerns.

*"We're working on developing a program for physicians that will address the main concerns that limit physicians from accessing care,"* Holes-Lewis said. *"We know the problem exists and want to provide a confidential environment to provide necessary care so that the physicians in our community can find a balance of wellness and meaning in their work."*

Physicians also have access to the most popular way of completing suicide in the medical field – medication.

*"Everyone knows of someone who committed suicide and in retrospect states that they never even knew there was a problem. This happens with physicians and students as well, as they are very often trying to hide the problem from colleagues and family members,"* Holes-Lewis said. *"The two most common ways physicians complete suicide are medication overdosages and firearms. As physicians we have ready access to medications, and it amplifies the problem."*

*The problems Holes-Lewis is helping students manage within the CAPS Program are what Constance Guille, M.D., assistant professor in the MUSC Department of Psychiatry and Behavioral Sciences, has decided to research.*

*Guille said that over the course of medical internship year, about 40 percent of interns from multiple specialties become depressed. When asked when their first episode of depression occurred, they answered "sometime in medical school."*

*This finding is consistent with a large body of literature that recognizes that medical students are at a much greater risk for depression in comparison to the general population, and they are less likely to seek mental health treatment.*

*"Prevention programs can be effective in lowering rates of depression and mental health problems in high-risk populations," Guille said. "Medical students are an ideal population for a prevention program in that we can intervene with a prevention program prior to the start of their academic year and prior to the potential for their mental health to deteriorate."*

*Ashley Barker, Public Relations, September 5, 2013*

To find out more, visit www.musc.edu/caps. To learn about the Department of Psychiatry and Behavioral Sciences, go to www.musc.edu/psychiatry/.

It makes me feel very good that medical schools are beginning to take these steps to help medical school students with any anxiety, depression or mood disorders without fear of the stigma. If more programs were put in place in medical schools, there would be fewer students going around hiding their severe depression.

254

There is also an organization that I feel very passionate about and that is The American Foundation for Suicide Prevention. According to their website, these are some of their education and prevention programs:

## Our Education and Prevention Programs

Our efforts to prevent suicide begin with increasing public and professional awareness of suicide as a mental health and public health problem.

Our innovative educational materials help teachers, parents, youth, and community leaders to understand suicide risk factors and warning signs, and support their efforts to assist those at risk for suicide to get the help they need.

We also collect and disseminate the latest research on suicide causation and prevention to physicians and mental health professionals so that they may more easily recognize and reduce suicide risk. And we work to reduce the stigma that deters so many people from seeking help.

AFSP seeks to reduce suicide and suicide attempts by developing and implementing our own innovative approaches to suicide prevention.

## The Interactive Screening Program

AFSP's signature prevention program, the ISP, is a web-based method for anonymously connecting people at risk for suicide to a counselor who provides information and support for help-seeking.

## Programs for Teens and Young Adults

- More Than Sad: Teen Depression
- After a Suicide: A Toolkit for Schools
- Suicide Shouldn't be a Secret PSAs

- The Truth about Suicide: Real Stories of Depression in College

## Community Programs

- Depression and Bipolar Awareness: From Diagnosis to Remission
- Living with Bipolar Disorder
- Billboard Program

## Programs for Professionals

- More Than Sad: Suicide Prevention Education for Teachers and other School Personnel
- Physician and Medical Student Depression and Suicide
- LGBT Suicide and Suicide Risk: From Knowledge to Prevention
- Best Practices Registry for Suicide Prevention (BPR)"

As you can see, the organization not only strives to help individuals, but provides education for professionals who are in a position to help and educate people about mental illness.

AFSP sponsors walks across the United States called Out of the Darkness walks, which raise funds for this organization and help raise awareness of mental illness and suicide prevention. Many members of my family, friends and I participated in this event in Myrtle Beach, SC in October 2013.

This organization focuses on suicide prevention, education, and the fight against the stigma of mental illness and their website has a vast amount of information. The link is included in my resource section.

## Blog entry 1-1-14: The Winds of Time

*The cool winds blow across your stone, which move the leftover leaves and straw from the past fall across the dates carved into it. A tiny wet piece of leaf clings to the date of your death, 4-11-13 and on this very first day of 2014 that act screams out into the quiet of this field of stones that you have been left behind. 2013 is no more and 2014 starts with a dagger of pain into my soul. How can it be that 100 funerals, 100 Thanksgivings and Christmases could not compare to the pain that that tiny leaf on 2013 represents?*

*The winds of time blow across this field that represents broken hearts and broken dreams and makes me know that time will continue to march on.....without you. How dare it?*

*How unfair is it that such beauty can be taken away and force the world to continue on without it? How utterly incomprehensible it is to realize that so much can be given and so easily be taken away? How horrific it is to love someone so much and have them lost to you? How unspeakable the pain is that comes from realizing such beautiful things and beings simply do not last in this world and we are left with anguish. How confusing it is that someone who had so much to give did not have a chance to continue giving? How wrong it is that the gifts of deep thought and ability are the very things that sometimes make people unable to live here on this earth?*

*So this is 2014 and how it feels to be forced to move on without you. The world is turning, everyone continues laughing and going about the business of living. This is what you wanted, but I can't bear the thought of you being forgotten. I don't begrudge anyone trying to learn how to live again, but it tears up my soul to know that you are not here moving on as well. I know your troubled mind wanted to leave, but I knew the real you and that you wanted to make a mark on this world that no one would ever forget.*

257

*You did make a mark, an indelible mark, on my soul and to
all who knew you.*

*So the winds blow across your grave my daughter and
the grass has veiled the soil. The winds of time take me
farther away from you but closer to the time when I will see
you again.*

Kaitlyn in 2012

# Chapter 19

## Special Memories of Kaitlyn

*Thank you...for gracing my life with your lovely presence,
for adding the sweet measure of your soul to my existence.*

*Richard Matheson (What Dreams May Come)*

Kaitlyn and I always had a special relationship. We had so many inside jokes with each other, so many special things that we would only do or say to/with each other. These things endeared her so much to me up until the very last time I saw her.

In this chapter I want to reflect upon all those memories of Kaitlyn. Everyone has their own special memories of Kaitlyn, but here I will share my own. All of these things were so special to me and I will never forget them for as long as I live.

Some of these memories are happy and sweet and some of them are tainted with sadness.

### No Words Needed

Whenever we were travelling in the car and I was the front passenger, I would often put my arm over the backrest, without looking behind, and hold my hand out to Kaitlyn as she was riding in the back. She would slide her finger into my palm and I would squeeze her finger for just a few seconds and then I would let go. We did that all her life. Nothing was ever said when we did that. It was our special way of saying we loved each other and we were kindred spirits. We did it on her last visit to us.

259

## The Story of Night-Night Baby

Kaitlyn received a stuffed lamb type toy (I think it was supposed to be a child dressed like a lamb, I don't know) for her first Christmas when she was 11-months-old. It was very soft and cuddly. From that day on, Night-Night Baby always slept with her every night. If we went somewhere overnight, the toy went with us. Kaitlyn took it with her everywhere she went except for church and school. One day someone made a little blanket for Night-Night Baby, so that came along too. Night-Night Baby accompanied us to countless Disney World vacations, to the mountains, her one stay at the hospital and everywhere else.

Then, all of a sudden one night, she put Night- Night Baby in a tiny wooden crib at the end of her bed, along with the little blankie, and never slept with her or took her anywhere again. I guess she was about 10-years-old at the time. Even when she was upset about something or was unwell, we'd fetch Night-Night Baby to try to comfort her, but she would put her back. She had outgrown Night-Night Baby and never looked back.

I still have Night-Night Baby packed away in Kaitlyn's trunk. I almost buried it with Kaitlyn, but she was a young woman and had left Night-Night long ago.

## "Sit Savannah, Sit!"

We own a hyperactive chocolate Labrador retriever called Savannah who, at the time of writing, is 4-years-old. I had always wanted a Lab and it had been several years since I had owned a dog, so I bought her when she was a 6-week-old pup.

Why did I think Labs were placid, gentle dogs? Every one I've ever seen was. I've seen them riding on the passenger side of convertibles, complete with a scarf around their neck. I've also seen them riding around in golf carts, sitting still, remaining calm and enjoying the scenery as they were escorted around the campgrounds we visited. That was my vision.

What I actually got was the most energetic dog in the entire world!! She was also a nipper and I have scars all over my hands and arms to prove it. I trained her to be an indoor dog, so I trained her to "potty" on command outside. Not an easy feat, especially at 4am on cold mornings. I trained her to sit, fetch, lie down and shake hands. This was the extent of our training. However, no matter how hard we tried, we were unable to teach her not to jump up on us. We took her to two different training schools and practiced with her religiously at home, but we could not teach this dog any manners whatsoever. She was just a big old friendly dog, so we gave up and she is what she is.

I bought her a nice Dogloo dog house and an invisible fence around a large area of yard. Being a house dog was long abandoned as she would have torn our house apart, even though we love her to bits.

When we return after a trip out, we always go to her fence boundary and give her attention. (We play with her twice a day too). It takes us forever to settle her because she is always so excited. Her butt just cannot seem to touch the ground for more than half a second.

When Kaitlyn came home to visit, which was not often, she would always go to Savannah to pet her. As soon as Savannah saw her, she would wag her tail, go to where Kaitlyn was standing and look her straight in the eyes. Kaitlyn would say "Sit Savannah, sit!" and immediately Savannah's butt hit the ground and she would sit there as still as a house gazing at Kaitlyn. Kaitlyn would pet her and love her and talk to her, while Savannah stayed put. Kaitlyn was the only person that Savannah would "mind" like this. It didn't matter how long between visits; Savannah never forgot her, or how to mind her. There was something about Kaitlyn. Unfortunately, we will never get to see that again.

I guess she'll just sit there like that dog Hachi (from the movie Hachi: A Dog's Tale), forever waiting for Kaitlyn to come back.

## The Story of Harry

When Kaitlyn was young and we took her to elementary school each day, she would watch a group of squirrels playing in the yard there. Sometimes there was only one whom she named him Harry. Sometimes they would appear to be pecking at the ground like birds, and she took great delight in telling her teacher about them. Harry was there every day.

Thereafter, every time we ever saw a squirrel, we said it was Harry, no matter where we went. This was not only Kaitlyn doing this; it was all of us. Even when we went on vacation, the squirrels we would see would be Harry and if there were any with him, those would be his brothers, sisters, cousins, etc.

Once when we were vacationing in the mountains, we saw Harry with a red bushy tail! He was trying out a new fad I suppose.

It has been many years since Kaitlyn named Harry, and we have seen thousands of Harrys since. Even on trips that Allyn and I would make by ourselves, if we saw a squirrel, it would be Harry and even up to this day Harry lives on.

Kaitlyn, Harry will always be here, just for you.

## Sea Monkey Has My Money

We both always liked the movie Finding Nemo (yes, even after she was grown; it's a great movie and so funny). My favorite part in the movie is something we always quoted and it would always be just out of the blue. I could be passing by her and say, "Sea Monkey has my money." And she would say, "Yes, I'm a natural blue." And no one else would ever know what we were talking about. For those who are familiar with the movie, it was the part where Dory was talking in her sleep. We did this the last time she was here.

## Kaitlyn's Apartment

After a year and a half in undergrad at Campbell University, Kaitlyn moved into her own apartment in Cary, NC, which she decorated it beautifully. She was living alone and this apartment would be totally her own creation. No compromising with a roommate; she could do what she wanted.

Before she moved everything in, there was something she had to do. Of course all the walls were white and this was totally unacceptable to her. She could not bear the thought of plain white walls and wanted to paint them. Her father and I tried so hard to talk her out of it, telling her it would be so much work for her, because she had never painted a wall in her life. But she would have none of that. She cleared it with the management, but the only criterion was that she would have to paint it white again when she moved, or alternatively pay a fee to have it painted.

She picked out the paint and bought the brushes and masking tape etc. and painted that apartment herself, except the bedroom and bathroom, which she left white. She did not pick out what we thought were "normal" colors. She picked out green, burgundy and dark brown and painted each of the walls a different color. When we heard she was going to use these colors we were horrified. Again, we tried to talk her out of it, thinking she'd never be able to match anything to those colors because they were too dark. Again, she would hear none of that and went about painting it the colors she wanted.

263

The results of her work and the vision she had in her mind turned out to be nothing less than absolutely beautiful. Once again I was reminded that my simple, conservative taste was nothing to her creative, brilliant mind and good taste. The furniture matched perfectly. She bought pictures to match her color schemes and decorated her apartment so beautifully. Her father and I were both amazed. But then again, Kaitlyn always amazed us.

She lived there for a couple of years before she was accepted into medical school. That meant she had to move to another city, Winston-Salem, NC. This time she went on her very own and found an apartment herself, signed the lease and took care of everything on her own. We did get a U-Haul and helped her move everything into her apartment along with the help of her boyfriend.

Again, the walls were white. Although we had already moved the furniture in there, she still wanted to paint it. We tried to tell her it would be too much trouble for her to cover the furniture and then have to paint, in addition to her medical school preparations. Again, she didn't listen to us and did what she wanted. This time, her boyfriend helped her. Again, it turned out to be beautiful. She used the same colors, but chose only to use the burgundy and the brown this time. She left the bathroom and her bedroom white.

Every time we went to her apartment I would walk around it and admire it, often finding new things she had purchased. I loved going to see her and she was proud of her place.

When she died, her father and I had to go to her apartment and painstakingly take down each and every painting, wrap up and box all her glasses, pots, pans, kitchenware, clothes, bedding and all her other possessions. This was one of the most painful experiences of my entire life. Bits and pieces of her life being taken down and put in boxes; all the things she loved and took such time and thought into buying all put in boxes. We literally packed up her life and moved it away.

Her living room suite now sits in my living room and sometimes, just sometimes, in my mind, I still see her sitting on that beautiful green couch, feet on her table, laptop in her lap, studying. And then she is gone.

## Seagulls in a Parking Lot

From the time Kaitlyn was a little girl to the end of her life, if we were ever in a parking lot where seagulls were sitting and flying around, we would ponder over this. We live one hour from the beach, so why would seagulls be in a parking lot so far away? We would notice this mostly in the K-Mart parking lot. We would feel sorry for them, knowing they were existing on trash and bits of discarded food. How and why did they fly so far from home? We decided they were displaced. Sitting there on a hard parking lot, landing on something that perhaps looked like the sea, but then discovering a hard, hot surface with no fish available. All her life we would see this and say, "Poor displaced seagulls."

I hope you didn't feel like a displaced seagull Kaitlyn. Existing in a place that looked like it may have been just for you, only realizing once you landed, it was far from the place that you belonged. Now, you are in another place flying high somewhere I hope, and happy with your wings spread wide, soaring and diving for the food that will sustain you. I love you.

I will always think of you when I see the seagulls. Always.

## Easter 1996

On one occasion when Stephanie was here, we viewed some old video footage of the family. I had recently had all my VHS tapes converted to DVD and Stephanie wanted to see some of when Kaitlyn was little.

We watched a DVD from Easter 1996 when Kaitlyn was 6-years-old and Stephanie was 10. It was of the Easter egg hunt we had at my mom's every Easter. Oh the spectacle it was! The two of them, along with some of their cousins, were running around searching for Easter eggs. Kaitlyn was running around so fast that we could hardly keep the camera on her when we were trying to video her. She wanted so many eggs.

At one point, she and Stephanie saw an egg at the same time, but Stephanie got to it first. Kaitlyn was not at all pleased and started crying and having what we call in the South "a hissy fit". Her daddy said, "Now Kaitlyn, Stephanie got to it first." And Kaitlyn replied, "Well I wanted it!" A second later she was over that and continued to fly around the yard. The Easter basket was almost as large as she was and was so heavily laden with eggs that she had to drag it on the grass. During this process she fell down and ALL her eggs spilled out of the basket onto the grass. She stopped and hurriedly picked them up and put them all back in the basket. So there she went, dragging a basket full of eggs, knees skinned and bleeding, running like fury and still hunting more eggs.

That was Kaitlyn. I forgot how very determined she was as a child. I had forgotten that she knew how to cry and get mad too. Kaitlyn was born determined and stayed that way.

We laughed all the way through the video. Even though Kaitlyn was not there to share it with us, we still enjoyed the memory and reminder of her personality.

# The Room

Every day I go into the room; the little spare room into which I put many of Kaitlyn's possessions. I go in there daily because there are more than just her belongings in there; there is my printer, my picture albums, some of the items we buy from Sam's in bulk and a closet containing some of my clothes. Every day I am at home, I open up the mini blinds to let the light in, as I do throughout the rest of the house.

That room has so much of Kaitlyn in there. It's the room that was Kaitlyn's when she was born, until the day Stephanie left home and Kaitlyn moved into her big room. That's where Kaitlyn's bassinet was, then her crib, then her little bed. Bedtime stories were read in there every night until she became too old.

"Hush little baby, don't say a word….." was sung many nights by me to soothe her to sleep. (Though she never had trouble sleeping, we just liked to do it).

A piñata was hung in there, just because she thought it was pretty, but never to hold candy, and the sombrero from Disney World's Mexico showcase hung on the wall after she finished wearing it. The SpongeBob Square Pants' characters that she drew hung on the walls for years. Harry Potter books were read in the little bed that was in there. A bookshelf with all the books she loved was and still is there. (We love books in our family and there are bookshelves everywhere).

Every single night before bed she prayed, "Down I lay me down to sleep, I pray the lord my soul to keep. If I should die before I wake, I pray the Lord my soul to take. Amen."

After Stephanie moved out and she moved into the bigger room, the little room still contained so many of her things; the medals she won, the pictures she drew, awards, old books and all the things I didn't put away. Eventually, I packed all those things away when I redecorated the room after Kaitlyn went away to college. It took me 3 years to be able to do that.

Now it's still Kaitlyn's room. Instead of all the things that she kept in there as a child, there is now a multitude of attractive items with which she decorated her apartment; pictures she once hung on the walls, ornaments, and pictures of her family in beautiful frames, including her trip to Africa. There is a beautiful antique-style cabinet on which the tiny Vizio TV sat and her desk at which she studied for her medical exam, complete with the lamp and the metal cat her friend Neal bought her. Also on the desk is a wind up clock with the time fixed at 12:20. We haven't wound it up since. In the corner are stacks of containers, storing belongings of her young adulthood that should not be there. They should all be in her apartment. Her dirty clothes basket is beside those, complete with all the clothes she left in there, never to be washed. On top of the containers are albums of her pictures of her young adulthood, and memories I typed in my blog and put in binders. On the floor lie her purple running shoes. They look as though they are waiting for her to step back in them and run several miles. Beside them is a brand new pack of socks that have never been opened. These are special socks for runners I suppose because they are designed to keep your feet dry. She probably bought them at a specialist store. They could not have been old because she ran all the time and they would not have stayed in that pack long.

I look at these things that should not be in there every single day. Sometimes I pause to smell her clothes, look through her pocketbook or billfold. Sometimes I just stop in front of her desk, put my hand on the back of the chair and just breathe in her scent. Sometimes I don't, because I can't bear it and sit on the floor crying about the unfairness and injustice of such a person not being on earth anymore.

At the time of writing, it's been six months since Kaitlyn took her life and I still cannot grasp why. My beautiful, sweet, intelligent daughter, who was so easy to love and who gave love so easily, who was at the launching point of a great career and appeared so content, was not happy at all. My world has turned upside down and I have no equilibrium, no course of action and am unable to believe that whatever I perceive is true...ever again.

The pain of loving someone so intensely, wrapping your world in hope for their happiness, to feel such a bond with your child and then to lose them, is a pain that defies description. The person is gone. You can't do anything with them anymore. You can't hope for their future anymore. They are GONE. And that truth and that realization is the worst pain that any human being can endure, or at least attempt to endure.

Everyone who reads my blog who suffers from depression or suicidal ideation, please try to think of what you will leave behind. No matter who you are, someone loves you and more often than not, many people do. Look at my blog and try to understand the gaping holes in the hearts of those who are left behind following the loss of a child to suicide. There is however, something inside the gaping hole, and that is pain that will never go away as long as I live. I am not angry with Kaitlyn. I know she continued on for as long as she could, but that her pain was all she could focus on eliminating. I know by her note that she tried for many years not to do this thing because she knew it would hurt us, but she could bear it no longer. So to some of you who maybe thinking of taking your own life, please seek help urgently. If you have done so, but still feel the same, please think about what you will leave and find another avenue of help. Hopefully, it won't be too late to make a difference.

Recently, I looked at her documents on her computer and I found one entitled, "Bucket List". There were ten desires on the list. Top of the list was to become an MD, then get married, then have children, then to write a book of poetry. I can't remember the others offhand, but those were the main ones. She never got to do one single one. But she was working towards some of them and would have completed that list if she had lived on. It tortures my soul that she could not finish these things; a young woman who rarely gave up on anything.

So I look at the room; the room filled with so many goals, ambitions, dreams and memories - all packed up in containers and stowed away. My bright, wonderful, beautiful, ambitious daughter; her sweet scent permeating that room and nowhere else. That room and all it signifies makes life so hard, painful and intolerable. No such thing should EVER be.

**The Alligator is Going to Get You!**

One of the countless special memories I have of Kaitlyn was when she was little and I would give her a bath in the tub. I guess when she was around two-years-old or so we used to play this game. I would hold one end of the washcloth and move it along in the water. I would say "Here comes the aaaalligator.....he's going to get you." She would feign fear as I pretended it was vicious, making it thrash around in the water as it moved towards her. I would do that for a while, getting closer and closer to her, become more ferocious until, all of a sudden, it was at her!! However, instead of biting her, it would start giving her kisses. We would laugh and giggle and would play this game at each bath time. We actually reminisced about this on the last weekend I saw her before she died.

When Kaitlyn was a little older she finally said, "Momma, I can wash myself, by myself." I thought she was too young to be able to do an adequate job but I agreed and said that I would supervise her for a couple of nights to make sure. Well, the girl could wash herself better than I could, complete with washing her hair, so that was the end of our tub times. You only had to show Kaitlyn something once and she remembered it.

## The Hats

Kaitlyn, I remember when you were a little girl and you went through a phase where you LOVED hats. You just had to have many hats. I remember we used to go to Belk's and there was a section there where there was a standing rack with hats on it. But these hats were the type that old women wore to church 50 years ago. You were just fascinated with these hats and you begged me to buy you one, but I always refused. For several months, you pleaded for one of these hats each time we went to Belk's. I tried to explain to you that they were not hats for young children, young girls, or young women, but were for old women. You still wanted one. I never bought you one.

Why didn't I just buy you the hat? I wish I had.

## Burned End French Fries

On the drive with Allyn to our last grief counselor session, it was still daylight, and I was struck by the realization that the world was no longer a pretty place to me anymore. I'm a lover of scenery and always look out the window and think about the places I see. They hold no charm to me anymore. The light and beauty has gone out of the world for me without Kaitlyn anywhere in it.

Before we arrived at our session, we stopped at McDonald's and ate, so we wouldn't be so late getting home later. As I sat there and ate my Big Mac Meal (something Kaitlyn would never eat anymore, and something I seldom ate before she died), I looked at the French fries before me. I remember one occasion when she was a young teenager, maybe a little younger, when we were sitting in a McDonald's and she said there was a secret about the French fries that only she, her sister and her cousins knew. The French fries with the slightly burned ends were the best apparently and you were lucky if you got some of them. Those were the special ones.

From then on, if we ever ate French fries, Kaitlyn would grab one with a burned end, glance at me with a knowing look and eat it. I would do the same and we would pretend it was a huge secret that no one else must ever know. No one else would have understood the humor and silliness of things we did like this sometimes. But we got it; we got each other.

So, when I ate those French fries in McDonald's, I grabbed the ones with the burned ends first and I thought of Kaitlyn. Ever since the day she first told me this, I have always done this.

Kaitlyn's humor was so subtle, but so funny. We had inside jokes galore. I am so thankful we had all these special experiences that would make no sense to anyone but us.

So, I ate those special burned end fries; I always will. I so long to see Kaitlyn at the other end of the table eating them with me, but that will never be again.

**The Memory Jar**

When Kaitlyn was a little girl, I adopted two kittens from a work colleague. One was black and one was white. Stephanie named the black one Salem after a cat on a TV show. Kaitlyn named the white one Friend-a-Lee (not Friendly, because Kaitlyn had to be unique).

Friend-a-Lee was a rather placid female cat. She wasn't overly playful, but she was a good cat. Salem, on the other hand, was quite a clown and he just charmed us from the beginning. We would see him on the girls' swing set (the two-seater) out in the backyard with his leg flopped over the side like he was the King. He was just such a funny, loving cat and rather handsome. He was large and totally jet black. Kaitlyn and I adored cats.

One day, just as Salem had reached full adulthood, he was hit by a car and killed. When Kaitlyn came home from school I had to tell her and she cried her little heart out and I cried along with her. I guess she was around 9 or 10-years-old.

Allyn dug a grave for Salem at the edge of our yard and we held a funeral, but that was not enough for Kaitlyn. She came up with the idea of a memory jar. We would write out separately on little pieces of paper the things that were so special about Salem and put them in that jar, which became full of memories.

I kept that jar in my den for years. Finally, several years after Kaitlyn went away to college, I either threw it away or stored it in a trunk with all her other childhood memories, I'm not sure. But I looked at that jar many times and read its contents, and I let it remain just where she put it in my den until that time.

In a way, my blog and my book is my memory jar for Kaitlyn, containing all the wonderful memories of her and how special she was to all who knew her. Sure, it's filled with grief, because she's not here anymore, but her memory will live on in my mind, other people's minds, and in this memory jar. I never imagined I would make one for her.

## Rock Piles and Bridges

We live in about an hour's drive from Wilmington, NC, a town rich with Revolutionary and Civil War history, not far from the ocean. It's also near Fort Fisher, one of the last forts to fall in the south during the Civil War. When it fell, Wilmington became fully occupied by the Northern troops and all the southern supplies were cut off. Wilmington is also full of lovely restaurants, fun places to visit, and an historical district called The Cotton Exchange that we always loved to go to via the Cape Fear River front. It is named after the cotton that used to come in and out of the area. Now it's full of quaint shops, eateries, bars and a beautiful area called the River Walk. You can stroll along the Cape Fear River as you watch the boats sail back and forth. Looking out from the Cotton Exchange area, you can see the bridge that crosses over the Cape Fear River to get to Wilmington.

When our daughters were younger, we made many, many trips to Wilmington, which we all loved, especially The Cotton Exchange. Many a day we walked through the shops and unique places there. You felt as though you had been transported through time. Many of the original buildings remain and most have been revitalized into usable businesses.

On our visits to Wilmington when the girls were small, we always drove past a company that sold a multitude of rocks; decorative rocks, gravel and rocks you could use for anything I suppose. There would always be piles of rocks, but there was always this one pile in particular, always in the same place that was so high and inviting looking. I think it was gravel. Kaitlyn once said when she was tiny that she would love to be able to climb that rock pile and from then on it became Kaitlyn's rock pile. Every single time we passed this place we would all say, "There's Kaitlyn's rock pile!" Even when Kaitlyn had long moved away from home, if any of the rest of us ever passed that pile we would say, "There's Kaitlyn's rock pile!"

In the year prior to Kaitlyn's death, I noticed that the pile wasn't replenished like it always had been before and eventually it dwindled away to nothing. When Kaitlyn was home for the final time before she died, she and I went to Wilmington and looked for the rock pile as we drove past, but there were no longer any rocks. I told Kaitlyn I guessed it was the end of her rock pile. She said she supposed it was. But it was rather sad.

Our visits to Wilmington also included going over the Cape Fear River Bridge. Ever since Kaitlyn was a little girl she would always say, "Ok everybody, when you get to the beginning of the bridge, start holding your breath, and let it out at the end, for good luck!!" And she would start counting down before we got to the beginning, "One, twooooo, threeeeee......three and a haaaaalf......" We would all suck in our breaths very loudly at the beginning and feel like we may explode by the end of the bridge and let it out again, noisily, as we crossed the end and all laughed. The very last time Kaitlyn and I crossed this bridge, she did this. She said we should hold our breaths just as we always had. We did, and we laughed as always when it was over.

Kaitlyn always did these special things, these inside jokes, little things that were so distinctive to her. And even though the last time we did these things, she was a mature, 23-year-old woman, she still indulged my need for her to be my little girl, even when I didn't ask. These rituals were dear to both of us, and no amount of being "grown up" could change that. She was never too good or too grown up to take pleasure in them.

We would then resume talking about the ways of the world, the universe, science and other adult topics, but she could revert back to being my little girl at will.

For the rest of my life I will look over to see if that rock pile is back, and I will always and forever, hold my breath across that bridge.

## Falling Water

"Falling Water". As I wash my hands in the bathroom I see the words there on a piece of soap that I have never used lying in a soap dish. I will never use it, for using it will mean that it will be gone one day and I don't want that. I don't want anything that Kaitlyn ever had, that she ever gave me, that she ever made, to be gone. I must keep the material things, for they bring back the bittersweet memories so clearly.

Falling Water is the name imprinted on a special, scented soap that was the last material thing that Kaitlyn ever gave me. Every time I'm at the bathroom sink, I look at the words, I smell the beautiful scent and I am transformed back to the time when she was sitting in the back seat of our car while Allyn was driving and I was turned around looking at her. We had just picked her up from the airport after she had visited her boyfriend. She said, "Oh Momma, I have something for you and Stephanie. Pick out the one that you want." She produced a paper bag that had 2 special soaps in different colors and different scents, with "Falling Water" imprinted on them. I smelled each of them, then smelled them again and picked out the one that I wanted. She asked me if I would give the other one to her sister Stephanie the next time I saw her and I said I would. She had bought them for us in Ann Arbor, Michigan.

"Falling Water". Each time I inhale the beautiful scent, I see her in the back seat of our car. I see her pretty blonde hair that she had cut short less than a year previously. She told me she was growing it out and it had become a tad longer. I see her fair skin that was so much like mine, except hers was youthful, smooth and without blemishes or scars. I see her pretty smile and beautiful eyes as she looks at me in happiness because I loved my gift. I look at her in the way I have looked at her since the day she was born; the intense, unconditional, heart swelling love that I have always felt for her.

"Falling Water". It was the last material thing she ever gave me and the last experience she ever gave me was on that same day. She gave me a kiss, a hug, and a smile with a promise to see us next month. On that same day she drove off as she had done so many times before. The only difference being that it was the last time I ever saw her alive. Within four days I was told she was gone.

"Falling Water". It always takes me back to that last day. The last day I hugged and kissed my youngest daughter Kaitlyn goodbye.

## The Swamp Room Waits

There is something about swamps to me. There are many of them where we live. They have beautiful cypress trees and areas of water that have Lily pads. Some are a little dry, others are covered with water, and sometimes in the midst of it all are streams. But what I love most of all are the birds that inhabit or frequent the area. I've spent a little bit of time trying to research what the names of these birds are, but still have not come up with the exact species. They belong to the egret or crane family. Many are white and so elegant looking and sometimes you can spot them easily in the swamp, sometimes gathering in large groups and sometimes alone. However, they are not always spotted easily. Sometimes I see the lone solitary gray one that is larger than the rest and his long beak reminds me of a stork, but I know that's not what he is. He's a different type of bird to the white ones. These are harder to see and rarer to find.

I pass a swamp like this on my way to my mother's and used to pass it at least twice a day when I worked in a neighboring town or took my girls to school.

There's something about these birds. The girls and I always made a point of trying to see the birds as we passed in the car. Every time we saw one we would cry out, "BIRD!!!!" We would try to see who could spot the first one.

As time went by, Stephanie obtained her license and no longer rode with me, leaving Kaitlyn and I to drive back and forth via these swamps. It became a very special thing to us. It was always fun to spot these birds and we would still call out "BIRD!!!" when they were spotted. The last time she was home, we spotted these birds and continued our ritual.

When Kaitlyn was 18, she left home to go to college. This was really hard for me because she was my youngest, my baby, and my kindred spirit. It's always easier to let the first one go because you have one left, so when Kaitlyn left it was really hard. I experienced the empty nest syndrome big time, which was strange, because I didn't ever think I would. My husband and I ensured that we would have plenty to do once she left. We had a motorhome and a motorcycle and often took long weekend trips and vacations. Those things were fun, but I still had an empty hole in my heart. I never told Kaitlyn how bad it was; I didn't want her to know. She knew I missed her, but wasn't aware to what extent. I didn't want her to worry about me. Her presence was illuminating. We shared so many things and she was always so interesting to talk to. The times when we exchanged visits were some of the greatest highlights of my life.

After she left for college, it took me two or three years to do anything with the room she left behind. She left so many things, especially after she moved from a dorm into her own apartment. I kept asking her to do something with all she left, but she never did. Finally, one day she said, "Momma, just do what you think is best with them." I felt I had to change her room and clear out her old things, because it reminded me of when she was still there; a high school girl. Not only that, but her original, smaller room was full of the things she had as a child. I was stuck in a time warp that made my empty nest more severe. I had to do something.

A few years after she left for college, I finally sorted through her belongings. Some sentimental items were put away in chests or boxes, the things I knew she didn't want were put in the trash and the rest was given to my mother-in-law for a garage sale or to goodwill. (This was a hard process too and took me several emotionally-draining days). I then totally redecorated the room, but kept the furniture, because it was beautiful and of high quality. Guess what my theme was? Yes, a swamp. Sounds ugly doesn't it, but it's not.

It all started with the matching curtains and bedding I selected first, based on a swamp-like/water theme. I had no intentions initially of making it a swamp room, but it all evolved from that bedding. So then I went to a home furnishing store and bought a painting of a swamp, a metal hanging of three dragonflies for the wall and a few other decorative swamp-like knick-knacks. The two things I wanted most of all for the room were rather elusive; two small white egret statues. I searched the internet, stores and eBay, but I could not find them. Instead, I settled for two water birds of some type, perhaps they are egrets, but they are not white. I never found a white one. They are grayish/blue. They are beautiful carvings. But these are still beautiful and serve the purpose of the theme I have for the room. I think it's beautiful.

I don't feel that I have much taste creatively, certainly not decorating, unlike Kaitlyn who was gifted in this area and many others. I do however recognize and appreciate good taste. However, I became completely absorbed in this project and the theme evolved as I progressed, even though I didn't originally plan it that way. I was simply going to buy new stuff and hope it looked ok.

This room is now a spare room where Kaitlyn always slept when she came home. Her only possessions that remain in there are the books on the bookshelf and a picture of her. I felt better after I did it. It helped decrease my empty nest syndrome and made me realize that she was pursuing her dreams, which I ALWAYS wanted for her. I never wanted her to stay around for my sake. I let her go because her needs and ambitions were more important than mine.

Though few of her things are left in this room, I look at those egrets and I think of her. I look around the room and see the swamps I love. I think of her and say "BIRD" just as I still do when I pass those swamps.

One of the saddest things I experienced after she had gone away to college was seeing a beautiful white egret flying at the edge of the swamp one day, as I drove past alone; so beautiful, so elegant and so graceful. I watched it as it glided around the periphery of the swamp, transfixed by its beauty and its apparent love of the glide. All of a sudden, it flew into a power line that ran next to the swamp, fell into the swamp and I assume lost its life. I've never erased that image from my mind.

The final Facebook entry I sent Kaitlyn was just before she came back home for the last time. It said, "The swamp room waits" and she replied, "Yay! So excited!"

My special egret fell from her beautiful glide, but the swamp room still waits.

## When Kaitlyn Went Away To College

When Kaitlyn graduated high school and was about to go away to college in 2008, I felt like most mothers do when their youngest leaves the nest. I felt I would miss her so much that I wouldn't be able to bear it, but I didn't tell her how much because I wanted her to fly away to continue to mature and be successful.

I wrote to her; not a letter or a poem, but a list of some of the many things I would miss. I never confessed just how much I missed her. Here is what I wrote for her before she left.

I'm Going To Miss.......

- All the talks we've had about the world, the universe, and the politics of our country.

- All the times you came home going straight to me with a giant hug and smiling face.

- Visiting East Wind with you (a Chinese restaurant)

- The times you came to me wanting to change the rules because you thought you were too mature and grown up for the ones that were in place at that time.

- The times you talked to me about your plans for the future and house you may have one day.

- All the times I sat in the bleachers to watch you in the band at games and at contests. The times I sat in the audience as you received your many, many awards and honors.

- Ann of Green Gables, Dr. Quinn, & The Universe.

- The awards you won in art, and going to see them on display.

- All the books and movies of Harry Potter and how you would buy the book at midnight when they came out, and then stay up all night reading on into the next day until you read it all. The excitement and anticipation you had before each book.

- All the times I read in the paper of your achievements.

- Waking up in the morning, peaking in your room and seeing your blonde head lying on that pillow and you all snuggled under the covers.

- The sound of your car as it comes driving up after school, work, or anywhere you have been.

- Your "courtesy calls" because you are too old for a curfew.

- All the times I discovered that you had Mythie (our cat) in the house before I got home from work.

- Hearing you say you love me in person many times a day.

- Knowing you're here.

- Looking in the crib and seeing you playing with your mobile.

- Seeing your little head bobbing up and down on the floor as you try to learn to crawl.

- The way your head always smelled when you were a baby.

- When you were only two, when you gave me hugs, would linger in my arms, squeeze me tightly and didn't try to get away.

- The way you would get in my lap and like to be there.

- "The monster is going to get you....." in the tub.

- The way we would "lay up" when we watched TV together.

- The way you would fall deeply in love with every kitten we had and insist on naming each and every one of them, no matter HOW many we had, and expecting me to remember all the names, and then drill me on it frequently.

- Pokémon, SpongeBob, Barbie, and Lizzie Maguire,

- How you always beat me at any game, even at age 5....maybe younger.

- The way you were so competitive and my trying to teach you to lose gracefully, even though losing anything was rare to you.

- THE monopoly game.

- The times you would try to get me to buy you hats everywhere we went.

- Your little girl voice.

- How you were brave enough to get on any ride at any amusement park, even braver than all of us.

- The way you would crawl in my bed on Saturday morning and how we would lie there and talk long periods of time about any and everything.

- All of these things, but I look forward to the many new special moments to come as you enter your college years and young womanhood and I can hardly wait to experience them with you. They will all be as special as the memories so far.

You are truly a special person and a wonderful daughter. Thank you so much for all the memories you have given me in your life so far. They're all in my mind and in my heart and will be there forever.

I'm going to miss you....... here.

Love, Mom

# Chapter 20

## Dear Momma and Daddy

*The sun stopped shining for me is all. The whole story is: I am sad. I am sad all the time and the sadness is so heavy that I can't get away from it. Not ever.*

*Nina LaCour, Hold Still*

As I have stated, before Kaitlyn took her life, she also wrote suicide notes to a few of her closest friends as well as her family and one to her apartment manager.

After her funeral, I sat in the living room and announced I was going to read the note Kaitlyn left for us, to anyone who wanted to listen. Most people there were family and I know all were curious to hear the reasons Kaitlyn gave for taking her life, because it was something that no one could ever conceive her doing. So, I sat there in the middle of my living room, about 10 people around me, and somehow managed to read her note. I felt as though I was revealing something that was private to me and her daddy, but I also felt the need to let others know what she was thinking.

Since that time, however, I have not read it to anyone else, but I have read it over and over again, perhaps a hundred times, hoping one day to fully understand. Only occasionally would I paraphrase a few remarks, or quote a few words in one of my blog posts. I swore that the note would thereafter remain private. I finally moved it from my bedroom dresser into a decorative box that Kaitlyn had left in her bedroom when she went away to college.

One day I decided to share it with a friend, Randall, who contributed to an earlier chapter and whose son was so much like my daughter. His son only wrote a terse note, but he at least wrote something. I just felt a great need to share it with someone whom I trusted and knew would understand. I'm glad I did. Many people who take their own lives do not leave notes, which was really surprising to me. I knew some did not, but thought most did.

I felt that Kaitlyn's note was meant for our eyes only and I swore I would share it with no one else after this. However, as I have found occasionally since Kaitlyn's death, I sometimes change my mind about things for various reasons.

I thought long and hard about this, in the same way that I thought long and hard about publishing this book. Eventually, I decided to include her note that she left to us. Though it contains her last words to us, I feel it important to let the world know what goes on in the mind of a truly tormented soul; someone who appeared as though she had her life so well planned. I do this out of respect for my daughter, knowing that if she knew it would help someone, that she would not mind my sharing it.

*Dear Momma and Daddy,*

*I am so dreadfully sorry for the unimaginable pain and hurt that I have caused you by taking my life. I am sorry for hiding from you that I was so deeply sad. I am sorry for not letting you know that I felt like I simply no longer wanted to live my life. I am sorry that I didn't let you in on the perpetual despair I lived in. Depression is nothing new to me. I can't remember a time in my life in which I didn't feel like I was barely treading water. I never told you how pervasive it was because I wanted to protect you from it, and I wanted to protect myself from it. But I have finally decided that I'd rather just not exist. I have found myself happy on occasion, and I have had many pleasurable things in my life, but mostly I feel overwhelmingly sad and exhausted from the weight of it. I would just rather not endure it any longer. I would have died years ago, but I couldn't bring myself to cause you such sadness and heartache. I still can't bear to think of the hurt this brings you, but I just can't go on.*

*You both are the most wonderful parents on the face of the earth. Please do not blame yourselves. Please don't wonder what you could have done. The only thing wrong is me. I love you deeply. I respect you immensely. I wish I could have waited until you both had gone peacefully many years in the future, after you've fully lived you own beautiful lives, but forgive me that I couldn't. This is the worst thing I will ever do to you. I am sorry I cannot ever make amends. I just want you to know that I love you so very much and that even though I don't want to live, I still wish you all the happiness in the world, and I wish I could be able to have it with you.*

*I know you may not understand why I didn't seek help. I don't know if I can really explain why. I just want you to know that I may be incomprehensible and you may be angry with me, but I am not angry, and while it eludes me why I was to be destined to live the way I've lived and to feel the way I've felt, this choice makes sense to me. I know I had such a seemingly bright future, and I know I would have been such a successful doctor and wife and mother. But all I have ever desperately wished for is to not feel like not existing would be preferable to being who I am and living the life I live. But that's never been true. And that's deeply sad and horrible and possibly terribly unfair. But that is how I feel and how I've felt for longer than I can remember. It may be inadequate and it may not justify my action, but it is the best explanation I have.*

*I hope you will forgive me. I hope you can be happy again. I hope you can find the strength to endure this burden I've placed upon you. And I hope you will never doubt how much I love you.*

*Please take care of Gatito. If you can't bear the thought of him living with you, please find him a good home. I know this will have hurt him, but I want to limit that hurt as much as possible.*

*Please make sure the people to whom I have left letters are notified and that they receive my letters. Their phone numbers are listed below their addresses. You do not have to call them, but please make sure someone does.*

*I love you both so much.*

*Your Daughter,*
*Kaitlyn*

This letter from my precious daughter who I thought was so happy and had the world in her very hands. My mere words in this entire book cannot portray the unutterable grief at losing my daughter and reading these words.

Many times I write to Kaitlyn as if she can hear the words that I write. I really think she can. It helps me to get my feelings out about her and it makes me believe she will hear just how much I love her and how proud I still am of her. I've always told her this and need to tell her still.

As the song Diamond Rio sung years ago goes: "Every now and then, soft as breath upon my skin, I feel you come back again......"

So I write to her and the following letter is in response to the last note she wrote us:

*Dear Kaitlyn,*

*As of this writing, you have been gone for a little over 7 months. I have written about you and this horrible thing that happened to you in my blog and book, and the words themselves would fill an Olympic sized pool. Though I have written so much, I still cannot form with mere words the severe blow to my spirit, my body, my mind, my heart, and my outlook, that your death has caused. I speak for myself, but know that all of your family and friends feel the same.*

*I cannot adequately put the intensity of my grief into words, but I could not have seen what would come to pass with you in a million years. In my eyes, and to all who knew you, you had a better grasp on the world than we all did. Your talents and goodness made you stand out from the time you were very little. As your mother, I felt so blessed to have you for my daughter. You gave me more joy than I could possibly ever imagine. Our connection was strong and special.*

*I have spent endless hours writing about why and how and the injustice of it all since the day I found out about your death. This book was my journey into trying to figure out why. But what it all comes down to Kaitlyn is that you suffered from a mental illness called depression. You wrote you had this all your life, but I don't know if it just seemed that way when you were in your depths of despair or not, or if it was in fact true. You always acted like such a happy child. How can a child hide their sadness? How can someone hide their sadness an entire lifetime? But I must take your last words written to us as truth because it's all I have.*

*Your death has shaken so many things I held to be true. It makes me question everything that I see in this world as being true, possibly not being true after all because all I saw in you was happiness and a pure joy in accomplishment. My heart is forever broken and can never, ever be repaired. In this book I cannot even give readers hope for the future, because I can't see it. They will have to go to other books for that.*

*But the one thing I do know Kaitlyn is that you enriched my life so very much. You brought a beauty to my world that I feel so very lucky to have had. I saw a person with* the heart of an angel and the gifts you possessed were innumerable. For those 23 years that I had with you, I will be forever thankful. But it hurts so much to have to give that up.

I question so many things in life; why was I given the gift of you, why were you given the life of such a gifted and good person only to have it taken away? I see no sense in this. I see no sense in any person being taken away by any means. I will never understand this, nor be accepting of the fact that "we will all know someday".

But thank you Kaitlyn. Thank you for being in my life and the lives of so many others. You were so very special. And as you similarly put in your letter, it eludes me why you had to live a life of such sadness, that it took away the wonderful future you could have had.

I'm never mad at you Kaitlyn, never. But I despise the horrible thing that took you away from us....depression. That horrible thing that cares not who it takes; it just takes and takes.

I will never, ever forget any single thing about you Kaitlyn. Until the day I die, my memories of the beautiful person you were here with us will remain in my heart as clearly as the days I was experiencing them, for no one can ever forget someone as wonderful as you.

Your last act on this earth will not define you Kaitlyn. You were so much more than a suicide statistic. Your life was a wonderful gift that was tragically ended by a disease. You were all that was good and special in this world. No one who has ever known you will ever forget you.

Sometimes I find myself saying "My daughter killed herself; she killed her beautiful self". But Kaitlyn, in my journey to this point as I have written this book and researched, I have come to realize that you did not kill yourself; a disease killed you but it used your hands to do it. You did not want to leave us and your life but the pain of this unbearable disease became more than you could *endure after years and years of its unrelenting torture. It's depression I blame, not you.*

*I would say, "Rest in peace Kaitlyn", but the word "rest" indicates being inactive and not striving for anything and rest is something that is needed only between doing things. I do wish you peace Kaitlyn and I hope with all my heart that you are in paradise so much more wonderful than anything that we have here on this earth of ours. I have no conception of what kinds of things one can achieve in heaven, but I know you deserve something so exciting and things that would stimulate your beautiful mind as it did on this earth, just a thousand times better.*

*I wish with all my heart that you are in a place where sadness does not exist, for if anyone deserves all happiness and goodness it is you my dear, wonderful daughter.*

*And always remember my bright shining star.....I love you bigger than the universe.*

*Your mother that loves you more than life,*
*Momma*

One day, during the first week of October, I was in the yard playing with our dog Savannah. We live in the country and our yard is partially surrounded by thick woods. At the back, to the side of our yard, is an area of underbrush and briars. On that day, I looked over and saw something colorful in the underbrush. I moved closer and I saw that it was a single purple flower. In all of the brush, in all of the woods that I could see, in no part of my yard were there any other flowers because it was the Fall. I had planted no flowers there and there had never been any flowers there before. I didn't know what kind of flower it was, but I had seen it before and knew that it had something to do with Kaitlyn, but what? It was beautiful and perfect and signified the brilliance of a unique being. It was growing in the midst of dead brush. I immediately went in to get my camera, took a picture of it and went inside to look it up on the internet. I found out that it was a Morning Glory. Thank you Kaitlyn for this sign when I so desperately needed it. I will love you forever my precious daughter.

### Falling Into Being

*You, you with the clovers in your hair, your braided sun beams.*

*Flowers and winged things. How you'll never know the species of them, but you know them by their colors - their tiny reflected sunlights. You call them cousins by their hues: this one is robin red, this one is lily white.*

*You touch them with your bluebird eyes.*

*What is the final truth, then? Is it that they live, that there's beauty in existing as you are?*

*Before the sun had risen, you cupped your hands around your mouth and whispered to the spiraled bud of a morning glory: why will you bloom?*

*No answer until the morning, and then it unfurled its petals; its greeting to the day, to a lifetime.*

*You sat and watched this little being bloom with the magnificence of purpose. It was beautiful in its silence, in its pride.*

*You gave it the honor of breathing softly, of acknowledging its vulnerability. You knew it was weaker, less protected as a softly petaled bloom than as a bud.*

*You saluted its courage.*

*And when it died in the dusk of fading lights and fading colors, you stood in reverence as you do at the funeral of a man who lived well. Shed a tear but smiled in acceptance of a gift you never intended to receive.*

*And by morning, you had discerned the colors of yourself. You had fallen into being.*

*Kaitlyn Elkins*

**Kaitlyn aged 15**

293

# Chapter 21

## Books and Resources

Below is a list of resources that can offer information and understanding about mental illness, help in surviving the loss of a loved one from suicide and helpful books on the subject.

**If you are in crisis, call 1-800-273-TALK (8255)**
**National Suicide Prevention Lifeline**

### Websites & Organizations

**The American Foundation of Suicide Prevention**
http://www.afsp.org/

This site offers a wealth of information on suicide prevention, personal stories, statistics, and ways to help and contribute to suicide prevention. They also offer Out of the Darkness Walks across the United States where groups get together to walk and raise money for suicide prevention. We took part in one such walk in Oct 2013 in Myrtle Beach, SC.

**The Compassionate Friends: Providing Grief Support After the Death of a Child**
http://www.compassionatefriends.org/home.aspx

An organization for the support of people who have lost children to death by any means. They also have support groups all over the US.

**NAMI  National Alliance on Mental Illness**
http://www.nami.org/

Information on Mental Illness, awareness, education, support and advocacy.

**Supporting Emotional Needs of the Gifted (SENG)**
http://www.sengifted.org/

SENG is dedicated to fostering environments in which gifted adults and children, in all their diversity, understand and accept themselves and are understood, valued, nurtured, and supported by their families, schools, workplaces and communities.

**Black-bile.com**
http://www.black-bile.com/

This website is dedicated to physicians suffering from depression, and those who love them.  Depression is a surprisingly common, but frequently unrealized diagnosis among health professionals, and it is immediately treatable if recognized.  Yet far too often, it is not.  Suicide is the most serious result of untreated depression.  The loss of a healing professional to a treatable medical disease through ignorance, fear or denial is a travesty.  Help us to spread knowledge about physician depression and physician suicide by visiting and referring others to this site.  If you are a professional suffering from depressive symptoms, please know that you are not alone.

# Online Support Groups, Websites and Forums

## Child Suicide
http://www.childsuicide.org

A support website for people who have lost children to suicide. This site was started by Jan Andersen who in 2002 lost her son Kristian to suicide when he was 20-years-old. It is full of resources, stories, facts and figures, poems, photos, memorial sites, a meeting place page and so much more. I found this site soon after Kaitlyn died and it has been so helpful to me.

## Alliance of Hope for Suicide Survivors
http://forum.forsuicidesurvivors.com/index.php

A forum where all suicide survivors can come to read about others' experiences, post their own experiences and receive a tremendous amount of support. I belong to this forum and post regularly.

## My Bright Shining Star
http://welding81.wordpress.com/

My blog that I started after Kaitlyn died. It may not help you, but you can read about the feelings of a mother that lost her daughter to suicide.

## Books

## Books about Experience of a Loved One's Suicide

Chasing Death: Losing a Child to Suicide by Jan Andersen

Melissa: A Father's Lessons from a Daughter's Suicide by Frank Page with Lawrence Kimbrough

Grieving a Suicide: A Loved One's Search for Comfort, Answers, & Hope by Albert Y. Hsu

Goodbye Jeanine: A Mother's Faith Journey after Her Daughter's Suicide by Joyce Sackett

No Time to Say Goodbye: Surviving the Suicide of a Loved One by Carla Fine

Dying to Be Free: A Healing Guide for Families after a Suicide by Beverly Cobain and Jean Larch

**Books about Personal Experience with Mental Illness**

Night Falls Fast: Understanding Suicide by Kay Redfield Jamison

Touched with Fire: Manic-Depressive Illness and the Artistic Temperament by Kay Redfield Jamison

Darkness Visible: A Memoir of Madness by William Styron

Hyperbole and a Half by Allie Brosh

I must explain the suggestion of this book. Though it is mostly a very comical book with amusing illustrations, this author, who also has a blog by the same name, http://hyperboleandahalf.blogspot.com/ had a severe experience of depression before she was able to publish this book. When she did publish it, she added two stories about her experience "Depression Part 1" and "Depression Part 2", which give the most accurate description of how someone feels when they are depressed that I have ever read. When I read it I thought it brilliant. Then I went on to read her other stories and I laughed harder than I ever have since losing Kaitlyn. It felt good.

## Books about Grief and the Death of a Loved One

Safe Passage: Words to Help the Grieving by Molly Fumia

Living When a Loved One Has Died by Earl A. Grollman

Tracks of a Fellow Struggler: Living and Growing through Grief by John R. Claypool

## Books about the Special Needs of Gifted Children

Searching for Meaning: Bright Minds, Idealism, Disillusionment, and Hope by Jim Web PH.D

Kaitlyn aged 18

Kaitlyn and her cat Gatito

# About the Author

Rhonda Elkins lives in North Carolina with her husband Allyn. They have two cats, Dagny, and Kaitlyn's cat Gatito who they adopted when Kaitlyn died. Unfortunately, their other family pet Savannah, a chocolate Labrador Retriever escaped her invisible fence and was hit by a car and killed on 1-19-14, Kaitlyn's birthday.

They also have another daughter, Stephanie Alford, and a son-in-law, Steve Alford, who also live in North Carolina.

Rhonda is a registered nurse, but at the time of this book's publication has not returned to work since Kaitlyn's death. She is an advocate for suicide prevention.

Rhonda can be contacted via her email address of welding81@intrstar.net or her Facebook page at https://www.facebook.com/rhonda.s.elkins?fref=ts

CPSIA information can be obtained at www.ICGtesting.com
Printed in the USA
LVOW13s0522030414

380150LV00003B/449/P